THE VOICE OF THE TRUMPET

*For Medwin, Lois,
Paul, Caroline, Justin,
and Camille White*

" . . . let the family follow softly after us . . . "

—Tobias 11: 3

DAVID ALLEN WHITE

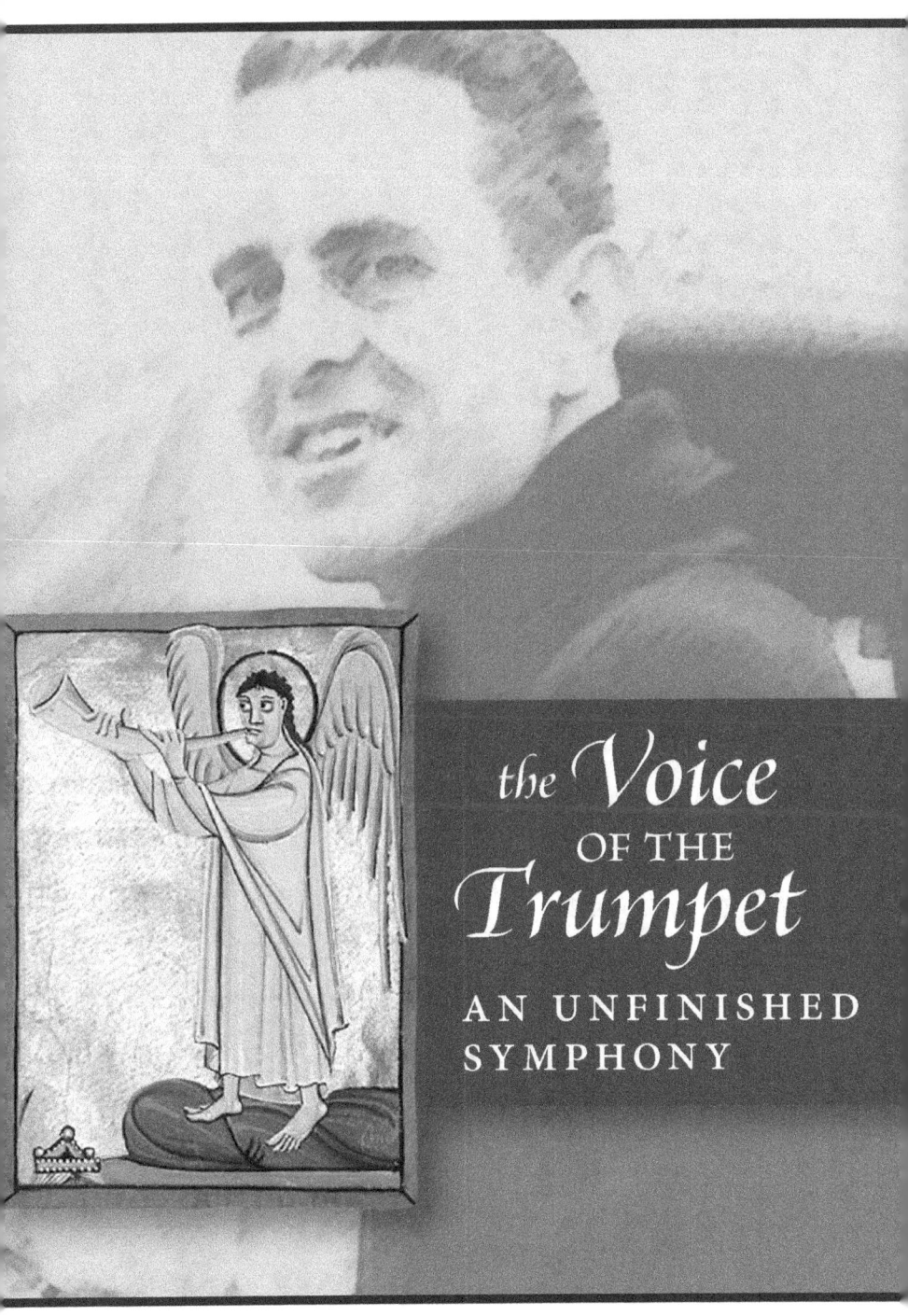

the *Voice*
OF THE
Trumpet

AN UNFINISHED
SYMPHONY

A LIFE OF BISHOP RICHARD WILLIAMSON
〰 IN FOUR MOVEMENTS

© 2018 BRN Associates, Inc.
All rights reserved.

ISBN (paper) 9781940306162
ISBN (Kindle) 9781940306179
ISBN (ePub) 9781940306186
ISBN (PDF) 9781940306193

For more information,
or for additional titles, contact:

Marcel Editions
An Imprint of the St. Marcel Initiative
www.stmarcelinitiative.com
c/o BRN Associates, Inc.
9051 Watson Rd., Suite 279
St. Louis, MO 63126
(855) 289-9226

St. Louis, Missouri ~ 2018

NOTE

Direct quotations throughout the text are, unless otherwise noted, of His Excellency Bishop Williamson, from extensive interviews conducted with the author. Citations to *Letters from the Rector* and *Eleison Comments* refer to works authored by Bishop Williamson; the numbering of the former follows that of the True Restoration Press edition. The front image is the "blast of the fifth trumpet" from the early 11th-century Bamberg Apocalypse, an illuminated manuscript containing the Book of the Apocalypse and a Gospel Lectionary. A high-resolution image of the original is available online via the Bamberg *Staatsbibliothek* (Msc.Bibl. 140).

The episcopal coat of arms.

Contents

I
A Portrait of the Bishop as a Young Man ❧ 3

II
From Seminary to Seminary ❧ 97

Selected Photos ❧ 176

III
Explosive Missives ❧ 193

IV
Veritas Variations ❧ 237

Coda ❧ 349

Williamson as subdeacon in procession, Mass of priestly ordinations, Argentina, Dec. 1, 1985.

"I was in the spirit on the Lord's day and heard behind me a great voice, as of a trumpet."

—Apocalypse 1: 10

Aus unser Taten
Steigt ein Gericht!
Aus unsen Herzen
Ruft die Posaune,
Die uns lädt.

—*Die Frau ohne Schatten,*
Hugo von Hofmannsthal

The medallion marking the site of the Tyburn martyrdoms.

PART ONE
a Portrait OF THE Bishop AS A Young Man

"Music is a natural language of the human soul."

—Bishop Richard Williamson

"Thanne longen folk to goon on pilgrimages..."

Allegro moderato

FROM THE THIRD CENTURY FOLLOWING THE Sacrifice of Our Lord on the Cross on Calvary, the soil of England has drunk the blood of Catholic martyrs. The first of these martyrs, St. Alban, stood trial at an undetermined date in the third century; no contemporary account exists. He was charged with allowing a priest to escape from Roman persecutors by means of an exchange of clothing and identities, a sacrificial gesture that may have inspired the dramatic conclusion of a classic tale of two cities by England's greatest novelist some fifteen hundred years later. St. Alban at his trial fearlessly and publicly proclaimed his faith in "the true and living God who created all things"; so the Venerable Bede recounts four centuries later, the words of the proto-martyr having been handed down over those centuries by fellow English Catholics. The verdict handed down by the Roman authorities – death by beheading. The "thirsty entrance of [the] soil" on the hillside outside Verulamium, the Roman name for the present city of St. Albans in Hertfordshire, lay in wait for the sacrificial libation. St. Bede tells us the local river that separated the city from the hill divided Red Sea-style, allowing Alban to march dryly to his death, and then a spring effervesced suddenly on the hillside, a last gift of water to slake the martyr's arid throat before his blood sanctified the earth. The executioner who felled the axe on the Saint's neck had his own eyes fall from their sockets as he dealt the deathblow. His blindness pre-figured that of many previous and subsequent executioners and functionaries, who knew not what they did.

From the axe that hewed down the first English martyr to the knightly knives that gashed Bishop Thomas Becket in Canterbury Cathedral in 1170, and to death instruments and martyrs' blood beyond, England may boast of a proud parade of victim souls. These martyrs and saints asserted the Right and Rule of God over and above the rule of governors and the "rights of man." Faithful Catholics have for centuries honored these sacrifices by making pilgrimages to the sites of these selfless oblations. The pilgrims honor the saints, those dead to earth but alive in heaven; the pilgrims affirm their belief by imploring the holy martyrs' intercession and thanking them for prayers that have been answered.

> The hooly blissful martir for to seke,
> That hem hath holpen whan that they were seeke.

Even in the present "progressive" modern Age of Apostasy, this urge to make a pilgrimage survives in countless souls, for what is this life but a pilgrimage?

The Bishop as a Young Man

> This world nys but a thurghfare ful of wo,
> And we been pilgrymes, passynge to and fro.

In ancient Lud's Town, now called London, such a destination still exists. Modern souls from around the world, the instinct of pilgrimage not yet dead in them, journey to a spot sacred to them to pay tribute to those they revere and adore. This spot, worshipped by multitudes, has gained such fame and fired such enthusiastic devotion that modern technology has come to the aid of those distant, home-bound souls who cannot make such a journey. In its god-like capacity to fix an all-seeing eye, electronic wizardry has situated a permanently-planted camera on the site to afford the whole world a twenty-four hour, three-hundred-sixty-five day a year animated icon of the pilgrims coming reverently to their "holy place." Devoted ones dwelling seas or continents away may witness on their votive-light-like screens the new pilgrims. The devout stand frozen in homage, recreating for an instant an indelible and irrecoverable bubble of glory. They stand reverently today where four mop-headed youths from Liverpool years ago stopped the flow of traffic, transversed the zebra-marked crossing, completing their ascension as human deities to "secular immortality," an earthly paradise of celebrity and status and cash. This apotheosis occurred on Abbey Road.

The famous album cover photo for *Abbey Road* was taken in 1969, on Friday, August 8 – the day when in 1570, Blessed John Felton, layman, was martyred in St. Paul's Churchyard and when in 1586, Father John Finglow was martyred at York. The record album became a record-breaking success and the cover itself became both renowned and controversial. The hairy quartet first flew into the entertainment world with the name "the Blackjacks," then they transmogrified into "the Quarrymen," then, at the suggestion of an art school friend of John Lennon, they metamorphosed into "the Beatals," then "the Silver Beetles," then "the Silver Beatles," and finally landed on their renowned simple buggy appellation – "the Beatles." The *Abbey Road* album, released in 1969, came as the boys neared the end of their life-cycle of insectile musical eminence. The "bubble reputation" would soon pop; the singing coleopetras would chirrup together for the last time on this album.

The controversy over the album cover sprang from the rampant rumor that the ambulatory line of pop stars represented a funeral procession, mourning the departed Paul McCartney. John Lennon religiously led the procession in a heavenly white suit, Ringo Starr followed in black as the mourner, George Harrison clad in denim would be the gravedigger and Paul McCartney, barefoot, out of step, stood as a seemingly animated corpse, a member of the walking dead. "Is Paul dead?!" The world waited confirmation or final denial; for years the airwaves buzzed with contentious debate, fan clubs broke into sects over the momentous question, the faithful debated and feared and hoped and mourned.

Many decades have passed. Those still holding to the beliefs of their hippie ancestors, and many of the old balding geezers themselves, assemble from the four corners of the globe, ending their pilgrimages at the lineated pedestrian crossing where the weevily superstars once walked. A webcam broadcasts to the world the images of the staunch zealots who dash into the roadway and for one brief moment stand "in alter Beatle," having retraced the steps of those departed exoskeletons whose sheathed wings have flown away.

Fewer than two miles away from Abbey Road is a small triangular traffic island at the corner of Edgware and Bayswater Roads, just above Hyde Park. A concrete memorial plaque surrounded by brick simply reads "The

The Bishop as a Young Man

Site of Tyburn Tree" with a small cross at its center. The plaque in the center of the traffic island marks where Tyburn Tree stood, the Triple Gallows made from wood with a flat triangular top that allowed multiple criminals to be hanged simultaneously and from which were hanged more than 350 Catholic martyrs, executed by Henry VIII's "new church" of Anglicanism. When most of the victim bodies were drawn and quartered, to the delight of many in the gaping crowd, their blood sank into the English soil. These "rigid" faithful would not worship at the protestant "new mass" of Thomas Cranmer, concocted for the adulterous monarch, nor accept the phony "Virgin Queen" Elizabeth as a substitute for the Blessed Virgin Mary, the Mother of God, Queen of Heaven; they would not bow a knee to political leaders who with satanic pride placed themselves above God's anointed, the head of Christ's Church on earth. They willingly sacrificed their physical bodies for their belief in the Mystical Body of Christ – One, Holy, Catholic, Apostolic.

Hundreds of mechanized motorized machines, insect-like, crawl or fly by the holy site every day without a glance, without a nod, without a prayer; only the occasional rare visitor will brave the oncoming vehicle swarm to race to the spot, kneel and pray his beads in honor of those martyrs. Given the continued apostasy of England and the decline of the "blessed plot" into modern debauchery and decay, a mind fixed in time might question the efficacy of all that sacrifice, all that shed blood. But certainly those hundreds of English souls above wearing martyrs' crowns delight with joy that in an age when apostasy has entered the Roman Catholic Church like "the invisible worm/ That flies in the night/ In the howling storm," the most outspoken, detested, persistent, outrageous, implacable, unyielding, forthright, kindly and charitable Catholic Bishop, the rightful heir to a strong, adamantine, saintly French Archbishop, a true faith warrior, comes from their "precious stone set in the silver sea." "He is an Englishman."

He is an Eng·lish·man

The roots of Richard Nelson Williamson's family tree sink deep into the soil of England but also reach out across the "herring pond" as far as the New World. His father John's family had always been as English as afternoon tea and cricket; his mother Helen's family as American as apple pie, baseball and the Revolutionary War, a conflict in which an ancestor fought. In both branches of the family tree, the genealogy carried revolution, in the paternal line with the Anglican revolution against Rome and in the maternal line with the liberal rallying cry of "freedom" and "independence" from the Motherland of England. Some of his critics might suggest that the future Bishop of Tradition never escaped his revolutionary heritage but remained a rebel all his life (Benedict XVI would one day level this charge against him), but the same accusation was brought against the most prominent Traditional Catholic of the post-conciliar twentieth century, Archbishop Marcel Lefebvre, who would become Richard Williamson's spiritual father, a model for truth-telling and fierce determination in defense of the Catholic Faith. No sensible mind could seriously claim the Archbishop, Catholic and French and traditional to the core, could ever seriously be branded as "revolutionary," other than by those confused Catholics who themselves thwacked the Church topsy-turvy.

The Bishop as a Young Man

The charge can, and should be, dismissed at the outset. A quick glance at the unholy trinity of heretical wreckers who attacked the Mystical Body, sowing tares, crushing the life out of souls and toppling every tower of the civilized world, shows clearly that neither the Archbishop nor his spiritual son could seriously be tarred with the brush of that radical catastrophic juggernaut. Both became notorious in the Age of Apostasy for remaining Catholic to the core and purveying in all its purity Catholic doctrine, whereas the three fathers of the anti-Catholic rebellion rejected the Catholic faith fully and deliberately. The mad monk Martin Luther rejected the idea of pilgrimage to heaven and the moment to moment drama of the individual soul leading to salvation or damnation at the moment of death in favor of a one-time "coming to Jesus" moment where the Man-God's sacrifice washes away all sin in one fell swoop, blind "faith" obliterating any need for "good deeds"; the lecherous monarch Henry VIII, praised in his saner days by Pope Leo X as a "Defender of the Faith," founded his own religion based on libidinous vanity and pronounced himself the head of that "church"; the maniacal John Calvin simply turned God into Ibsen's Button Maker, selecting some buttons from their origin for preservation and tossing others aside as worthless and dispensable; for Calvin those "buttons" were living human souls. God whimsically saved some and damned others.

These fatuous ideas – life without moment to moment spiritual drama, life based on satisfaction of personal desire, and life rendering individuals helpless and dependent – over time gorged on the abundant harvest of Catholic civilization, and, swollen with lunatic pride, set the rotten and false foundation of the modern liberal, i.e. godless, governments. The Archbishop and the Bishop had no commerce with such vagaries of demonic inhuman ideas. They were genuine Defenders of the Faith, especially the immutable doctrines of the Faith, and remained so, despite all obstacles and derogation.

◙

The most ancient of Richard Williamson's recorded ancestors, a great-great-great grandfather James Nelson of McConnellsburg, Pennsylvania (1757–1828) fought as an ordinary soldier against the English during the American Revolutionary War. The last name of Nelson passed down the family tree to the future Bishop's maternal grandfather. The Bishop suggests whimsically, "If I wanted to be a Daughter of the American Revolution, I could be" (especially in the mad modern era's phony construct of so-called "gender fluidity").

The Nelsons had been an established family in Pennsylvania for many generations but Harry Nelson, the maternal grandfather, grew up on a farm in Monroe, Michigan, then an agricultural area, now swallowed and digested by devouring suburbia. Harry Nelson did not pursue farming, however, but became a manager in the leather goods business, eventually being sent to Paris to set up a new shop in the City of Lights. Before the Second World War, he began running his own independent leather goods shop in Paris and became the proprietor of a successful leather factory, noted for making fine saddles. Harry's wife, Olive Nelson, had been a native of Toledo, Ohio. Of Welsh ancestry, she found herself far from the "Buckeye State," living in Paris in the 16th Arrondissement, one of the smartest areas of the city.

Helen Nelson, Richard's mother, thus came to be born and bred in Paris and grew up in a fashionable Paris neighborhood. An only child, she received an education not just from her schooling but also from her rich cultural surroundings and the special attention her "only child" status received. Between the two world wars, she had an opportunity to visit one of her cousins, then living in England. At a party she attended during her visit, she made the acquaintance of Jack William Williamson, Jr., as he had been christened; some years later, displeased with the redundancy in his name, he officially changed it to John Blackburn Williamson, Jr., eliminating the appellative echo and simultaneously honoring his Scottish heritage. John Williamson had grown up in the English Midlands where his ancestors had settled in Nottinghamshire after leaving Scotland. John's mother also had Scottish blood, and came from a line of Blackburns, so his choice of a new middle name paid homage to his mother's side of the family, as his future son's middle name Nelson would honor his mother's family line – Richard Nelson Williamson.

John Williamson along with his two siblings, a brother and a sister, were popular among their peers and had a special gift for organization and skillful administration. The three Williamsons were able to "boss" those around them because they never appeared in the least "bossy," possessing dispassionate objectivity, calm directness and genuine pleasantness. They could manage affairs and direct subordinates without making noise or raising a fuss, probably because they lacked that element that causes so many supervisors to create turbulence around them – ambition.

The Bishop remembers his Aunt Jean with great fondness and speaks of her as a "good woman." Her gift for leadership allowed her to advance high in the ranks of the WRAF, the Woman's Royal Air Force. Her brother John, the father of Richard, began working for Marks and Spencer, the English firm founded in 1884 that gained its success with stores selling clothing, household goods and luxury food items. John rose rapidly through the ranks of the company because of his excellent managerial skills and remained with the company until his retirement at the age of sixty-one. John Williamson had an especially high regard for Sir Simon Marks, the son of the one of the founders of the store, Michael Marks, and expressed a special admiration for the talents and skills of many of the Jewish employees with whom he worked. He passed this admiration on to his son, though many contemporary media-polluted minds might find that fact hard to believe.

John Blackburn Williamson, Jr. lived his life as a middle class gentleman. He was quiet, reserved, intelligent, and non-ostentatious, qualities he passed to his son. Other paternal characteristics that passed to his famous offspring include a lack of ego, profound humility and a reluctance to talk about himself. An affable and outgoing man, John made a point of focusing on the "other" in social situations. After his retirement from Marks and Spenser, he worked as a hospital administrator; precisely because of his genuine interest in individuals, as well as his refusal to become embroiled in medical politics, he had great success in dealing with the "prima donna" doctors who processed along the hospital corridors.

In the 1920s, John had spent time living and working in the Far East but he returned to England in the middle of the 1930s. Shortly after his return he encountered Helen Nelson at the party she graced on her visit from Paris. The sociable middle class gentleman of Scottish ancestry from Nottinghamshire and the cultured expatriate American lady from Paris who spoke perfect French married in 1936 in a civil ceremony. The husband settled into middle class routine, devoting himself to his work at Marks and Spenser, supporting and overseeing his family, and religiously playing golf on Sunday mornings, a modern man dedicated to sport as a sacred pursuit ("And the wind shall say: 'Here were

The Bishop as a Young Man

decent godless people:/ Their only monument the asphalt road/ And a thousand lost golfballs.'") Helen had little interest in things domestic but devoted herself to her home out of love for her husband and her three sons – John Harry, Richard Nelson and Thomas George. The family embodied everything solid and decent in middle class life in the mid twentieth century, a father working diligently to support his wife and children, a mother creating a home of comfort and order and refinement for her husband and her three sons, a Tom, Dick and Harry, who were raised with morality, civility, custom and culture.

Helen filled her free time when her daily chores were completed with music, directing her heart and intellect toward the keyboard. She possessed very fine musical gifts and played the piano with love and excellence, with special fondness for that composer whose genius flowered in the garden of ivory and ebony keys – Frederic Chopin. Her son, recalling her private performances says, "She played much better than I ever played. . . . I never played properly." She did plant a seed by providentially priming her son for future musical inspiration, a providential moment that would open his ears not only to majestic sound but "harmony, heavenly harmony, with which the world began."

The couple got along well and their home created an island of quiet and calm, without quarrels or rows or fracases; those confrontations, common to many "modern" marriages, were not their style. The religious bedrock may not have underlain family life but the soil from which faith could sprout did define the home – order and art, manners and morals, devotion and tranquility. Richard Nelson Williamson began life in this household of harmony in Hampstead, London, on March 8, 1940 – the feast day of St. John of God and the thirtieth anniversary of the founding of International Women's Day, which was to become a national holiday in Soviet Russia shortly after the revolution.

Trumpet Solo

Sacrifice in the family . . . . For heaven's sake, what can the family be without sacrifice? The head of the family is the father, so the sacrifice must start with him. "Husbands, love your wives and be not bitter towards them" (Colossians 3: 19). The husband and father must give up his independence, selfish pursuits, and, all due proportion observed, career and money, to make time for his family, quality time, because by how much time he gives them they will accurately gauge how much he cares for them. In particular his wife needs from him attention, time, and affection, not disproportionately much, but certainly more than many husbands today come up with.

> Love in a man's life is a thing apart,
> 'Tis a woman's whole existence . . . .

Let the woman then sacrifice her own will, her emancipation, her trousers, her money and pseudo-career in order to attain the glorious freedom of motherhood to bring into the world and raise whatever children God sends – "The woman," says St. Paul again, 'shall be saved through childbearing; if she continue in faith, and love, and sanctification, with sobriety" (1 Timothy 2: 15).

—*Letters from the Rector*, No. 192

The Bishop as a Young Man

"The child [who] is father of the man" has fixed as his earliest and longest lasting memory the sound of bombers advancing overhead. The buzzing of the incendiary swarm spoke to the boy and told him that this was not a world in which one could "play with mammets," but, rather, a place of contention, danger, and potent death. The war of false words and phony diplomacy had been replaced by the detonation of real bombs. Germany unleashed the "blitz" one month after the second son arrived in the Williamson household and the planes overhead began to "Pitch like King Billy bomb-balls in," hoping that the enemy island would "lie beaten flat." The attacks continued throughout the summer months of 1940. Marks and Spenser, in preservation mode, moved its company operations out of London to Leicester. John Williamson accompanied the firm to Leicester, not far from his birthplace in Nottinghamshire, settling in a small house in Kibworth, south of Leicester. The "blitz" ended in May 1941, but the sound of planes kept echoing overhead for the remainder of the war years.

Pleasant memories also sealed themselves on the malleable young mind. Visits to and from the boy's maternal grandparents stand out. He fondly remembers his maternal grandfather, Harry Nelson, as "a tall, generous, expansive man." Grandfather Harry loved films and would regularly take his grandsons to the movies during his visits to England; afterwards, he would slip them half a crown. Mother Helen would play along with her father's surreptitious generosity, feigning surprise and asking, "Now where did you get that from?!" In Paris the grand old gentlemanly grandfather would take the family to a restaurant and in a charitable mixture of generosity and trust would hand his wallet to the waiter with a simple instruction, "Look after us," an action recalled many years later by his grandson as being "typical of Americans."

Harry Nelson also had the deep-seated and now sadly vanished American love of card playing and he passed that fondness to his grandson Richard. Card parties were for decades a source of entertainment, social bonding and good fellowship for millions of Americans, even those living abroad. And when no party could be arranged, playing solitaire was an acceptable substitute. Grandfather Harry transmitted to his grandson a love of "spider solitaire," a game played in the modern technological age with cards appearing on a computer screen rather than being held in the hand. The temptation to indulge in this hereditary delight still maintains its strong appeal, forcing the removal of the game from more than one episcopal computer and proving that some of the seemingly smallest sacrifices may indeed be the most onerous.

One visit to Paris stands out in his memory. One night the boy received permission to sit with the "grown-ups" at a dinner party. Before the event, he had been given a small toy gadget with an inflatable tube that when pressed would expand in size. When no one was looking, the young trickster would hide the device under a dinner plate and then press the tube, inflating it and causing the plate to move suddenly and unexpectedly. Such a prank would delight most children; here the delight was doubled as the adults, kindly, pretended not to know what had caused the plate to be set in motion. One might say that years later the innocent joy of a playful imp would be replaced by the knowing truth-telling of a dedicated man that would upset more than dinner plates on the world-wide table.

The Williamsons returned home to London from Kibworth following the war. They bought a larger house so the Nelsons from Paris could live with them but have their own separate apartment. The older couple, however, had come to love Paris and had no desire to leave.

The Bishop as a Young Man

Harry Nelson died in France in the early 1950s and his wife spent her last years, as so many of the elderly do now, in a home, her mind faded and confused. When she would ask after her husband, "Where's Harry?," the gentle and comforting response would be, "He's on a business trip to Belgium."

The post-war Williamson domestic life remained simple, calm and serene. John Williamson possessed woodworking skills and enjoyed building, so he had a carpenter's shop at home, stocked with tools. His son Richard learned to saw and hammer and sand. Though he never reached, he says, his father's level of excellence (just as he never matched his mother's ability at the keyboard), nevertheless, he learned enough to build years later when he taught in Ghana a solid stool and a functional gate.

But before teaching, one must be taught oneself. The modern world has so debased education that the students lack basic skills and the teachers, themselves once students mired in the morass, have not acquired them either. What can they pass on? Such was not the case in England in the late 1940's. A solid, beneficial and rewarding traditional classical education existed for many students. From his earliest years, Richard Williamson benefited from such an education.

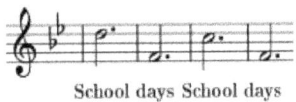
School days School days

"While spending the Christmas time of 1085 in Gloucester, William [the First, the 'Conqueror'] had deep speech with his counsellors and sent men all over England to each shire to find out what or how much each landholder had in land and livestock, and what it was worth." So relates the *Anglo-Saxon Chronicle* in describing what many have called the first official government census. The survey upon completion had the imposing appellation the "Domesday Book" placed on it, for as Richard FitzNigel would write nearly a hundred years later in 1179, "the sentence of that strict and terrible and last account cannot be evaded by any skillful subterfuge, so when this book is appealed to . . . its sentence cannot be put, quashed or set aside with impunity. That is why we have called the book 'the Book of Judgment' . . . because its decisions, like those of the Last Judgment, are unalterable."

In that impressive and ominous sounding tome, mention is made of a church located at Leatherhead. No mention is made of a town or citizens, cattle or landholders, flocks or forest. Leatherhead in Surrey, south of London, is designated only as a "Church." Nearly 900 years later, young Richard Williamson at the age of six went to the town of Leatherhead where the local church, Catholic in 1086, was now occupied by rebels of a false religion, a religion the boy had been handed as his own.

Leatherhead had another distinction bestowed on it by religious revolutionaries. On February 23, 1791, John Wesley, a lapsed Anglican who sowed and nurtured the tares of Methodism (and who first coined the phrase "agree to disagree") delivered his last public sermon in Leatherhead, appropriately enough on a bluff named "Bull Hill." Less than a week later, Wesley stood before God for judgment.

Over the years, Leatherhead also acquired some artistic fame. Edmund Tilney, the Master of the Revels to Queen Elizabeth I and who thus approved all the plays penned during her reign by the "upstart crow" from Stratford-on-Avon, lived in the Leatherhead Mansion House. Some two centuries later, Jane Austen visited relatives in Leatherhead at the time of the composition of *Emma* and many claim that "Highbury," the novel's prominent setting, is modeled on the town. In recent years, the Surrey Sound recording studio has given to the world the pop musical excrescences of the Police, Siouxsie and the Banshees, the Lotus Eaters, Alternative TV (all larvae laid by the Beatles), as well as the most famous burble of the local punk band named Head – "Nothing to Do in a Town like Leatherhead."

bb

The six-year-old boy Richard Nelson Williamson arrived in Leatherhead in 1946 to attend Downsend School. Looking back from the perspective of age, the elder Williamson describes the small educational establishment as "a very good preparatory school." The seven years of study laid the foundation for what he calls in retrospect "a very good education." Downsend School, established in 1891 as a "first school" for boys to the age of thirteen, has as its motto "Nihi Virtuti Invium," "Nothing is denied to valour," a sentiment that one of its most famous, or infamous depending on one's perspective, students would exhibit to a remarkable degree in later years.

Downsend provided the bedrock for solid future education because it was, in His Excellency's words, "a well-run school." Cedric Lindford, the headmaster, a tall, straight, silver-haired gentleman of no ego, knew who he was and what he was expected to do, so he did it well. Headmaster Lindford would tell parents that he knew his trade and knew how to handle boys, thanks to the "automaticness of the basic assumptions." The school existed to make boys learn the basics, to teach them discipline, to promote natural decency and courteous civility, and, most importantly, to prepare them to receive scholarships to prestigious public schools, the name the English give to their private schools. Of course, no education is possible without real regard on the part of the educators toward the pupils entrusted to them. The faculty at Downsend acknowledged the ultimate goals, but also displayed the necessary affection toward the students. The Bishop remembers fondly an array of genuine personalities and demanding teachers – Mr. Sykes, the French instructor, Mr. German who taught Latin, Mr. Straker and Miss Sykes the mathematics teachers, and especially Miss White, an unmarried, towering, matronly figure with a booming voice who oversaw the junior school with a kindly, motherly manner, caring for the boys who became the children she herself never birthed.

None of the personalities could ever be called "professional educators" in the modern, pseudo-scientific sense; they held no abstract theories from education courses that have taken the place of the study of real academic subjects, theories that have cracked the bones of real education and devoured the marrow of schools. Those who stood before the classes at Downsend "simply taught boys. Period." The teachers knew boys; when necessary, they would knock them around, but given the nature of the school and the leadership, such measures were only slight and occasional. The headmaster and the teachers, the parents and the boys knew why the school existed and what work was worth doing. No tinge of Catholicism touched any corner of Downsend which was Church of England from dormers to dustbin, but a natural value system, universal at that time, defined every part of the school, so all shared a common purpose and worked together toward a common civilized goal. "More than a mechanical conveyor belt, more than an educational military march, Downsend was human, filled with the power of shared and unquestioned principles," says the former pupil.

No such commonality exists today. The obligatory "Mission Statement" of Downsend in 2012 states, "We encourage our pupils to become well-rounded individ-

The Bishop as a Young Man

uals in a modern society." One cannot help but be reminded of the exchange that concludes Evelyn Waugh's novella *Scott-King's Modern Europe*, published in 1947, a year when the young Master Williamson was studying at Downsend. The headmaster of "Grandchester" tells the classics teacher Scott-King that the new school year will begin with fifteen fewer classical studies students. The reason?

> "Parents are not interested in producing the 'complete man' any more. They want to qualify their boys for jobs in the modern world. You can hardly blame them, can you?"
>
> "Oh, yes," said Scott-King. "I can and do."
>
> . . . .
>
> "I wonder if you will consider taking some other subject as well as the classics?
>
> History, for example, preferably economic history?"
>
> "No, headmaster."
>
> . . . .
>
> "Then what do you intend to do?"
>
> "If you approve, headmaster, I will stay as I am here as long as any boy wants to read the classics. I think it would be very wicked indeed to do anything to fit a boy for the modern world."

a - ny-thing goes.

The bright young student devoured learning with relish, digested the solid material being offered and grew in knowledge and alacrity of intellect; he quickly climbed the Downsend success ladder, arriving in the "top class" with a year to spare, and so spent an extra year absorbing added benefits. He concluded his Downsend years well-drilled and well-prepared. As the Downsend school had as one of its main goals to prepare boys for further education, the ideal was for a boy to win a scholarship to one of the most prestigious schools in England – Eton, Harrow or Winchester. Of the three, Winchester had the most glowing reputation as a challenging and rewarding center of intellectual study. The young Williamson, being a bright lad who had demonstrated his ability to use his special gifts, was put forward by Downsend to try for a scholarship at Winchester.

Headmaster Lindford notified the Williamson family of the potential honor. John Williamson took time away from his Marks and Spencer work to take his son to Winchester where the young scholar would sit for several days for multiple exams, exams that could provide the key to unlock the entrance to Winchester College, as it was called. Winchester College did not use the Common Entrance Exam used by the other prestigious public schools; this guaranteed the Winchester "experience" would be viewed as very selective and very demanding from its start. Boys who wished to enter a 'Commoner house" could take an exam with the headmaster of the house, followed by an interview; those boys who wished to apply to the College had to sit for a different, more difficult exam, called an "Election." Success in the three or four days of exams, such as Richard Williamson undertook in 1956, could result in a scholarship that would reduce the tuition and boarding fees by two-thirds. The exams were thus understandably not only highly formidable but also highly competitive.

The exams completed, days of waiting followed, but culminated in the arrival of good news. Richard Nelson Williamson received a scholarship to Winchester and became the pride of Downsend. Little did the young student suspect that this success would be the pinnacle of his scholarly achievement in a worldly sense. He would soon be distracted from school work and further achievement in his studies by serious and disturbing questions pertaining to lived life. The golden worm of doubt gnawed its way into the academic apple.

Winchester Cathedral, begun in 1079, is one of the largest cathedrals in the world, having the longest nave and overall the greatest length. It rises majestically in the city of Winchester in the county of Hampshire in southeast England. In 642, just north of the present structure, an earlier cathedral was erected known as Old Minster, but that ancient edifice was demolished in 1093 when the new Cathedral was consecrated. Old Minster saw the coronation of King Edward I, St. Edward the Confessor, the only English King to be canonized, "sundry blessings hang about his throne/ That speak him full of grace." The monastic buildings, the cloister and the chapel house of the Cathedral were demolished in the mid-sixteenth century when Henry VIII imposed his new apostate religion. The Cathedral witnessed the marriage of the King's Catholic daughter Mary Tudor to King Philip II of Spain in 1554 and watches over the bones of St. Swithun, the patron saint of the Cathedral who died in 862, as well as the grave of Jane Austen who died in Winchester in 1817. It is certainly the only Cathedral to be memorialized in two pop music hit songs, the first – "Winchester Cathedral " by the New Vaudeville Band ("You're bringing me down/ You stood and you watched as / My baby left town . . . . Oh-bo-de-o-do, oh-bo-de-o-do . . . ," etc.) which climbed to #1 on the pop charts in 1966, and the second by Crosby, Stills, Nash and Young in 1977, a song simply called "Cathedral."

The cathedral city of Winchester grew out of a Roman settlement and served as the capital of the old Kingdom of Wessex from the late 600s until it was sacked by the Danes in 860. The old Roman street plan, cross-shaped, remains to this day in the system overlaid on it by Alfred the Great, the King of Wessex, in the ninth century; a City Cross, known as the Buttercross as farmers sold their wares at its base on market days, dates to the fifteenth century. The Buttercross is surrounded by statues of the Virgin Mary, as well as statues of saints and other historical figures. Fewer than two years before his death from tuberculosis at the age of 25 in 1821, John Keats resided in Winchester where he wrote "Isabella," "St. Agnes Eve," sections of "Hyperion," and one of the greatest of his "Odes," one of the most exquisite of all English poems, "To Autumn."

Verbal Music Interlude

I.

Season of mists and mellow fruitfulness,
  Close bosom-friend of the maturing sun;
Conspiring with him how to load and bless
  With fruit the vines that round the thatch-eves run;
To bend with apples the moss'd cottage-trees,
  And fill all fruit with ripeness to the core;
    To swell the gourd, and plump the hazel shells
  With a sweet kernel; to set budding more,
And still more, later flowers for the bees,
Until they think warm days will never cease,
    For Summer has o'er-brimmed their clammy cells.

II.

Who hath not seen thee oft amid thy store?

The Bishop as a Young Man

    Sometimes whoever seeks abroad may find
      Thee sitting careless on a granary floor,
    Thy hair soft-lifted by the winnowing wind;
    Or on a half-reap'd furrow sound asleep,
      Drows'd with the fume of poppies, while thy hook
        Spares the next swath and all its twined flowers:
    And sometimes like a gleaner thou dost keep
      Steady thy laden head across a brook;
    Or by a cider-press, with patient look,
      Thou watchest the last oozings hours by hours.

III.

Where are the sounds of Spring? Ay, where are they?
    Think not of them, thou hast thy music too –
White barred clouds bloom the soft-dying day,
    And touch the stubble-plains with rosy hue;
Then in a wailful choir the small gnats mourn
    Among the river sallows, borne aloft
      Or sinking as the light wind lives or dies;
And full-grown lambs loud bleat from hilly bourn;
    Hedge-crickets sing; and now with treble soft
The red-breast whistles from a garden-croft;
    And gathering swallows twitter in the skies.

In the springtime of his years at the age of 13, young Richard arrived in Winchester in the county of Hampshire, seat of Winchester Cathedral and home to a public school for boys, Winchester College, an educational establishment with the longest unbroken history of any school in England.

WIN–CHES–TER CA–THE – DRAL

The Voice of the Trumpet

William of Wykeham, Bishop of Winchester and Chancellor to both King Edward III and Richard II, founded the *Collegium Sanctae Mariae prope Winchester*, Saint Mary's College near Winchester, in 1382. For centuries the renowned school for boys had sent out its graduates to higher education and distinguished positions in all areas of English life. The alumni rolls can boast of prominent political figures, statesmen, lawyers, businessmen, sports stars, doctors, actors, poets, essayists, journalists, novelists, theatrical producers, archbishops and bishops and priests (genuine and apostate), Lord Chancellors, Poet Laureates, Prime Ministers, composers, museum directors, shipbuilders, media moguls, field marshals, ambassadors, literary critics, archeologists, codebreakers, economists, historians and a host of cricketers. In its long list of distinguished alumni the school includes the name of Richard Williamson, identified as "controversial bishop."

By 1953, Winchester College had been stewed in Anglicanism for centuries, and as in an overcooked meal, the defining flavors had long since been steamed and simmered away. Only the memory of its tangy past informed the habitual mandatory worship of its bland present.

In its earliest centuries, however, Winchester College had been steeped in the true faith and had produced great Catholic leaders. None were more eminent than those "Wykehamists," as graduates were called, who held firmly to the Catholic faith as the apostate poison of Henry VIII seeped throughout the land. A few should be remembered and honored by their later fellow Catholics in the Mystical Body:

- Father Henry Cole (1500–1580), the Catholic priest who preached the sermon on the occasion of the

The Bishop as a Young Man

execution by fire of Thomas Cranmer; Fr. Cole elucidated why a repentant sinner should nevertheless still be burned at the stake for gross heresy; Elizabeth I, her father's obedient apostate daughter, upon her ascension to the throne, imprisoned Fr. Cole in Fleet Prison where he remained until his death in 1580

- Bishop John White (1510–1560), the devout Bishop of Winchester who was removed from his position by Elizabeth in 1559 and died in prison the following year

- Father Nicholas Sanders (1530–1581), the faithful priest who wrote the first account of the suffering Roman Catholics in England during the protestant persecution, *De visibili Monarchia Ecclesiae*

- Father Henry Garnet (1555–1606), the superior of the underground Jesuit priests in England, referred to by Shakespeare in "The Phoenix and the Turtle" as the "treble-dated crow [1555]/ That thy sable gender makest [who ordains new priests into the black-robed Jesuit order]/ With the breath thou givest and takest . . . [by speaking the words of ordination]"; Father Garnet spoke of the "intolerable burden of loneliness" he carried during those difficult years; he was executed by hanging, drawing and quartering in St. Paul's Churchyard on May 3, 1606, for his alleged role in the Gunpowder Plot (perhaps one of the earliest and most successful "false flag" events); at his death, he professed his innocence and noted that his execution was taking place on the Feast of the Holy Cross (this feast day was removed from the calendar by John XXIII in 1960).

Honor does not accrue to all Winchester graduates during the time of persecution. Winchester College also educated Archbishop of Canterbury William Warham (1450–1532), who wrote to Pope Clement VII, urging the Pontiff to accede to King Henry VIII's demands for separation from his legitimate spouse; Archbishop Warham also was appointed as counselor to Queen Katherine and offered her little spiritual or practical assistance, later excusing his behavior by stating he did not want to enrage the King for *ira principis mors est* ("the king's anger is death").

In the twentieth century, Evelyn Waugh tweaked the education and resulting pride of graduates of Winchester College by saying, "These Wykehamists have the kind of mind that likes to relax by composing Alcaics on the moving parts of toy trains."

Winchester College also educated men as varied and influential as John Davies and Sir Thomas Browne, Thomas Otway and Anthony Trollope, Rupert D'Oyly Carte and Christopher Dawson. Richard Williamson never found a home at Winchester College. He arrived at the school founded during the reign of King Richard II as a successful young student filled with promise, but departed five years later, during the reign of Queen Elizabeth II, a cynical, confused, uncertain young man; he had also become an atheist. The young man who graduated from Winchester could well have descended into pessimism and isolation or exploded with anger and virulent liberalism, but grace spared him. Perhaps during those less than happy years, the Blessed Mother looked down on him with benevolent eyes. A statue of the Virgin Mary stood unmolested over the entryway into the College, looming too high for the Anglicans or the puritans to have it torn down during their years of apostasy and revolution. Her motherly gaze would hold the student until the day when he would become her devoted son, and for many years beyond.

The Bishop as a Young Man

1. A -ve Ma-rí- a,

The student never felt completely at home at Winchester because he sensed that he was out of place socially. Most of the other boys had rolled in on the same easy street that had brought their fathers to the prestigious school. These gilded boys came from privilege and breathed headier social air. Young Williamson inhaled the common breath of the middle class.

His earlier education at Downsend had been an unquestioned process – values were to be accepted, thinking was to be rote learning, schooling was drill: translate this sentence from the Latin, translate that sentence into French, solve this problem in geometry, memorize these dates in history. He had been a docile boy and managed the drill well. Winchester offered more of the same. As his new housemaster instructed the newcomers, "Winchester combines Athens and Sparta, Athenian study, Spartan drill." Drill for the mind, drill for the body, drill, drill, drill . . . . What had been accepted without question by the boy at Downsend proved insufficient for the young man at Winchester. Drill was not enough to sustain a mind whose switch had been turned to "on," a mind whose horizons were expanding as rapidly as dawning day could provide new light. Young Williamson began asking questions, of himself and his actions, if not directly yet of his superiors.

During the first year or two, the boys had to be "processed through" the Anglican church. This unquestioned assumption supposed that all the boys came from Anglican families and therefore would be formed along Anglican lines, an end easily accomplished by more drill, in this case, drill for the soul. At first the young man, having been trained to accept and follow, went along unquestioningly with the unquestioned assumptions. He was "confirmed" in the Anglican sect. Slowly, however, and not consciously at first, uneasiness set in and dissatisfaction gripped him, even as he made himself go through all the required motions with proper public piety. Then the uneasiness began "to heat the deep" and kraken-like began to "roaring . . . rise." Specific questions demanded answers: "Why Anglican?" "What does it mean to be 'Anglican'?" "Why am I pretending to be 'Anglican' when I don't know what it is or what it means?" He continued to study as an Athenian and to sport as a Spartan. The student applied himself to Greek and Latin, the athlete went to the playing fields, the seemingly-pious youth attended chapel. The internal turmoil, however, lasted not only for a "winter of discontent," but festered and metastasized during all five years at Winchester.

    None of the teachers ever saw the symptoms or diagnosed the onset and spread of the "malaise." They never saw the strengthening spiritual discomfort. They felt no need to be close to the students or form the personal bonds that allow young men to ask questions of their elders, to seek guidance or find direction from them. The instructors taught their subjects, and some taught very well. The Bishop speaks highly of Classics Master Colin Badcock whom he remembers so fondly that he has visited the elder teacher on two or three occasions in later years. The best teachers tried to inspire, some with genuine fervor. One, an old stooped instructor, gave a fiery talk in the chantry one day, words of passion and strong convictions, spoken from the heart of his deepest beliefs; unfortunately, those beliefs centered on the values and glories of the British Empire, known by young Williamson to be shrinking and dying as he had observed on the history maps at Downsend; with the passing years, the red washes of the Empire showed themselves diminish-

The Bishop as a Young Man

ing so precipitously that the sun would clearly soon set on it. The teachers understandably tried to prepare the boys to endure life as they had endured life. The brilliant classicist John Stowe who taught Hobbes, Locke and Rousseau to his students also taught them how to spice their essays with the pungency of cynicism. He was a molder of youth who was himself kind and decent and brilliant, but godless and spiritually depleted.

Williamson began to absorb the negative modern outlook. The heartfelt sentimentality of his early essays, such as one recounting the melancholy felt on sailing away from the White Cliffs of Dover and the subsequent joy on seeing them again on the return, soon crumbled to sandy cynicism; the last few bluebirds flew far away. Sarcasm washed away sentimentality; youthful optimism expired under newly learned worldly-wise pessimism; the larger acute questions went unanswered.

At the same time, on a stage in the West End of London, the theatre district, a new character appeared. His name was Jimmy Porter and the play by playwright John Osborne was called *Look Back in Anger*. Osborne captured the rage rising in many young men of all classes throughout England. At Winchester, a young scholar began to look around and his anger grew. He looked forward with hopelessness. He took his stand and unfurled his banner in the manner countless young students would for years to come – the banner of unbelief. He began to let his classmates know his chapel attendance was merely *pro forma*. He had by this time in his stay at Winchester risen to the level of prefect, but his discomfort and irritation at chapel services became more noticeable. He intended to be noticed; he would no longer pretend piety but would sit coldly, unmoved and unmoving, with his eyes tight shut. His demonstrative and ostentatious denial resulted in a reprimand from the Headmaster, Sir Henry Desmond Pritchard, a classics scholar and the translator of Plato's

The Voice of the Trumpet

Republic for Penguin Classics. The Headmaster pulled the ornery prefect aside and said, "Well, my boy, you know, you have been seen at chapel . . . and your behavior has been noticed. . . . Faith, my boy, is like a chessboard; there are black squares and white squares. And sometimes you believe and sometimes you don't believe . . . . " Such was the single response to a multitude of doubts; this was the answer age and wisdom offered to questioning and doubting youth. This was the spiritual nourishment on which a young man was meant to live?

So Jimmy Porter in the West End stormed about the stage, looking back in anger, and Richard Williamson at Winchester gloomed about the school, the beliefs and values of the past, having been dwindling down to a precious few over the years, existed only as moribund words. The young, despairing of such nonsense, turned to the theatre of anger and absurdity; they turned to the music of rock and jazz; they found that the underworld of the beats and the hip in its protest and rejection at least possessed life and energy. And thus the time was ripe for four mop-headed rock stars emerging from Liverpool shortly thereafter to sweep the board, knocking all the pieces to the ground in a decisive endgame; they became the new idols of the young; they would be worshipped for years.

I-mag-ine there's no heav-en.

Trumpet Solo

Of course Rock can make its stars into millionaires, but money is never the ultimate explanation, the question being mere-

The Bishop as a Young Man

ly pushed one stage further back – *why* does this kind of music and not that kind make so much money? Answer, because it is "hitting the spot," it is filling a need.

Nor may adults dodge the accusation that Rock flings in their face, by saying that skillful managers like Brian Epstein of the Beatles see an opportunity to exploit, and merely create the kind of music to exploit it. For indeed musicians are creators, and all down history they have created new kinds of music. But they do not create in a vacuum. What they create is to a considerable extent shaped by what they sense in their audience. Brian Epstein did not create the Beatles out of whole cloth, but out of the vibrations he was picking up from British youth in the early 1960's, and it is because he read the vibrations correctly that the Beatles achieved wealth and fame . . . .

Western adults, if they care at all for their youth, must pay attention to the message. Surely the message is, precisely, that the adults do not care! "Rock music is one long, unheard, scream for help . . . ."

—*Letters from the Rector*, No. 158

Help!

Help arrived unexpectedly.

A common saying among musicians states that when the angels play music for God, they play Bach; when they play music for each other, they play Mozart. Pope Gregory the Great says in a homily, "It avails nothing to take part in the feasts of men, if we fail to take part in the feasts of angels." Surely we are first attracted to the "feasts of angels" by the beauty that echoes from their joy and their glory. Mozart, perhaps more than any other composer, captured that joyful beauty, the glory of the feasting angels. And to take in those unique sounds is to be brought closer to the Divine Nature itself. The Angelic Doctor says, "The human soul is moved in various ways according to various melodies of sound . . . hence the use of music in the divine praises is a salutary institution, that the faint-hearted may be the more incited to devotion."(*Summa Theologiæ* II-II, Q. 91, Art. 2). And so more than a century and a half after his death the small man and gentle soul from Salzburg began to pull a distraught youth up from out the "slough of despond" and place him on a pilgrim's path, leading upward.

In his second year at Winchester, the fourteen year old Richard Nelson Williamson, starved of soul and souring inside from the lack of spiritual nutrition, turned to music. "It was nourishment I needed and I found it in Mozart." None of the studies, none of the teachers, none of the chapel services had provided the necessary sustenance; Mozart did. Helen, his mother, had filled the home with music and had seen that her son learned the rudiments of "tickling the ivories." He might protest in later years that he could never play as well as his mother, but he could play. Within the calm comfort of the nest she had created, notes sounded, and the nest and the maternal love and the lessons and the music had prepared the interior terrain of sense to allow the seed to grow, illumined by sunlight and watered by a mist of melancholy; love of Mozart grew in the well-cultivated garden of the heart.

The Bishop as a Young Man

Trumpet Solo

In 2005 at a meeting of seminary professors at Écône, Father Puga stated, 'Today all of the seminarians need personal, psychological tender loving care.' When I arrived at Écône in 1972, no such personal care was needed; in 2005 it is essential. There is something lacking in the family. Mothers aren't mothers, fathers aren't fathers. They are all running around like chickens with their heads cut off and they have neither time nor understanding. The family is gone. The television has destroyed the family. The young men coming to the seminary have the faith, they have good will, they have courage, all precious qualities, but they are lacking in what the Germans call (*Nestwärme*), the warmth of the nest. They are emotionally deprived. This is a widespread condition – something is missing. It is analogous to what I was looking for at Winchester.

The seeker found what he was looking for and found it first in Mozart, perhaps because he had known (*Nestwärme*), built by a sacrificing mother with the support of a governing father, or, perhaps, because the Blessed Mother herself saw this soul needed her intercession to become fully her child. The young man found a refuge, not a hiding place but an elevated peak, at the keyboard. "From harmony, from heav'nly harmony/ This universal frame began . . . " and the fingers turning notes on the score into such harmony caused reverberations in the soul.

The time at the piano also led to a greater love, devotion to the music of another composer who Mozart himself had predicted "one day will make a great noise in the world" (—Ludwig van Beethoven). In the College at

The Voice of the Trumpet

Winchester, five halls had been set aside for study. Each hall had a cubicle where a student could retreat for some leisure during study time. Each separate cubicle had in it an old gramophone and a stack of 78 rpm recordings. One day during a study break, the young scholar picked up a stack of twelve 78s and put them one by one on the gramophone. He could not identify the composer, Ludwig van Beethoven, nor did he know what the music was; he placed the first disc on the old gramophone, lowered the needle onto the record and the bold, forceful opening chords of the Symphony #3 in E-flat Major, Opus 55, grabbed him instantly. The music held him then and still holds him today; the "Eroica Symphony," as it is popularly known, remains his favorite work in the vast musical repertoire. A stack of six 78s of the Symphony #5 in c minor, Opus 67, hit the turntable immediately after the "Eroica." A life-long bond of deep devotion had been born. As the older man once quipped, "When they exhume my corpse, they will find Beethoven still written on my heart."

If Mozart had given the young man a glimpse of higher realms with its classical order, bold innocence and gentle melancholy, Beethoven in the "Eroica" Symphony marched forth with heroism and courage, the bold steps in sound asserting both glory and defiance, as poet John Berryman phrased it in his poem "Beethoven Triumphant": "This world is of male energy male pain." The Fifth Symphony exuded titanic struggle, the battle with fate, wrestling with anger and despair, but with the rage and rebellion structured and ordered, and, most importantly, promising at the end a glorious victory over the arrogant self and the disdainful world, expressed through music proclaiming the nobility of the spirit and the triumph of truth. The grey shallows of the everyday life at Winchester, the duty and drill, the dead classes and the dying ideals, the wispy husks of a burned out

The Bishop as a Young Man

apostate "faith" could all be forgotten in the promise of the music; the ideals survived in the great art and promised the greatest glories could never be lost for good. The call of those trumpets summoned him.

For a time, the student had taken some comfort stewing in the grim pessimism of the novels of Thomas Hardy, the architect turned novelist who at least offered well-structured narratives to order a dark vision. But with the infusion of renewal found in the fruitful oases of Mozart and Beethoven, the appetite for understanding moved beyond the gramophone and the piano to the bookstalls for further study.

In his 70's, the Bishop could look back on his early formative years and name five specific titles that were essential milestones in his pilgrimage to Eternal Rome and Holy Mother Church. The first two were purchased when he was fourteen, after he had discovered the power and the glory of great music. Both were volumes in the Master Musicians series, *Mozart* by Eric Blom and *Beethoven* by Marion Scott. He still carries both books with him and can still, over six decades later, praise them as "very well done." Each of the landmark books "marked" him and contributed to his formation. As each of the five appears in this account of his early development, appropriate excerpts seem in order.

Book 1.

The fact is . . . that his music has an infinity of meanings. Mr. W. J. Turner has suggested that you cannot tell whether in the last resort Mozart's music is sad or merry, and the observation is perfectly just. The only thing you can tell, it may be added, is that it is never purely joyous in the way that, for instance, Haydn's finales so often are. It may be *expressive* of joy, to be sure, but it is never *productive* of it without some alloy of sadness, not to say bitterness. Listen to anything of his that is apparently purely pleasurable – the bubbling finale of this C Major Symphony last mentioned [K. 338] is as good an example as any other – and you may at any moment feel like bursting into tears. And the more perfect the composition happens to be, the nearer will you come to that strange well of bitter waters. But then, could anything be more poignant to human beings than perfection, unattainable in life even by such a being as Mozart himself, but magically conquered by him in art?

—Eric Blom, *Mozart*, London: J. M. Dent, 1935, pp. 195–196.

"[An angel] inclines the will as something lovable, and as manifesting some created good ordered to God's goodness. And thus he can incline the will to the love of the creature or of God, by way of persuasion."

—*Summa Theologiæ* I, Q. 106, A.2

The Bishop as a Young Man

Book 2.

Whether he was so ill that he anticipated death, or whether he had not altogether mastered the temptation to suicide, no one will ever know; but on 6th October [1802] he wrote the "Heiligenstadt Will" – a document designed for his brothers in what he felt to be the near event of his death. Every sentence vibrates with profound feeling:

> O my fellow men, who consider me, or who describe me as, unfriendly, peevish or even misanthropic, how greatly do you wrong me. For you do not know the secret reason why I appear to you to be so. Ever since my childhood my heart and soul have been imbued with the tender feeling of good will; and I have always been ready to perform even great actions. But just think, for the last six years my hopes of being cured [of deafness] have gradually been shattered and finally I have been forced to accept the prospect of a *permanent infirmity* . . . . I must live quite alone and may creep into society only as often as sheer necessity demands; I must live like an outcast . . . . *Patience* – that is the virtue, I am told, which I must now choose for my guide; and I now possess it – I hope that I shall persist in my resolve to endure to the end . . . . Almighty God, who look down into my innermost soul, you see into my heart and you know it is filled with love for humanity and a desire to do good.

—Marion M. Scott, *Beethoven*,
London: J. M. Dent, 1934, p. 49.

The Voice of the Trumpet

Interviewer: "What do you think of Beethoven?"
Ringo Starr: "Great, especially his poems."

> —First Beatles' press conference upon their arrival in the United States, February 7, 1964

Blessed Thomas Sherwood.

> —layman, martyred at Tyburn, February 7, 1578

"Roll Over, Beethoven."

> —The first number played at the Beatles' first live U.S. concert in Washington, D.C., February 11, 1964

Father Francis Levison.

> —priest, starved to death in prison at Worcester, February 11, 1679

The music and the books, the struggle and the heroism, the joy and the bitter sadness, the lift and the resolve,

The Bishop as a Young Man

these new-found escape routes from the drill drudgery and stultifying disillusionment prevented a descent into permanent atheism. And the blessing of friendship supported the spirit as well. One of the brightest boys in the school, sharp but modest, became a life-long friend. Nicholas Richardson had also found a means of sustenance in music, his taste at that young age influenced by an American teacher, Anita Blake, whose love of Puccini kindled a similar passion in her pupil. The friends walked through their Winchester years behaving as expected and learning what was required, but living internally with the emptiness of routine filled with the mystery and majesty of sound.

Such life-long friends are a special gift. Nicholas, an eventual convert to Catholicism, now married with four children and a retired Don of Classics at Oxford, stepped forward in 2009 when the world had its heyday savaging his old friend, now a "controversial bishop" as the Distinguished Alumni List at Winchester names him. Responding to an attack in the English *Catholic Herald*, Nicholas Richardson stated in a letter that the hateful character the *Herald* had presented bore no likeness whatsoever to the man he had been privileged to know as a friend for many, many years.

The five years at Winchester passed. Subjects mastered, Latin and Greek especially well learned, much music absorbed, but the underlying gnawing of discontent did not entirely disappear. Friend Nicholas had distinguished himself at his studies and carried off eight or nine prizes at graduation ceremonies. Richard did not repeat his Downsend success. The only laurel garnered by him was awarded for French recitation, a speech from Victor Hugo's drama *Ruy Blas*. The speech, an angry tirade by the hero-statesman directed to the corrupt politicos around him, offered an opportunity. The young Williamson had the heat in him to deliver it with appropriate burning fire and barely controlled rage, fueled as he was by resentment against those assembled Masters who had deprived him of something intangible he gnawingly knew he desperately needed, even if he could not identify the yearning at the time.

> O ministres integres!
> Conseillers vertueux! Voila votre facon
> De servir, serviteurs qui pillez la maison!
> Donc vous n'avez pas honte et vous choisissez l'heure
> L'heure sombre oùu l'Espagne agonisante pleure!
> Donc vous n'avez ici pas d'autres intérêts
> Qui remplir votre poche et vous enfuir apres!
> Soyez fletris, devant votre pays qui tombe,
> Fossoyeurs qui venez le voler dans sa tombe!

> [O virtuous statesmen!
> Most faithful senators! This is the way
> You serve! False stewards who loot your master's house!
> And lacking shame, you choose the darkest hour,
> The time when Spain cries out and sinks toward death.
> You have no other interests, you traitors,
> Who pillage, fill your pockets and fly away.
> Wither and die, before your country falls –
> Gravediggers! Coming to rob him in his tomb!]

Ruy Blas, Act 3, Scene 2.

The speech, some thirty lines of French verse, allowed ample opportunity to display an expertise in French recitation, but surely the angry subtext contributed to the award.

The Bishop as a Young Man

In the late 1960's, Richard Williamson returned to Winchester to visit the decent upstanding Headmaster who still oversaw the school.

"Oh, yes, you were here in the 1950's. Well, the school is somewhat different now, you know. Back in the 1950's, the school was easier to run because the lower boys admired and imitated the upper boys and the upper boys admired and imitated the adults. But now since the Beatles, instead of the lower class admiring the upper class, the high society boys want to imitate the boys in the street so values are completely upside down. Back in the 1950's, it was easier to get the boys to try to be perfect, easier to teach them, but now . . . ."

What next?

"I didn't know what to do. I stayed on the conveyor belt because I had no other conveyor belt to step onto."

So the young man moved forward not by an act of the will but because the manufactured social conveyance moved one forward. The University became the next stop because the belt moved Winchester graduates on to the University. Why go to the University? Because that is what everyone does.

Before his first term began at Cambridge University, however, the recent graduate and his friend visited Salzburg, home of Mozart and of one of the finest summer music festivals on the continent. Besides luxuriating in the great music, the visitor purchased all the Mozart postcards he could find and, the purchases being made in Salzburg, they were abundant. Upon arriving at his rooms at Clare College, Cambridge, he covered the walls with the pictures of the musical genius. Anyone entering the room witnessed at once that the young man did believe in something – the music of Mozart. This was a milestone on the journey. Music is the most spiritual of the arts. It is sound – formed by creating vibrations that pass sightless through the air and arrive on the drum of the ear where the invisible oscillations are transformed into patterns; with its combination of material and non-material elements, music becomes a bridge to higher (or lower) realms. The love of Mozart and the public assertion of that affection was a step upward in a spiritual journey.

Having first applied to Oxford University and having been rejected, RNW went to Cambridge which had accepted him to study languages, a field that seemed to open new interests for his future. But the Cambridge years proved empty years for none of the discontent that had erupted at Winchester could be finally quelled there. During the University years, the doubts and questions increased, despite the honored history of Cambridge as a superb educational institution. Founded in the thirteenth century on the Cam River in a town with many Catholic churches, the University had quickly become a noted learning center where young scholars could study under old masters and head on to careers in the Church,

The Bishop as a Young Man

canon law, civil law and government service. The Cam River still flowed through the grounds but the life blood of the University, the nurturing sustenance, the true faith, had been drained dry.

Evelyn Waugh in his masterpiece *Brideshead Revisited* has the narrator Charles Ryder describe the deadly vacuity of modern education:

> The view implicit in my education was that the basic narrative of Christianity had long since been exposed as a myth, and that opinion was now divided as to whether its ethical teaching was of present value, a division in which the main weight went against it; religion was a hobby which some people professed and others did not; at the best, it was slightly ornamental, at the worst it was the province of 'complexes' and 'inhibitions'... and of the intolerance, hypocrisy, and sheer stupidity attributed to it for centuries. No one had ever suggested to me that these quaint observances expressed a coherent philosophical system and intransigent historical claims; nor, had they done so, would I have been much interested.

Boston: Little, Brown, 1946, pp. 85–86.

Cambridge, as with all the other once great centers of learning, had been turned upside down, the founding religious pursuits now laid in the dust and the mundane and trivial exalted, promoted and sanctified. But, then, the symbol of Satan has always been an upside-down man as the dark destructive agent seeks always to invert God's order. The "father of lies" had one of his greatest triumphs in turning universities on their heads and in upending poor students, leaving them with their heads in the mire.

What could a young, questioning, aspiring soul hope to find in such an inverted setting? One simply shuffled on, going through the motions, while continuing to fester inwardly. In his last two terms at Winchester, the young student, finding no fire in studying Greek and Latin, had switched his major studies to French and German, knowing they would be easy to learn and allowing him more time to explore the inspiring and healing energies of Beethoven and Mozart. Arriving at Cambridge, he continued with French and German, but after one year decided such study offered nothing to him. He decided to change to the Law, finding some interest in the study of Jurisprudence, the Principles of Law, but little to attract him in other aspects of the subject. Little time was required before he realized he was not, nor could he be, suited to become a lawyer.

In frustration, he sent two letters of disappointment and disgust to his then Housemaster, Tom Howarth, whom he considered to be a good man. The response – simple, direct, contemporary. "Dear boy. Enjoy yourself." At Cambridge, as at Winchester, no ideal existed. What was a young man to hope for or work for or struggle for? He knew some such ideal existed for it rang out in the dynamic opening chords announcing the heroism expressed in his beloved Beethoven "Eroica"; it showed itself rationally and with beauty of design in the sonata form that shaped the creations of Mozart; it gave its glow to the 'season of mists and mellow fruitfulness' and bounded down the centuries in the sublime thoughts of highest human contemplation. Where was it now? Where had it gone?

Having swallowed a bite of Jurisprudence and still being gnawed with hunger, Williamson went to the senior tutor at Clare College, Dr. John Northam, an Ibsen scholar, and said he wanted to change his course of study again. The tutor responded, "If you ask to change again, I am going to think there is a psychological problem." After passing his exams that year, he revisited the tutor and his definite desire to change resulted in the

The Bishop as a Young Man

promised response: "Alright, I'm going to ask you to see a psychologist." Dutifully, the confused and center-less young soul took himself to a modern mind-bending pseudo-shaman. After only one or two sessions, young Williamson surprised himself and his mental medicine man by suddenly asking, seemingly out of the blue, "Do you believe in God?" The young "patient" did not himself believe but for some reason, clear in retrospect but concealed at the time, he wished to know if this man who was probing into his mind and, yes, his soul, had such a belief.

Such a question was *verboten*. The precious balance between "doctor" and "patient" had been destroyed. Any modern young man who could ask such a question of a high priest in the Temple of Science had to be either playing the fool or dwelling beyond help or hope. The sessions ended, but the fire to formulate and answer serious questions that the University, the Language Studies, the Law Studies, the Housemaster, the Senior Tutor, the Psychologist, could not answer, still burned within.

Switching studies again, Richard Williamson moved to English Literature and read, he remembers, Jane Austen, with side roads taking him as far afield as Ariosto and St. Paul. He passed his exams and was awarded his degree; he officially could now be called a Master of Arts.

And he had no idea where to go or what to do or why.

What to try his hand at? Perhaps journalism? He had a decent education, he could write, he had a special interest in the arts. So what was available? The Cardiff *Western Mail* in Wales advertised for an art and music critic.

The Voice of the Trumpet

This could be a first job to gain experience, hone critical and writing skills and put some bread and cheese on the table. The wandering Cambridge graduate reinforced by his Master of Arts degree applied for the job.

A very sympathetic Scotsman conducted the interview for the Welsh newspaper and after two interviews Williamson landed the job. The new cub reporter would do ordinary reporting as well as the art and music criticism. And so in the autumn of 1961, the young man embarked on his new career in journalism. He immediately ran into difficulties. The greenhorn pressman kept getting his legs knocked by the editors at the paper. The problems arose because the novice reporter refused to garnish stories, to add puffery or to pump out extraneous and unimportant detail to fill up his columns. He may have been new to the job, but his no-nonsense character compelled him to report only the straight, unadorned facts as he collected them; he felt an imperative urge simply to tell the truth as he saw it.

The editors more than once forced him to re-write articles and reviews with suitable journalistic adornment – "words, words, words." His overseers demanded satisfaction, but were barely satisfied. The reporter/critic went through the motions and turned out copy for print but his work gave him no more gratification than it gave his editors. He retreated into "digs," bought a second-hand piano for his living quarters and escaped once again into a Beethovenian refuge. The amateur pianist had begun exploring Beethoven's Sonata in B-flat Major, Opus 106, the "Hammerklavier," a Mount Everest in the piano repertoire. Bored with his day job, the climber scaled the peaks of the first and third movements of the piece, but even this haven which had previously offered consolation began to fail. The old satisfaction refused to reappear. Was it the piece itself? His world weariness? What was missing?

The Bishop as a Young Man

The small skirmishes at the newspaper led in time to a major battle. The town fathers in Newport near Cardiff had in the early 1960's commissioned a set of twelve murals from an exiled German painter, Hans Feibusch. The large paintings would adorn the entrance of the newly-constructed City Hall in Newport. In 1930, Hans Feibusch had been awarded the German Grand State Prize for Painting, but by 1937, with the advent of the Nazi regime, he found his work held up for contempt as "Degenerate Art." His paintings were banned in public and some were destroyed. Being Jewish, Feibusch saw the swastika on the wall and left Germany, taking up residence in England. There he converted to Christianity, Anglican style, and resumed his career as a painter and muralist. Over the next few decades, Feibusch would become one of the most prominent figures in British art, executing more murals in churches in England than any other twentieth century artist.

Feibusch began working on the commission in 1961 and labored on the project over the next two years. The twelve murals depicted the history of the Newport area and the city of Newport in northeast Wales over the course of its existence. The official dedication of the murals naturally became a major civic event. Local government officials, state officials, business leaders, and artists, all attended the gala affair, politicians, profit-makers and painters all celebrating together. Critics came as well. The art critic for the Cardiff *Western Mail* had expressed his opinion some months before the ceremony, viewing them when they were first completed in 1963, before the public event. He wrote a review; he did not admire the murals.

Heavy with expressionism, the murals depicted faded or transparent human figures gliding through pastels of blues and oranges and pinks. The machines and construction gear that had entered the local scene in more recent time received the strongest and most dynamic presentation. The murals may have agreed with the art deco style of the building but they were not agreeable to the critic. His review, a sardonic piece on the quality of this expressionistic art and in fact the whole expressionism movement in general did not sit well with his editor. The boss commented simply and straightforwardly, "This won't do. This won't do." What the editor read as snootiness about provincial art rather than a criticism of a popular art movement could not be published as written. The order: "Rewrite it." Being a paid employee, the critic did rewrite the piece to the editor's satisfaction and the revised review did appear in the paper. The experience drained the last drop of pleasure from the writing of criticism; journalism had proven a dry land. He knew the time had come to move on.

In an odd epilogue, the painter Feibusch left the Church of England in 1992, some years after the critic had done the same. Feibusch returned to his Jewish roots and said of himself, "I am just a very tired old Jew." After years of painting Christian religious subjects, civic commissions, legends from myth and nature scenes, the old painter found a new subject. In the early 1970's, after watching the five-hour television mini-drama entitled *Holocaust,* Feibusch stated, "It moved me frightfully and gave me a wish to express new things." He ended his career by painting a series of "holocaust pastels." The critic for the Cardiff *Western Mail,* long since having departed the newspaper world, never had the opportunity to review these works. In time, however, he would have words to say about the historical event itself.

The Bishop as a Young Man

His old school at Downsend needed a teacher for the summer term of 1963 and the failed critic needed a job. The mutual needs allowed a return to the halls where his solid basic education had begun and he joined the faculty to pass on the heritage of learning to a new generation, if only as a temporary assignment.

The work proved an easy burden and allowed an opportunity to frequent music in London, often the opera and often in the "gods," the uppermost reaches of the top balcony where the most devoted fans gathered, the inexpensive tickets allowing them the benefit of regular attendance. The novice teacher became one of the "gang." Another member of the "gang," Alan Forsyth, pointed the way for the next stage of the providential pilgrimage. One night at the opera, the younger Williamson stated, "I don't know what to do," an honest admission to an older sympathetic soul. He confessed that his life lacked direction, goals, purpose. The older man replied gently and calmly, "People who don't know what to do usually go into teaching or the church." The True Church was hidden far in the distance but the temporary situation at Downsend had begun the movement to the classroom. The first teaching experience did present some problems, though not in the halls of learning but in the residence hall. The amateur pianist, having decided that the "Hammerklavier" Sonata, though a masterwork of his hero, had something cold and analytic at its center, turned to the last of the thirty-two Beethoven piano sonatas, the Opus 111 in c minor, and began learning the first of its two movements. On the summer nights, he would sit at the piano in the residence hall and thump out over and over again the heaven-storming mighty music of the Master. His inner storms found some release at the keyboard as the difficult music by repetition made its way into his fingers. It also made its way into the ears of the boys residing in the hall. The time being the 1960's, they had found their musical joys in the duller, more predictable rhythm of the four-square beat provided by the Beatles, who were gaining universal celebrity by wanting to "hold your hand" or assuring themselves and multitudes of adolescents that "she loves you" (ya-ya-ya). Between the teacher and the pupils, as between Beethoven and the Beatles, there was "a great gulf fixed." The novice teacher sensing the mismatch, beyond mere music preferences, realized he would not find a new home in Downsend. He would seek students elsewhere.

The Gold Coast in West Africa had been one of the first African nations to gain independence. After the nation merged with the Togoland under the leadership of Kwame Nkrumah, the new nation took the name Ghana and in 1957 President Nkrumah declared Ghana's independence from Britain; nevertheless, the British influence remained strong for many years and the country depended on the British residents in a number of significant ways for its continued civic, agricultural, commercial, cultural and educational life.

A friend of the failed critic had gone to Ghana to teach, the education of the locals relying heavily on British schools and British teachers. After a year, the foreign educator contacted his drifting friend. Why not come to the newly independent nation and join the "education team"? The salary was decent and the students, unlike the youngsters at home, were eager to learn; the climate proved very warm, especially to British blood, but the nearby bay offered pleasant relief and a chance for relaxation. William-

The Bishop as a Young Man

son signed a two-year contract, with the option for future extensions, and began teaching in West Africa.

He found the new nation to be still awash in the receding tide of colonialism, meaning the circumstances of daily life offered pleasant living. The school itself, located between Takoradi and Secondi, had as its headmaster a native African gentleman, honest, upright, disciplined, so as the defining element of any organization flows from the top down, these characteristics also defined the school. Most of the pupils were young boys, with a handful of young girls in the mix.

The teacher marched many miles away from his native land but took a sturdy pilgrim's staff with him, the great Artur Schnabel recordings of the first seven Beethoven sonatas. He also began to explore the Russian literary classics, carrying with him the Everyman Classics editions of the major works of Leo Tolstoy. "Graduating to Tolstoy," as he says, he wanted to understand the ideas of the modern genius who had so influenced the shaping of the Indian revolution through its leader, Mahatma Gandhi. Williamson had begun to suspect something was "not quite right" with this turning point in the history of India and thought insight might be gained by exploring Tolstoy's ideas, concepts that had helped inspire the revolt. As with most peripatetic assays into learning, the study of Tolstoy led him instead to a profound understanding of and appreciation for the importance of nature, how the land and the earth with its rhythms and seasons teaches men profound truths, and how easily we can wander astray when separated from those foundations of the earth that define our corporal being.

If Tolstoy had been the companion who journeyed with him to Africa, the teacher found himself being taught by a writer from his own heritage, one of the greatest of his countrymen; in the heat and foreign climes of the African continent, Richard Williamson discovered William Shakespeare.

The Voice of the Trumpet

7

The local library in Secondi had a collection that His Excellency remembers as "functional" and being "functional," it offered the occasional interesting volume to catch a reader's eye and prove worth the page-turning. One book rested on the shelf at the Secondi Library, waiting to be perused by the Williamson eye, dissected by the Williamson mind, and then allowed to germinate in the Williamson soul. Written in 1959 by a fellow Brit, John Vyvyan, the title on the spine read *The Shakespearean Ethic*. Vyvyan was neither an academic nor a literary scholar. Trained as an archeologist, he had along with most British students, including RNW, been exposed to Shakespeare's works, but over time and with increased familiarity, Vyvyan detected a pattern of action that informed and shaped most of the great tragedies, a pattern that created a clear ethical and moral system delineated by the author. Vyvyan wrote his book to outline the ethical system he discovered at the heart of the greatest of all English literary works.

Vyvyan's observations stated on page one of his book struck a chord with the library patron who had taken the book down from the library shelf; the words vibrated in accord with the dissonant vexations that had rattled his insides for years.

Book 3.

Shakespeare was himself a "perturbed spirit"! He was not satisfied with conventional answers; yet he needed answers, for his own peace, in terms of life. And his plays are part of the quest for them . . . .

—John Vyvyan, *The Shakespearean Ethic*,
London: Chatto and Windus, 1959. p. 9.

The Bishop as a Young Man

"Like a swallowed bait," these words hooked the teacher who needed answers himself. Vyvyan theorizes in the book that Shakespeare is not merely an outside observer who never takes any clear moral position in creating his characters and developing their actions in the dramas; rather, instead of the actions being "ethically neutral," Vyvyan asserts "Shakespeare is never in doubt as to whether the souls of his characters are rising or falling." Scholars long ago established that the medieval drama was of central importance in Shakespeare's dramatic designs. It is certainly providential that the last location in England where the medieval mystery plays were still performed was Coventry, close to Stratford; Shakespeare's father John, being a devout Catholic, would have taken the family at Corpus Christi to Coventry and the future playwright as a boy would have wondered at the Bible stories with their lessons depicted by local tradesmen that rolled by on the pageant wagons. He also would have been acquainted with the medieval morality plays, such as *Mankind* and *The Castle of Perseverance* and, the greatest and most famous, *Everyman*. These moral stories, assimilated at a young age, imprinted themselves on the artist's imagination.

Vyvyan delineates the basic pattern in the tragedies: the tragic hero chooses to be "untrue to his own self," casts out love, abandoning or inverting conscience, and permits the devil to enter in. "All [of Shakespeare's] doomed heroes sin in the same way – they betray the Best . . . the immanent divinity in themselves."

The thirsting soul of the young teacher received this flow of sense and truth with relief. Here was a clear, thoughtful mind asserting and succinctly delineating an absolute moral order in the highest accomplishments of England's greatest writer. The same wise commentator also advanced the concept of "soul," not as an abstract exhausted buzz word, but as an interior reality, a fundamental interior element of every human creature, a living divine verity that strengthened or weakened as it engaged in real relations and took real actions in a real world.

To this day, the knowledge gained from this one book and the seeker's re-entry into the worlds of Brutus and Hamlet and Othello and Lear and Macbeth remains an influential element of the episcopal understanding. Without a moment's hesitation, Bishop Williamson can enumerate the nine steps outlined by John Vyvyan that characterize the fall of Shakespeare's tragic heroes: 1) a noble soul, but with a fatal flaw that lays it open to temptation; 2) the "voice" of a tempter possessed of an evil persuasive nature; 3) a temptation scene in which the weakness in the hero's soul is probed and the temptation yielded to; 4) inner conflict, during which the nobility of the hero's soul fails – first fall; 5) second temptation and second inner conflict with mounting intensity; 6) second fall as the hero loses the "kingship of his own soul"; 7) the tragic fatal act, an act of darkness; 8) the realization of horror; 9) death.

Richard Williamson came away from this exploration of the Shakespeare tragedies and Vyvyan's helpful explication of their ethical construction with a clear idea – there *is* a moral pattern in human decisions and subsequent events, and there *is* a moral order.

One of the key elements in the loss of "kingship of the soul" according to Vyvyan is the casting out of love, in the tragedies dramatized most often by a rejection or brutalizing of the feminine principle. Brutus pushes away his wife Portia, Othello doubts then destroys Desdemona, Lear casts out Cordelia. Here is Vyvyan's examination of Hamlet's rejection of Ophelia:

> Ophelia symbolizes the love-star in Hamlet's soul – inspiring him, when he is moving upward; but an

irksome reproach now that he has sworn to sink. And his rejection of her is the rejection of his guiding self. Admirers of Hamlet have tended to veil his conduct towards Ophelia: Shakespeare, on the contrary, gives it prominence, showing it as a major symptom of the sickness of his soul . . . .

Ophelia is a dual character of this kind: she is the girl we all know, and she is an allegorical figure representing a quality in Hamlet's soul. When Hamlet speaks to her, he is sometimes talking to a girl, sometimes to an entity in himself, and often to both. As an allegorical figure, she is that point of love in Hamlet which is the centre of his true nobility; and therefore she coincides with his highest self, which he is about to fail, and is a symbol of the law of love, to which he cannot rise. Everything that happens to Ophelia is an allegory of what is taking place in Hamlet.

Ibid., pp. 36–37, 40–41.

With these ideas in mind one can better understand the profound revolutionary temptation and demonic fall of the protestant movement when it cast out devotion to the Blessed Mother of Our Lord, and in its irrational darkness denied her Virginity. Even the deliberate diminishing of the role of Mary by the post Vatican II Church makes sense with Vyvyan's words in mind. The five hundred year fall into heresy, horror and death has been inevitable as the rebels have denied and cast out "the law of love," the Divine Love embodied by the Virgin Mother of God. If as tradition has it, Satan rebelled when he learned that he, an angel, would be subservient to a Man-God, how much more hatred must he have felt for the "merely" human female who would be the Mother of God. So the final and decisive confrontation between Satan and the Blessed Virgin has its origins far back and high above. The years of satanic rebellion since 1517 have been a terrible tragedy, indeed, but we know whose Immaculate Heart will triumph – a glorious finale, indeed.

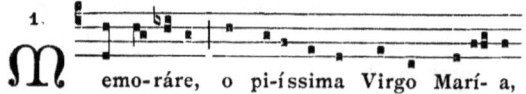
emo-ráre, o pi-íssima Virgo Marí- a,

> God speaks to us without ceasing by His good inspirations.
>
> —St. John Vianney, Curé d'Ars,
> Patron Saint of Priests

Providentially, the other book taken down from the shelves of a small local library in an obscure corner of the African continent also moved the convert-to-be toward a fuller understanding of the high station of woman and the deep spiritual significance of her role in the world. His ideas, traditional and rooted in common sense, would years later prove inflammatory and controversial to a world and Church sunk in mad modernism. These ideas were solidified from wisdom seared into his mind under the hot African sun. And, it should be added, his deep and intense devotion to the Blessed Virgin, Mother of God, Mary Most Holy, began to be shaped as well. The fourth formative book, the second of the African sojourn, was *The Flight from Woman,* the work of a Jewish psychiatrist who had converted to the Catholic faith, Karl Stern.

Book 4.

An undue emphasis on the technical and the rational, and a rejection of what for want of a better term we call "feeling," go

The Bishop as a Young Man

> with a neurotic dread of receiving, a fear of tenderness and of protection – and are invariably associated with an original maternal conflict. The poet Novalis made this confession after the death of his fiancée, in a letter to a friend: "Born with a softness of character, my intellect expanded more and more, and gradually displaced the heart from its domain. It was Sophie who returned the heart to its legitimate throne . . . . "[F]requently encountered today [is] the woman who finds it difficult to accept her womanly role . . . [this represents] . . . an over-evaluation of masculine achievement, and a debasement of values which one commonly associates with the womanly; a rejection, often unconscious, even of motherhood; an aping of man, associated with an unceasing undertone of envy and resentment . . . . [T]here is a flight from the feminine. If we assume, as many people do, that these disturbances are widespread today in comparison with other times in history, they entail far-reaching implications. Rationalism and positivism have influenced Western civilization during the past three centuries to an extraordinary degree; yet the rich benefits of technology inspire a wide-spread alarm that *human affairs* will be increasingly more programmed, and not in Marxist countries alone. And if we equate the one-sidedly rational and technical with the masculine, there arises the ghastly spectre of a world impoverished of womanly values.
>
> —Karl Stern,
> *The Flight from Woman*,
> New York: Farrar, Straus and Giroux, 1965, pp. 5–6

There is no doubt that the intellect reigned supreme in the young teacher who read these words. He had proven his capacity for high thought early in his academic career, slipping from highest honors only when that intellect began to question the point and purpose of the entire academic enterprise. Many of the rebellious youth who would upset the social apple cart and spill many rotten apples in the 1960's felt compelled by a rejection of the lies by which the world lived but, sadly, they ultimately

The Voice of the Trumpet

succumbed to them; this young man used his questioning mind and demanded answers. The poor fledglings of the 1960's became lost in an indulgent fog of pot smoke and were deafened by a driving beat and fell for the siren songs of phony gurus. Richard Williamson found real answers. Not only had his mind been prepared for the receptivity of truth, but his heart had been made ready as well. Raised in a home where the polarity and complementarity of the sexes had been easily balanced between the male father who provided a moral framework and the feminine mother who hovered over her piano, playing Chopin, and over her nest as the spirit brooded over the water, he had made his way through the "selva oscura," the dark wood of doubt and depression, and now could glimpse some genuine light. Mozart and Beethoven, Tolstoy and Shakespeare, prepared him to understand Vyvyan and Stern as they explained the most basic distinctions in nature – the different roles of men and women. These obvious truths became mental manna in the modern wilderness, or, perhaps more simply, crumbs of bread, but not like those crumbs left behind by Hansel and Gretel as they wandered unknowingly to a gingerbread house and a witch's oven. These crumbs of truth fallen from a rich table led to the ultimate solid glorious eternal home designed for the family of man.

Imagine the effect of the following excerpts from *The Flight from Woman* on the mind of a seeker after truth:

The Bishop as a Young Man

> [S]ince the French Revolution, the cry for *equality* has changed into an assertion of *sameness* [p. 14] . . . .
>
> Let us recall once more the very first account of man in Genesis, *before* Eve is taken out of the body of Adam, "And God created Man to His own image: to the image of God He created him, male and female He created them" (Gen. 1, 27) [p. 38] . . . .
>
> Faith, the most sublime form of non-scientific knowledge, is (if we consider its natural history, independent of all questions of grace) a form of swallowing or of being taken in. It goes back to an infantile, oral form of union. This is also true about Wisdom. *Sapientia* is derived from *sapere*, to taste, and *Sophia* is the she-soul of Eastern Christendom [p. 54] . . . .
>
> [W]hen one comes to look for what warps the minds of many Western Christians today, it is not hard to trace it all back to that double dose of Descartes and Jansenism which France got in the seventeenth century. Just as in the Cartesian concept of the world, nature can be understood *more geometrico* as an apparatus, in the Calvinist and Jansenistic religion God becomes a retribution machine which works with mathematical precision. Justice is autonomous, and severed from charity. All motherliness is taken away from the relation to God. The word of Isaiah, "I shall comfort thee as a Mother comforteth,' is as alien to this form of spirituality as though it came from some dead ancient religion [p. 108] . . . .

The reader who had carried Tolstoy with him to the dark continent would find the following brightly illuminating; how could this not be providential?

> All that is essential to [*War and Peace*], all that has given it and *Anna Karenina* their unique positions in the history of art, has been created with the same non-reflective sureness which characterizes Shakespeare or Vermeer or Mozart. *War and Peace* is a *Welt Theater* [Theater of the World] in the sense of Shake-

The Voice of the Trumpet

speare's or Mozart's work. Somebody once remarked that everything human occurs in this novel, and therefore we encounter the spirit not only as a supernatural glow which enlivens reality but also overtly. In other words, we encounter religion as it affects the everyday lives of some people. This appears particularly in the person of Maria Bolkonska. To me, Maria, with the hidden life of prayer, the anonymous radiance of love with which she affects the lives around her, has always been the image of the Mystical Body [p. 180] . . . .

The difference between a morality imbedded in the life of the sacraments and the Gospel on one hand, and a moral system on the other (as it is presented under pragmatic or positivist or Utopian or "scientific" forms) is the same as the difference between things *grown* and things *made*. Love can neither be planned nor managed, it can only be sown and nurtured. Here, too, the mystery of the womanly is bound up with the mystery of the supernatural life [p. 191] . . . .

Unlike the pilgrim of *The Divine Comedy* who was led by the child-virgin Beatrice, Faust and Raskolnikov are redeemed by women who have been broken by the world – the mad child-murderess and the prostitute. This emphasizes the tattered and bedraggled that are characteristics of our time. And yet, with all the devastation we may have wrought – the heart open to infused wisdom remains the heart of immutable virginity [p. 271] . . . .

History professors are fond of pointing out the parallel between the present time and that of the Roman Empire. As far as I can make out, they always did. The time of the Roman Empire presents, with stylized clarity, in model form, as it were, the dialectic tension of all history. At the historical moment of the Incarnation, Roman civilization was under the sign of power, philosophy under the sign of unaided reason, and the visible church of the Old Covenant was in danger of formalism and ossification. And this, of all times, was the hour of the poor in spirit, the little ones, in short of all those who, power-less, acknowledge their dependence of God. All this found its highest expression in the person of the Blessed Virgin. And with a strange *fiat* of God-like-ness marking the crisis of history then, it was the *fiat* of littleness which opened the curtain to the drama of Redemption [p. 302] . . . .

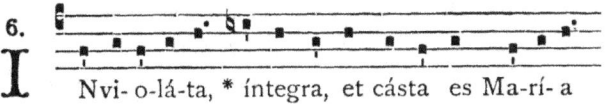

6. Nvi- o-lá-ta, * íntegra, et cásta es Ma-rí- a

Karl Stern points out that the word "vocation" is derived from "vox" which means "voice." A vocation is thus that which calls us to move on a specific path and we choose to answer that call or to block out that voice. Stern also suggests that the ability to hear that "calling" has become more difficult as the marital union and the family have become focused on the happiness of the individual, losing any sense of the transcendent. In a world where marriage is demeaned by divorce or degraded by illegitimate "unions," where family now extends to any group of friends or workers or neighbors, and thus barely exists at all, the higher calling can barely be heard; the calling voice is stilled and vocations wither like seeds that fall on rock.

A call came to Africa from the voice of an old friend. Tom Howarth, Williamson's former House Master at Winchester. Howarth had years before sought to help the troubled student under his care but did not know how to go about it. Good-hearted and genuinely caring for all the young under his care, he had remained in touch with Williamson and a friendship developed. Now an invitation came. Would the teacher working in Ghana consider coming to St. Paul's Boys School in London to teach languages? The call came, an internal debate ensued, the offer was accepted. In the summer of 1965, the teacher returned to his homeland.

The Voice of the Trumpet

St. Paul's School for Boys was founded in 1509 by Dean John Colet, then Dean of St. Paul's Cathedral in London, a Catholic Cathedral that was soon to be turned on its head by a lusty monarch. Dean Colet is remembered as a proponent of "Christian humanism" and his ideas influenced Erasmus who, indeed, Colet had hoped to make the first headmaster of the new school. The Boys School was dedicated to the Child Jesus and its primary purpose was to give young lads a Christian education. A trade association of merchants, founded in 1394, the Company of Mercers, exporters of wool and silk as well as importers of velvet, became the first trustees. The fabric guild thus became the first non-clerical overseer of education; in years to come, their kind would become legion.

Dean Colet's opinions aroused controversy in his day with many calling his devotion to the new "Christian humanism" heretical. The reigning Archbishop of Canterbury, William Warham, consistently supported the Dean, and King Henry VIII held him in such high esteem that the Monarch made Colet his Chaplain. Colet did not hesitate to criticize the Church of his day and seek reform.

In his famous Convocation Sermon that opened a gathering of the clergy of Canterbury at St. Paul's Cathedral in London in February 1512, Dean Colet spoke critically of the habits of life of the priests. These men of God, he stated, had been called by God to be beacons of light and if they became purveyors of darkness, the Church would be engulfed in darkness. He called on

The Bishop as a Young Man

them to turn to humility, charity, and sobriety, performing spiritual works, speaking the word of God with clarity, providing the sacraments, and making sacrifices for their sheep. He called on all to "return to the God of love and peace; return to Christ, in whom is the true peace of the Spirit which passeth all understanding; return to the true priestly life . . . . Be ye reformed in the newness of your minds, that ye may know these things which are of God; and the peace of God shall be with you."

Dean Colet died in 1519. God spared him the vision of devastation when the new "Church of England," fabricated by his King, fell into the slough of schism from which it has yet to emerge.

Originally situated near St. Paul's Cathedral, the school made four moves over the centuries. The new language instructor witnessed one of the moves, from out of the city to Hammersmith to its present riverside site in Barnes in 1968. The move changed the habitat from, as the Bishop now remembers, a "huge red-brick Victorian building to a sprawling steel and glass horror."

The boys had changed as well.

In 1965, while in Montreal for a Beatles concert, Ringo Starr, the drummer for the group, received a death threat by telephone. He shielded himself at the concert by placing the cymbals in his drum-set in a vertical plane to shield himself from potential gunfire.

Hap-pi-ness Is A Warm Gun

The Voice of the Trumpet

Arriving at St. Paul's School for Boys, the new language Master naturally reminisced about his school days at Winchester. He realized he had been given a very fine humanist education at his public (private) school, ranging over Greek and Latin and German and French, encompassing history and literature, grammar and rhetoric. English literature had been absorbed, as expected, on his own. The school days had been filled with courses of substance, but even as the clock ruled studies and activities, generous stretches of leisure remained to be filled with discovering great music and discovering dissatisfaction with the rote answers being provided to life's "big questions."

The lifestyle had been spartan with regular but spare meals, occasional baths in round tins that barely fit a boy's backside and that could not accommodate his lengthening legs. Boys had kicked other boys about as they learned to live in community, had stomped on new arrivals to push them in line, jumped on those who started to head too "far out"; the masters had disciplined the older boys and the older boys had disciplined the younger boys. Williamson recalled being "caned" a few times and wielding the cane on occasion himself when necessary, but such actions molded boys into men and not into sensitive plants.

> Mr. Langton one day asked [Dr. Johnson] how he had acquired so accurate a knowledge of Latin, in which, I believe, he was exceeded by no man in his time; he said, "My master whipt me very well. Without that, Sir, I should have done nothing." He told Mr.

The Bishop as a Young Man

Langton, that while Hunter was flogging his boys unmercifully, he used to say, "And I do this to save you from the gallows." Johnson, upon all occasions, expressed his approbation of enforcing instruction by means of the rod. "I would rather (said he) have the rod to be the general terrour to all, to make them learn, than tell a child, if you do thus, or thus, you will be more esteemed than your brothers and sisters. The rod produces an effect which terminates in itself. A child is afraid of being whipped, and gets his task, and there's an end on't; whereas, by exciting emulation and comparisons of superiority, you lay the foundation of lasting mischief; you make brothers and sisters hate each other."

—James Boswell, *Life of Johnson*,
London: Oxford University Press,
1957, p. 34

From Dr. Johnson's youth in the early 1700's to Williamson's schooldays in the mid twentieth century, the classical formula for education worked, although the healthy flesh of meaning and purpose had dried to the bone; the skeleton had remained, however, and the program for a while remained authoritarian, comprehensive and manly (with the girls being educated elsewhere where they could learn to be womanly). The vice "that dare not speak its name," a notorious problem in the boys schools, had only been evidenced one time during his schooldays when one boy was expelled, but he personally never encountered the problem ("[M]aybe because I scowled and growled too much, thank God, a saving grace . . . ").

Upon arriving at St Paul's, he discovered that not only had the very skeleton of the classical education crumbled but the boys had altered in profound ways as well. The boys he encountered in the classroom could only be described as "rough," sometimes resembling that "rough beast his hour come round at last." These boys were no longer docile, no longer accepting of correction or discipline, no longer interested in those studies handed down for centuries. The year was 1965 and their ears throbbed with the Beatles beat, foretelling upheaval, rebellion and revolution. The discontent had begun before the boys reached the school; many of them came from broken homes and the modern legal fiction of divorce had engendered rage in them and rightly so. They were no longer young gentlemen, nor did they care to be.

The Jewish boys, Williamson found, were not nearly as rough. George Bernard Shaw had once said that "Jews are born civilized" and the new language teacher found his Jewish pupils to be motivated, disciplined and docile, ready to digest what was fed to them. Too many of the other young pups would take the meat thrown to them, tear it to pieces and refuse to eat it. They had no interest in profiting from what was offered them.

The repeated attempts by the teacher to share his polished Winchester humanism proved futile. He realized he had two choices: he could either join them, as did so much of the education establishment at that time, pandering to them and praising their shallow interests with feigned enthusiasm, or he could try to engage them in battle, refusing to kowtow to the cultural collapse in which they rejoiced but in which they were actually suffocating. The decision came clear quickly: "I have got to find some way to lick these boys because I am not going to join them. They don't deserve to be joined. They tear

The Bishop as a Young Man

things to pieces. I have to find something that will stand up to their rampaging wrecking so that when they try to tear it to pieces, they will find it can't be torn . . . something that will catch in their teeth, that they can't spit out, that they will have to swallow."

But what?

Amplified Electric Guitar Riff

Christianity will go. It will vanish and shrink. I needn't argue about that; I'm right and I'll be proved right. We're more popular than Jesus now; I don't know which will go first . . . rock'n'roll or Christianity. Jesus was all right but his disciples were thick and ordinary. It's them twisting it that ruins it for me.

—John Lennon, Interview, March 4, 1966

O God, Thou didst strengthen Saint Casimir with the virtue of constancy in the midst of royal delights and the snares of the world; we beseech Thee, grant by his intercession, that Thy faithful people may despise the things of the world and ever aspire to those of heaven. Through Our Lord, Jesus Christ, etc.

—Collect, March 4, Feast of St. Casimir (who in the midst of the moral dangers of the court was an example of piety and preserved his

chastity), son of King Casimir IV of
Poland and Elizabeth of Austria

Father Christopher Bales.

—martyred in Fleet Street, March 4, 1590

Alexander Blake.

—layman, martyred in Gray's Inn Lane, March 4, 1590

Nicholas Horner.

—tailor, martyred at Smithfield, March 4, 1590

2. Hrístus re-súrgens * ex mór-tu- is

If reading John Vyvyan and Shakespeare's tragedies had convinced the teacher of the existence of a moral order, then perhaps a close examination of that moral order could provide an answer. This might be the meat to catch in the boys' teeth and make them chew on real viands. After a trip to a local bookstore, he returned to his room with a book on "non-religious ethics," because as a fashionable intellectual semi-atheist, he had been taught religion could never provide any serious answers to real problems. But the Lord God has His ways and not only knows what we need but knows how to provide it without our always recognizing the source. One afternoon, sitting in his room at the House of St. Paul's School – a cold room, drained of warmth – and reading the "non-religious ethics" book – a dead work, drained

The Bishop as a Young Man

of life, for all ethics must of necessity be rooted in religion – the inquiring reader had a thought enter his inquiring mind. The Bishop admits now that the thought was certainly a grace of God, but a grace sent to him anonymously "without telling me it was Him; if He had told me it was Him, I would have then said, 'No!' He was big enough to work around me – somehow." After coming to the realization that serious human problems had accompanied the explosion of the Industrial Revolution (Tolstoy having already taught him that a return to nature was a human necessity), the thinker hearkened to a newly voiced idea that simply said, "Maybe the real problem isn't the Industrial Revolution; maybe the problem goes back to the protestant reformation." The idea led him to deign to take a look at the Catholic faith with a genuine, though condescending, interest. He began reading some books on Catholicism and the Catholic faith, general introductions, quick surveys, basic beginnings. The cold room began to kindle with new warmth.

As he took the first tentative baby steps toward Rome, he found the classroom battles with the boys intensifying. As hard as they might hit him with their 1960's ammunition of cynicism, the language teacher would fire back bullets of certainty. One day, Tom Howarth, the Head Master who had issued the original job offer, asked to attend a class. Schoolmaster Williamson that day explored with the boys a French work by Antoine de Saint Exupéry. One of the usual heated classroom exchanges erupted. High top-level science students made up the class, youthful dilettantes and intellectual snobs puffed up with the pollution pullulating around them everywhere – pop music, pop movies, pop TV, pop psychology, pop art, pop pop pop. They began their assault on the work, attacking tradition and hierarchy and nature and order. Howarth blinked as he witnessed Wil-

The Voice of the Trumpet

liamson knock it all back at them, deflecting the boys' predictable pitches with hard-hitting assurances. The teacher was being dogmatic. Howarth later asked in all honesty some questions that Williamson could not yet answer but that propelled him further down the road: "How can you be so sure? How can you know? How do you think you can know?"

The searcher turned to one of the day's Intellectual Poster Boys – Albert Camus. He decided to explore Camus by teaching the boys Camus' novel *La Peste* – *The Plague*. The fictional work presents an "ugly" French port town on the Algerian coast in which the citizens work hard with the sole aim of "getting rich." Interested in "how [the citizens] love and how they die, the narrator chronicles the coming of the plague to the town and the reactions of the townspeople as they suffer and die." As Camus believed in no higher power or purpose, the devastation wrought in the town is grim, but alleviated by acts of kindness and generosity on the part of certain inhabitants, despite the absurdity of a life without meaning and the greater absurdity of death without meaning. The High Priests of the Literary Temple praised the novel effusively upon its publication in 1948, *The New York Times Book Review* going so far as to state that the importance of the book to the age was so great that to dismiss it "would be to blaspheme against the human spirit." The supreme import of the work to the time of its publication seemed to be that life is absurd and pointless but we can still be nice, be loving and be caring toward one another. A few years later a young Catholic lady crippled by lupus and living on a small farm in rural Georgia would give the lie to such sentimental nihilism. In her story "A Good Man Is Hard to Find," Flannery O'Connor would create the figure of the Misfit, a desperate soul seeking meaning, living in a country with a patina of phony faith, tortured by his inability to

The Bishop as a Young Man

verify if Christ *really* rose from the dead – an ultimate and life-changing question.

> Jesus was the only One that ever raised the dead . . . and He shouldn't have done it. He thown everything off balance. If He did what He said, then it's nothing for you to do but thow [sic] away everything and follow Him, and if He didn't, then it's nothing for you to do but enjoy the few minutes you got left the best way you can – by killing somebody or burning down his house or doing some other meanness to him. No pleasure but meanness.
>
> —Flannery O'Connor, *Collected Works*, New York: The Library of America, 1988, p. 152

Camus hauls up deep emotion from the empty well of life and luxuriates in its cool balm; O'Connor depicts the "furious rages" of a living soul burning with anger in the dead brush of a world dried by indifference and shallowness, as well as succinctly explaining the random outbursts of violence that she predicted would become part of American life.

Realizing that the nihilism and contrived consolation of the Camus work might appeal to the boys, Williamson put on the gloves and began pounding on the featherweight philosophizing. He attacked the book by pummeling its pomposity with humor. He produced a five page commentary for the boys, using a popular comic strip character of the day named Bristow.

"Bristow," created and drawn by Frank Dickens, is the longest running cartoon strip in the history of newspapers. Debuting in September, 1961, the strip still appears daily. The central character, Bristow, is a buying clerk in a monolithic office building. He longs for a better and higher life than drab office work, and spends his time imagining himself as a famous writer or a great brain surgeon or the like. A descendant of James Thurber's Walter Mitty, he is also the progenitor of Scott Adams' Dilbert. Bristow has succeeded in producing one major work – *Living Death in the Buying Department* – but he cannot find a publisher. Surrounded by an array of fellow misfits trapped in a pointless existence, Bristow and company live lives as devoid of significance as the characters in the Camus novel. Frank Dickens, however, finds humor in his creation and does not seek to reach existential heights or plumb dour nihilistic depths. The cartoonist is credited with inventing the device whereby action words are placed in bubbles next to or above the characters' heads, such as "Surprise! Surprise!," "Flinch! Flinch!," "Horror! Horror!," and the like. The teacher used the same device in his commentary to deflate the Frenchman's existential cream-puffery; Bristow mocked Camus.

Williamson showed his work to Tom Howarth who then wrote a counter-commentary, using five earlier writers, including Edmund Burke. Howarth sought to demonstrate the same device could be used to pop the balloon of almost any writer. He posed a question: "You are attacking Camus with a certain amount of depth. What would you have to say about these other classics, these that go further back? Would you grant to them something that you could not grant to Camus?"

The question had now been fully engaged. The switch had gone to "on" and Williamson had been forced to follow a path as a seeker after Truth from which he could not turn back.

The Bishop as a Young Man

Where to turn? In a world where the destroyers occupied the barricades, built from the rubble of western civilization which they gleefully continued to destroy, where could one find a thoughtful head that would speak rationally of preservation and morality and order?

As Williamson saw it at the time, only two such voices could be heard in the cacophony of the mad annihilators' rants that deafened all sense in the public arena. The barbarians had to permit a sane squeak to emerge occasionally so they could continue their fraudulent boast that they believed in "free speech" and "open debate." One of the voices belonged to Bernard Levin, the son of a poor Jewish family. Born in 1928 and raised in London, Levin rose to become one of the most famous British journalists of his day. Levin may have had a liberal bent, but his opinions were rarely doctrinaire, sometimes surprising, strongly stated and solidly supported. His public eminence, however, made him difficult to approach.

The other gentleman, also a noted journalist, had removed himself from the public sphere and the environs of London and lived with his wife in a cottage in the countryside of southern England. "A great man often steps forth from a humble cottage" and sometimes a great man will retreat to one, especially as the world around him goes mad. Malcolm Muggeridge had made such a retreat.

Malcolm Muggeridge was born in 1903 into a typical early twentieth century liberal family. His father co-founded the socialist Fabian society and served for a while as a Labour Member in Parliament. The father, being a good "man of the people," refused to send his son to an elite school, so Muggeridge joined the herd of boys who, as he later said, did not receive much of an education. Knowing his deficiencies, he taught himself and eventually went to teach in India for three years. He began a writing career there in published exchanges with Mahatma Gandhi on questions of war and peace. Returning to England in 1927, he married "Kitty" Dobbs and the couple remained together until Muggeridge's death in 1990. Being good modern liberals and supporters of the Russian Communist experiment, the Muggeridges traveled to Moscow in 1932 from where Muggeridge sent reports to the *Manchester Guardian*. Being an honest man, Muggeridge began to become disillusioned with the communist life and rule he witnessed on a daily basis. Rumors reached him of a famine in the Ukraine and without the approval of the Soviet regime he traveled there to investigate. His honest accounts of the horrors he encountered made their way to his paper secretly through diplomatic couriers, but the *Guardian* never published the full reports and the pieces that did see print did not carry Muggeridge's name. At the same time, *New York Times* reporter Walter Duranty, a shill for his Soviet bosses, received the Pulitzer Prize for Journalism for his fake news reports that proclaimed to the gullible American public that no such famine was taking place. Josef Stalin punished the Ukrainian farmers who would not submit to his rule by starving them to death; the estimated number of victims varies from three million to seven million. No one is punished for debating the actual figures. In 2008, Muggeridge posthumously received the Ukrainian Order of Freedom for his honest accounts of the national horror.

Fully aware of the phony nature of the "Communist utopia," Muggeridge returned to England and over time became conservative in politics, eventually writing a definitive piece entitled "The Great Liberal Death Wish," and increasingly became interested in the Christian faith, beginning his journey in *Jesus Rediscovered*, the first of his many books on the subject. During these transition years, he wrote, lectured and even edited *Punch*, the English humor magazine. His famous wit made him a natural for the job – "Never forget that only dead fish swim with the stream." In a famous talk given in January, 1968, Muggeridge resigned his post as Rector of the University of Edinburgh because of the distribution of birth control pills through the University Health Centre. He publicly railed against the increasing use by the young of drugs for pleasure. He excoriated a generation being allowed to destroy itself through "pills and pot" and being deprived of the most basic understandings of human life.

Having removed himself to a degree from the fray and settling with wife Kitty in a cottage in Sussex, Muggeridge appeared to be a source of possible assistance for Williamson. Here is an account written at the time of Muggeridge's death in 1990.

Trumpet Solo

When I returned to England in 1965 after two years in Africa, and, schoolmastering in London, found the schoolboys, like their country, ravaged by, notably, four unworthy 'mopheads' known as the Beatles, I looked around for a voice of sanity, or representative of worth, and standing out in his articulate, amusing but relentless condemnation of our worthless century, leaving it no chance of appeal, was Malcolm Muggeridge.

With crafted clauses and crafty glee, his articles that I would read went for the tin gods of Liberalism, and without mercy or malice tore them to pieces. Poor Liberals accused Malcolm of being 'negative,' of being 'destructive' (you know the whole silly line!) but for anyone with eyes to see or ears to hear there was more to him than that. Firstly, someone who has nothing to say does not usually bother with style or craftsmanship to say it, but Malcolm always had style and he was a craftsman with the English language.

And then secondly, behind all the impish mockery and iconoclasm there ran a coherent sense of there being some real values by which all the posturing poltroons who betrayed them stood condemned. Accordingly, although he was not a Catholic at the time, nor even, as I recall, professed himself to be a Christian, he attracted a large number of implicit and explicit believers who had nobody else to defend their minds and souls against the great lie of Liberalism with which their official leaders were, to a man, more or less going along.

So one day I got on a bicycle and rode over to his cottage in Robertsbridge, Sussex, to see him. I cannot remember whether I had announced my (completely unimportant) visit beforehand or not. In any case he and his wife Kitty received me very kindly, sat me down to lunch, and we talked, and he listened, and he essentially understood everything that 'my dear boy' had to say about the woes of teaching abandoned youth in mid-twentieth-century London.

I have fond memories of maybe half a dozen such visits to Malcolm and Kitty over the next few years. I am in no way boasting that I am a special friend of theirs, only that Malcolm was a good friend to me, a friend in need as I have no doubt he was to hundreds, maybe thousands, of spiritual derelicts of the twentieth century who made as I did the pilgrimage to the Sage of Park Cottage.

How good God is! I think had Malcolm been a full-fledged Roman Catholic at the time, I might not have gone near him. As it was, with his sharp and independent mind which had gone right into left-wingery and come out the other side, with his total refusal to buy into twentieth century illusions, and with his wisdom and goodness of heart manifested in his ready ear and warm hospitality, he greatly helped me towards the time when I left London and went ahead of him into the Catholic Church.

—Letters from the Rector, No. 89

The Bishop as a Young Man

The man who wrote these words of tribute could not be aware that besides the help he received in fanning away modern fumes choking his mind, Malcolm Muggeridge also provided an example of character that left an indelible mark on the formation of the personality of the green young fellow who cycled to Sussex. Those who know the Bishop in his later years would nod in agreement with anyone who described him as a serious "listener" of deep "understanding" with a "sharp and independent mind" who possesses "goodness of heart" and offers "warm hospitality" toward "spiritual derelicts of the twentieth century." Thus the light of character itself passes from generation to generation in the torch race of civilized humanity.

Malcolm Muggeridge at the age of 79 in the Year of Our Lord 1982 was received into the Roman Catholic Church along with his wife Kitty.

▃ ▃ ▃

> [F]our vacant youths . . . dummy figures
> with tousled heads [and] no talent.
>
> —Malcolm Muggeridge on the Beatles,
> *Esquire Magazine*, 1968

> They have become a religion in fact. The
> days of their ministry on earth seem to
> be over – they don't seem to perform
> so much – and they have been taken up
> into heaven preferring to conserve the
> holy mystery of the Holy Quaternity in
> a delicious incommunicado. All over the
> place though there are icons, devotional
> photos and illuminated missals which keep
> the tiny earthbound fans in touch with the

provocatively absconded deities.

—Jonathan Miller, *Partisan Review*,
Summer, 1964

And then like a pinball jettisoned by an unseen hand, Richard Williamson began ricocheting off bumpers Benedictine, Carmelite, Dominican and Jesuit, each lighting up briefly and sending him careening further in his seemingly random but surreptitiously providential way.

The boys at St. Paul's School had a debate society and formally argued the "hot button" issues of the day. In the mid-sixties, few of those "hot buttons" scalded more than the question of contraception, the topic becoming particularly incendiary following the promulgation of *Humanae vitae*, Pope Paul VI's controversial Encyclical on birth control. The boys had difficulty finding a teacher willing to speak against contraception and in favor of the Papal Encyclical, evidencing that already by that time schools had been hijacked by "educators" all possessing the same mindset. Teacher Williamson agreed to take on the task and agreed to speak against this "great advancement in science" and in support of the Catholic arguments. He began his research by trying to discover why the Church considered contraception a great sin; after all, the initial impetus for promoting and approving birth control had started its world-wide assault right there in England in an Anglican Conference at Lambeth in 1930.

The obvious contact point for research had to be a Catholic priest, for the Church stood as the one official public roadblock on the "Freedom Expressway," insisting an immoral impetus concealed itself behind this "scientific advance." The debater-to-be found a local Catholic priest who providentially held the Catholic Faith and could logically and coherently explain the reasons supporting the Church's teaching. Father Timothy Firth introduced Williamson to the long-held teaching on the natural law, admitting as he did so that the idea was not easy to teach, much less to a debating hall full of boys being shaped by a faculty of liberals. One example the good priest provided has remained in the Williamson mind to the present day. If a little boy or girl is playing happily with a toy and a brother or sister comes and grabs that toy away, the dispossessed child will send up a howl of protest, usually with accompanying tears. This is a simple and elemental example of natural law. An instinct placed deep inside of us tells us from the earliest age that such an action is a violation of justice, not fair, not correct, not proper. So throughout all aspects of our lives, those deep instincts toward the just and the right and the properly ordered, dwelling in our inmost being, reflect laws of natural justice fixed there by God to permit the proper functioning of His creation – man – on the planes of the life in nature and society. The idea walloped Williamson with its logic and sense. After years of seeking, he had been smacked with a supreme principle that made perfect sense and suggested the possible existence of a Creator, a Creator who imposed design and order for the sake of justice and the good of His creature, individually and collectively. The idea held his mind in an iron grip, striking it with a rod of authority and truth.

The two men through this initial conversation became friendly and began sharing thoughts and time and the squash courts. The good Father Firth perceived that this dry mind longed to drink in more of the ideas that appeared to be new but in fact were very old indeed. Father Firth suggested that the teacher, now turned student, visit the priest's old school at Ampleforth and meet the Fathers there so the conversations and accompanying discoveries could expand and deepen. The mine of wealth of Catholic thought had veins of rich ore for a lifetime and none of it was fool's gold.

A journey to North Yorkshire brought him to Ampleforth where since 1802 a college had educated young men and the attached monastery had exerted its religious influence. There Williamson met Father Anselm, one of the Benedictines, who considered himself an intellectual and, not surprisingly, handed the visitor a volume of Teilhard de Chardin. Williamson had already heard the name mentioned in a recent conversation with a Jesuit priest. The good angels, especially his guardian angel, did their work and the mind that was clearing and perceiving the dawning light of Catholic truth found nothing of interest in the modern philosophe-du-jour, the phony palaeontologist, the pseudo-evolution-promoting omega-point-posturing de Chardin. Williamson states simply, "He didn't grab me."

At this time, Williamson resided outside of London in Beaconsfield, Buckinghamshire, the home constituency of former Prime Minister Benjamin Disraeli (named first Earl of Beaconsfield by Queen Victoria) and the burial site of Edmund Waller ("Go, lovely rose . . . "), Edmund Burke ("All it takes for evil to succeed is for a few good men to do nothing . . . .") and G. K. Chesterton ("These are the days when the Christian is expected to praise every creed except his own . . . . "). In the same town lived a fellow Winchester graduate, Anthony Merer, whose father had chosen to live in the town for the same reasons the teacher had – pleasant surroundings combined with an easy train commute to London. Anthony Merer's mother had a cousin who was a Jesuit – Father Myles Lovell. Williamson made contact with this priest who in his kindness proved willing to contribute to the ongoing discussion. The Jesuit priest also suggest-

The Bishop as a Young Man

ed the eager reader explore the thoughts of Teilhard de Chardin, but Williamson admitted he had already made the effort, but found (*Deo gratias!*) little of interest there. Then Father Lovell proffered a simple but life-altering suggestion: "You should try Aquinas or Augustine."

The idea took hold in the burgeoning intellect. On a return visit to the Benedictine monastery in Ampleforth, he was again warmly welcomed by the monks, including Father Basil Hume who went on to become Archbishop of Westminster and a Cardinal. Williamson honestly admitted to being an atheist, but one interested in the ideas of the Catholic faith. The monks echoed good Father Lovell's suggestion – he should begin reading Aquinas and Augustine.

The teacher, being a good student, took the suggestion. He sought out the writings of St. Thomas Aquinas and "that has made all the difference."

The long and wind-ing road,

Book 5.

[I]t is possible to perform an excision of the purely rational organs incorporated in the living unity, and find oneself then faced with a prospectus of pure philosophy, coherent, consistent, and as complete as can be expected; an independent prolegomenon to belief which may be of special, and even urgent, interest to those who find themselves alien to the official organization of Christianity. Here also may be associated, if not for agreement then at least for conversation, not only Christians of different loyalties, but also those with no religious convictions but who would accept the reasonable life and are not insensitive to hints that there may be something more generous beyond it. A philosophical attitude may not be enough for health and happiness or for complete adaptation to reality, but it is a sound beginning.

—Thomas Gilby, *St. Thomas Aquinas: Philosophical Texts*, London: Oxford University Press, 1960, p. xxi.

Father Thomas Gilby, an English Dominican friar who taught at Cambridge, had done much work on St. Thomas Aquinas, including the translating and editing of a volume entitled *St. Thomas Aquinas: Philosophical Texts*. This volume consisted of brief paragraphs and snippets from the massive output of the great Catholic theologian and philosopher assembled under specific topic headings, such as "Science and Wisdom," "Existence of God," "Nature of God," and so forth. The eager reader found a copy and read it; then he read it again, finding it even more fascinating in a second reading. The acuity, clarity and wisdom of the Angelic Doctor manifested itself on every page. Williamson liked the book; it seized him and did not let go. Father Gilby had the correct sense of the power of Thomistic thought and even stated directly in the Introduction that the words of St. Thomas could appeal to non-believers.

In a world befogged by Descartes' mind/body dualism, Kant's unknowable and imperceptible reality, Camus' sentimental nihilism, the words of St. Thomas cleared the air. They opened a venue in the mind for fresh air, even pure oxygen, to stream in. This philosophy *was* "clear," *was* "consistent," and *was* "complete"; it dared to assert that an ordered and rational exploration of existence could come to reasonable conclusions. The truth existed *outside* the individual mind, not inside as Descartes had posited; the things of this world were real, substantial and knowable, not merely appearances as Kant asserted; life had design because it had been designed by a Designer and thus had meaning and purpose, not pointless emptiness as Camus proposed.

The questing Williamson shared his enthusiasm with his new mentor and friend Father Miles Lovell. Father Lovell simply replied, "If you're interested in St. Thomas, then you should read the *Summa*," a proposal instantly agreeable to the voracious reader. In a spirit of discovery, the teacher again became a student, this time at the feet of St. Thomas himself. He purchased a copy of the complete *Summa Theologiæ*, beginning to read it first in English, later in Latin, and during what came to be his last year of teaching languages at St. Paul's School, beginning to study it systematically, not with the rigors of grinding intellectual cerebration but rather with the joyful delight of a new found and endlessly inspiring hobby. He worked on an article from the *Summa* every day, exercising and training his mind with the intensity and dedication of a serious workout that most modern men display at their local gym. He would read the article of the day and discipline himself to summarise it in English. Readers in later years would wonder at the Bishop's ability to analyze and outline, condense and concisely explain in simple summary complex papal encyclicals, historical cycles, full orchestral scores or literary masterpieces; it was studying the *Summa* that had laid the groundwork and trained the mind for those subsequent tasks. One of his later catch phrases came from this study. He would advise the seminarians to pursue a healthy exercise: "If an apple a day keeps the doctor away, then an article a day keeps the trick-cyclist [psychiatrist] at bay." The *Summa* had begun to settle his troubled thoughts.

The summaries, produced daily, began to pile up. Though working away slowly day by day, the results over time created a complete and thorough Introduction to the Philosophy of St. Thomas Aquinas. These notes would one day be used as the basis for a course at a seminary nestled in a mountain post in Switzerland, though at the time of their composition, the author would have been shocked to learn of such an eventuality. In fact, in conversations with a good and kind Jesuit priest in Farm Street, Father Roger Charles, the Thomas-summarizing *Summa* explorer had stated, "Father, you have this Catholic thing; all very interesting, of course, and worth discussing, but don't come anywhere near me with the business of 'faith.'" The kind Father simply murmured, "W-w-well . . . y-y-yes . . . ," never pushing or proselytizing; in his wisdom, the priest knew that the on-going conversations combined with his persistent private prayers for his recalcitrant interlocutor could eventually result in a conversion, but that would be in God's good time, not his own.

Over time, the solid reasonable writings of St. Thomas removed the "chocks" from in front of the wheels of the plane sitting immobile at the end of the runway, its motor running, but not yet engaging in motion or flight. Williamson came to understand that the solution to the problems destroying the modern world could be found in the Catholic faith. He became so convinced that he even proposed it to the proud young players in the classroom banging and whistling away in Sergeant Pepper's Lonely Hearts Club Band:

Concertino for Muted Toy Trumpet and Fortissimo Amateur Combo

Teacher: "The solution to the problems of the Modern World is the Catholic faith."
Boys: "Really??!!"
Teacher: "Yes."
Boys: "Are you a Catholic?"

Teacher: "No. I am not."
Boys: "Then why are you telling us this?"
Teacher: "Because it is true."
Boys: "But you are not a Catholic?"
Teacher: "No. I am not."

(The trumpet repeats its one note; the band plays random squeaks, and blurts out raucous blasts. The two end on a note of discord.)

On August 20, 1969, the Beatles worked together for the last time as a foursome. That day's recording session at 3 Abbey Road marked the end; the dissolution of the pop giants became inevitable as the tensions among them had reached the boiling point.

At the mid-point of the 1969–1970 school year, the teacher decided he would stop teaching when the term ended. He very much enjoyed the boys, even in the constant combat, and enjoyed the school, appreciating his colleagues, but felt his career in the classroom was going nowhere. Feeling like a "nowhere man living in a nowhere land," he sensed no future as a teacher; he had no special female friend nor saw any likelihood of his being married. Tom Howarth had invited him to supper one night, a meal for three that included his daughter Frances, probably hoping for a future match. The guest found the daughter "fair-stockinged, civilizatress of dress" and even complimented the girl by composing a sonnet for her; deep inside, however, he had never thought that the great search on which he had embarked would find even a good woman at its end. Some other pursuit was in play.

His colleagues expressed disappointment and sorrow when he announced his decision to depart. He had been popular at the school, in the best sense of the word, with his students and his fellow teachers. One colleague, knowing of his recent interest in Catholicism, asked if he had ever met Father Robert Murray at Oxford. No, he had never met the priest and didn't know of him. Would he like to? Yes. The colleague arranged a meeting.

The meeting provided another providential milestone on the road leading to Rome, where all roads do – or should – lead, each path unique and not found on any map. During the course of their meeting, Father Murray asked a simple but heaven- and earth-shaking question: "Have you anything against the Mother of God?" The question took Williamson by surprise and in all honesty he responded, "No. Nothing particularly for, nothing particularly against." Father Murray presented the pilgrim with a chain that would bind him for the rest of his days to the Woman of Women; he gave Williamson a rosary and the beads were accepted. At that moment, the deal was sealed.

Father Myles Lovell had remarked that when he was going through his own "conversion event," he had gone away into the countryside for a few months on his own to think and pray. This seemed to be a sensible idea so at the end of the school year Williamson bought a car and packed it with books, a special place being reserved for volumes of the *Summa Theologiæ* given to him by St. Paul's School as a going away gift. Rosary in hand, he headed for the Scottish highlands to spend quiet time in a cottage loaned to him by a friend. For months he continued his study of Aquinas, one article a day, and even more importantly, prayed all Fifteen Mysteries of the Rosary every day. He recalls, "I thunk and I thunk and I sunk . . . "; sinking into the truth of the Catholic Church proved to be a very fortunate fall.

Music of the Spheres . . . sung by the Angelic Doctor

Did eternal mind not exist then no truth would be eternal.

—*Summa Theologiæ* I-II, Q. XVI, A. 7

The truth caused in our mind by things does not come from the mind's own ingenuity, but from the existence of things.

—*Quæstiones Disputatæ* I *de Veritate*, 2, *ad* 3

Having pondered on how God is apart from all and yet the cause of all, theologians sometimes have said that he is ineffable and at other times have attributed to him all manner of names. Such was demanded of the angel who had the appearance of God: Tell me, by what name art thou called? But he answered, to forestall misunderstanding that might come from naming God, Why dost thou ask my name? Truly this name is exalted and above every name that is named, not only in this world but in the world that is to come.

Yet God is praised in holy writ not only as ineffable but also as having many names. God calls himself, I am who am; the way, the truth, and the life; the light of the world; the God of Abraham. Prophets and apostles praise him as good, beautiful, the beloved of the beloved, the God of gods. As great and terrible, remaining for ever, thou who alone art, before the ages began. As the giver of life and breath, as wisdom, understanding, reason, righteous and mighty to save. As inspiring, and yet in whom are hid the treasures of all knowledge. As our witness, declaring his strength, the King of Kings and lord of lords, the ancient of days, without change or shadow of alteration. As God with us, sanctification and redemption, as greatness walking above the poles of heaven. As after the earthquake and the fire in a still small voice. He is in our hearts, and souls, and bodies; he fills heaven and earth, he is in the world, and above all his works. His knowledge is over all; heaven is his throne and earth his footstool. He is compared to the sun, the bright and morning star; to fire, water, wind, dew, cloud; to the corner-stone and the rock.

—Opusc. XIV, Exposition,
de Divinis Nominibus, I, lect. 3

At the time of his leaving his teaching position in London, the soon-to-be-retired language instructor spent some time at his parents' home. One day as his parents and their three sons gathered to do some painting in the house, brother Harry asked a practical question: "Where are you planning to go and what are you planning to do?" The lofty answer: "I plan on retiring to the wilderness and turning the world upside down by thinking." Harry: "Well, make sure you put the lids back on the paint pots before you do." A bubble of pomposity – popped by a practical elder brother.

The Bishop as a Young Man

On the road a-gain

The time spent in study, prayer and contemplation proved of great value, but surprisingly, the most important occurrence during that time came through the post. One specific fruit from the years of teaching blossomed forth unexpectedly. A letter arrived from a former St. Paul's lad, let us call him young Edgar. The seed that had been scattered in the classroom (and a teacher's ultimate mission is to scatter good seed and pray that it take root in good ground, germinate and grow) had fallen on fertile soil. "I found what you had to say about the Catholic faith very interesting. What should I do about it?" The reply, honest and straightforward: "I'm not a Catholic so I can't help you any further, but I did see in the newspaper an article that made a good deal of sense, written by a Catholic priest protesting against what is happening in the Catholic Church. Father Flanagan lives in Sussex, not far from you. I can't take you any further, but if you go see this priest in Sussex, maybe he can help you...."

Young Edgar made the six-mile pilgrimage from his home to St. George's Church in Polegate, East Sussex, to meet with Father John Flanagan, who had shepherded the parish since 1958. The young man and the older priest got on very well and soon another letter arrived : "Father Flanagan and I are getting on like a house on fire. He is offering to receive me into the Catholic Church. What should I do about it?" In his response the former language teacher quoted from Cardinal John Henry Newman's poem *The Dream of Gerontius*: " 'In the name of Princedoms and of Powers . . . go forth!' Go right ahead! If he is willing to receive you, go right ahead." Father Flanagan was a kind and also cunning old fisher of men and saw the opportunity of landing two souls by casting one line with one bait. The good priest suspected the former teacher who talked the Catholic talk but was not yet walking the Catholic road was primed to be pulled from the destructive waters of the world into the salvific bark; he encouraged young Edgar to invite his former teacher to the formal event that would take place near Christmastime in the Year of Our Lord 1970. The Bishop remembers his reaction. He simply thought, "Why not? Hey... in for a penny, in for a pound...," little suspecting what lay in store. So he threw everything from his Scottish digs into the back of his old car and headed south to Sussex.

Proficiscere, anima Christiana, de hoc mundo!
Go forth upon thy journey, Christian soul!
Go from this world! Go, in the name of God,
The omnipotent Father, who created thee!
Go, in the name of Jesus Christ, Our Lord,
Son of the living God, who bled for thee!
Go, in the name of the Holy Spirit, who
Hath been poured out on thee! Go, in the name
Of Angels and Archangels; in the name
Of Thrones and Dominations; in the name
Of Princedoms and of Powers; and in the name
Of Cherubim and Seraphim, go forth!
Go, in the name of Patriarchs and Prophets;
And of Apostles and Evangelists,
Of Martyrs and Confessors; in the name
Of holy Monks and Hermits; in the name
Of holy Virgins; and all Saints of God,
Both men and women, go. Go on thy course;
And may thy place to-day be found in peace,
And may thy dwelling be the Holy Mount
Of Sion:— through the Same, through Christ, Our Lord.

The Bishop as a Young Man

In the poem, the soul of Newman's Gerontius is leaving this world for good, but the words are appropriate for the two souls, one young, one older, who would die to their old lives and walk away from the fallen world, thanks to the work of Father Flanagan.

Go forth up-on thy jour-ney, Chris-tian soul!

Christmas Eve, 1645. Father George Muscot died, after being thrown into a filthy dungeon among felons and held there for three days. Nine of the ten men condemned to death who heard his last preaching were reconciled to the Catholic faith before their execution.

Christmas Eve, 1970. The unsuspecting Richard Williamson knocked at the door of the presbytery. A round and portly straight-backed priest of medium height with slicked back hair opened the door. Giving no evidence of his lofty plans, in all innocence he offered a warm and friendly and brogue-cloaked welcome, "Ach, come in Mr. Williamson, come in, come in. Sit down, sit down." In the corner of the priest's study sat young Edgar, a young man "with quite a bit of character," now unknowingly a bit of bait.

Duo for Muted Trumpet and Irish Harp

Irish Harp: "Ach, now, Mr. Williamson, what do you think of what this young lad is doing?"
Trumpet: "Well, Father, if I think about it . . . it does seem to me . . . sort of . . . all things considered . . . . if I weigh all the

factors ... and ... judge ... as best as I can ... it sort of seems to me ... that I'd have to say ... he's doing a good thing."

I. H.: "Ach, so you think so, Mr. Williamson. Ach. Well now, why aren't you a Catholic?"

T: "Oh, Father . . . oh, that's a completely different question. . . . if I . . . I have . . . that's not the same question . . . so if I . . . I have to . . . if I try to . . . if I think about that . . . . I am sure there are various reasons why . . . it's not something that I'm really . . . sort of seriously . . . to tell you the truth it's not something . . . . I've really seriously thought of . . . . it's not something I've really thought about."

I. H.: "Ach, Mr. Williamson, ach, is that so? Now Mr. Williamson, when do you want to be received into the Church?"

T: "Oh, Father, that's ... uh ... uh ... ooooh ... ooo . . . ."

I. H.: "Come back in three weeks and I'll receive you into the Church."

T: [mute, but humming, hemming and hawing, squealing, issuing tiny tinny toots of protest]

I. H.: " Look, just come back in three weeks. Think about it. Come back in three weeks and I'll receive you into the Catholic Church."

Three minutes. Hands flung in the air. Cornered. Feathers flying all over the room. Look of despair. Ripped fur and puncture wounds and the bite of steel.

No RCIA. No intensive instruction. The old priest knew from the boy's knowledge that the teacher had learned the basics and had passed them on and had even been doing a thorough study of St. Thomas Aquinas. The one thing necessary – a hearty and loving Irish Catholic shove into the frightening jaws of change that would prove to be a Saviour's kiss.

At that instant, a definitive and essential grace came from above. Richard Nelson Williamson, possessing free will, could easily have said, "No." But he said, "Yes." Looking back, he states unequivocally that the Rosary made the difference. The months of prayer bore fruit.

The Blessed Mother on this Christmas Eve offered God the Father two souls, one a young man named Edgar and a bonus soul named Richard, and not even Father Flanagan, wise as he was, could have seen God's design that one day both men would be Bishops.

Richard Nelson Williamson said, "Yes."

And that was that.

Ridgefield, May, 1987.

PART TWO
from Seminary TO Seminary

"Music is as natural to human beings as laughter."

—Bishop Richard Williamson

"In what space so ever you shall hear the sound of the trumpet, run all hither unto us; our God will fight for us."

—2 Esdras 4: 20

Andante

FATHER FLANAGAN RECEIVED RICHARD Nelson Williamson into the Catholic Church on January 23, 1971.

January 23rd is the Feast of St. Raymond of Pennafort, born in Barcelona in 1175 and one of the founders of Our Lady of Ransom, an order devoted to freeing slaves from their apostate captors.

On orders from Pope Gregory IX, he compiled five books of Decretals, papal decrees formulating decisions in ecclesiastic law that became vital parts of the Church's Canon Law. It is also the Feast Day of St. Emerentiana, the foster-sister of St. Agnes. The young girl was stoned to death by pagans when found praying at the tomb of Agnes. The day is also book-ended by martyrdoms, Fr.

William Patenson at Tyburn, January 22, 1592, and Fr. William Ireland and layman John Grove at Tyburn, January 24, 1679.

Also of note is that January 23rd had for many years been celebrated as the Feast of the Espousals of the Blessed Virgin Mary to Saint Joseph. Granted by Pope Leo X to the Nuns of the Annunciation, the special Feast Day is first recorded on August 29, 1517, two months before a mad monk in Germany nailed his theses on a church door. The Feast, widely celebrated throughout England in the nineteenth and early twentieth centuries, was suppressed by Pope John XXIII in his reforms of 1960.

A French proverb states, "One convert is worth two apostles." Characters in the novels of Evelyn Waugh who come into the Catholic Church or finally submit themselves to God's will have their conversions shrouded in secrecy. Waugh, a convert himself, believed such events are not explicable in "psychological" terms, but are the result of mysteries of grace and providence, far beyond simple expository explanations. Mysteries of grace and providence manifested themselves in the conversion of Richard Nelson Williamson.

Between the fledgling Catholic's Christmas Eve acquiescence and the January 23rd formal conversion, the soon-to-be Catholic received one manifest grace. The catechumen decided to pass the intervening time by visiting a Carmel shrine near London, the Aylsford Priory in Kent, known as "the Friars." The first General Chapter of the Carmelite Order to be held outside of the Holy Land took place at the site in 1247. That Chapter had changed its religious from the hermetic life of solitude and prayer to the life of mendicant friars. Over the next fifty years more than thirty priories were founded in England and Wales by the Order. The Prior General of the Order, St. Simon Stock, had been graced on July 16, 1251, with a vision of Our Lady who promised her protection

From Seminary to Seminary

to those who wore the Carmelite habit. In her hand she held a brown scapular that became a visible sign of Marian devotion. In our own time, the Blessed Mother assured the faithful that in the turbulent storms besetting the Church she would help them. Her aid would come to the faithful who would pray the rosary, wear the brown scapular, and remain devoted to her Immaculate Heart.

After the dissolution of the monasteries by Henry VIII in 1538, "the Friars" passed through the hands of many families down through the centuries until a fire in 1930 caused serious damage to the house. The Carmelite Order bought back their mother-house in 1949 and the first Prior at the restored site, Father Malachy Lynch, hoped to build an open-air shrine on the property. He gathered a group of artists, craftsmen and stonemasons to do the work. Fr. Lynch described the restored "Friars" as "a prayer in stone" and opened it to pilgrims. Faithful Catholics and one soon-to-be-Catholic convert "long[ing] to goon on pilgrimages" made their way to "the Friars." The strung beads of the rosary had brought the pilgrim thus far on his journey; the cords holding the scapular in place would bind him for a while to come to Mary Most Holy.

◖◗

During his stay at "the Friars," Williamson ran into a young American named Bob who was working on a new roadway on which pilgrims could travel to the "prayer in stone." The two men chatted as Bob cleared a ditch.

Duo for Folk Singer and Muted Trumpet

Bob: "I've been on the Continent recently, visiting shrines of apparitions of Our Lady. I even went to the recent one in northern Spain."

RNW: "Recent?"

Bob: "Yes. Our Lady has been appearing to four young girls in a mountain village called Garabandal."

RNW: "Pull my leg."

Bob: "No, really."

RNW: "Pull the other one."

Bob: "No, really."

RNW: "Spin me another yarn."

Bob: "Our Lady is very concerned about what is going on in the modern world. She is giving us warnings. I have visited there."

[RNW begins to listen seriously.]

Bob: "There's a book about it in the Visitors Library. *Garabandal*... It's by Francisco Sanchez Ventura y Pascual. Check it out."

Curiosity carried the catechumen to the library shelves where he located the book. He read the narrative describing the events that had occurred and the messages that had been given in the seemingly insignificant village in northern Spain from 1961 to 1965. Something extraordinary appeared to have taken place in the mountain village location.

But those particular library shelves were weighed down with other chronicles recording other apparitions:

- Rue de Bac, Paris, 1830: "Times are evil in France and in the world."

- La Salette, France, 1846: "Rome will lose the Faith and become the seat of the Anti- Christ."

- Lourdes, France, 1858: "I am the Immaculate Conception."

From Seminary to Seminary

- Pontmain, France, 1871: "But pray, my children. God will hear you in time."

- Knock, Ireland, 1879: The Lamb on the Altar.

- Fatima, Portugal, 1917: Three Messages; "Oh my Jesus, forgive us our sins, save us from the fires of hell. Lead all souls to heaven, especially those most in need of thy mercy."

- Beauraing, Belgium, 1932: "Pray, pray, pray . . . Do you love My Son? Do you love me? Then sacrifice yourself for me."

- Banneux, Belgium 1933 "I come to relieve suffering . . . pray."

Recalling the many books and the days of reading, the Bishop now states simply, "It all hung together."

On January 23, John and Helen Williamson, the always supportive parents, attended the ceremony at St. Joachim's Church in Polegate, Sussex, albeit in a "decent understanding liberal way." Father Flanagan had raised the funds and supervised the building of the new Church that had opened on May 14, 1960, the Feast of All Blessed English Martyrs, appropriately observed as Father Richard Reynolds, Priors John Houghton, Robert Lawrence, Augustine Webster, layman John Haile, and a soul simply named "Brigettine," had all been martyred on that day at Tyburn in 1535. Father Flanagan had wished the new Church to be named "Our Lady of Perpetual Succour," but his Bishop overruled him, saying the name would be St. Joachim's. On the occasion of the reception of Richard Williamson into the Catholic Church, Father Flanagan also offered a mass, the new mass of the new order, but the devout father, obedient to his superiors in celebrating the *novus ordo* mass, displayed his adherence to the faith by using the First Canon.

The new Catholic returned to "the Friars" at Aylesford for more prayer, more solitude, more reading and more conversation with Bob. One evening as he prayed before the altar, he sensed something "very special" in the Blessed Sacrament, "somebody." He denies that it was a "mystical experience"; he rather views it as a "reassurance," a heightened conviction. In fact, the Bishop denies ever having had a "mystical experience." "The Lord doesn't deal with me on that level. He's dealing with a bloody-minded Englishman so it's all pretty solid stuff."

As a result of his reading during those days at Aylesford, he decided to visit the shrines of the apparitions of Our Lady on the continent. He purchased a few travelers checks and filled a ruck sack. He stopped to see Father Flanagan before his departure and the good priest stunned the young man once again by a direct, unexpected exhortation.

Second Duettino for Irish Harp and Trumpet

I.H.: "Young man, you should be a priest."
T: (Stamping foot on brake and fumbling for mute) "Oh, Father, wait a minute . . . wait . . . "
I.H. "Ach, all right, all right. Off you go, young man."

And off he went.

From Seminary to Seminary

The first stop on his Marian "Mystery Tour" took Williamson to the Rue du Bac in Paris and then he proceeded to the south of France to visit Lourdes. His old friends Malcolm and Kitty Muggeridge were staying in the south of France at this time so he went to renew his acquaintance and tell them the good news. The Muggeridges received him graciously, as always, and upon learning of the younger man's conversion, Malcolm quipped, "Oh, so now you're a card-carrying member." The Muggeridges would "receive their cards" ten years hence. Also visiting the Muggeridges was English novelist Graham Greene. Greene had begun his career as a devout communist but had stunned the intelligentsia when he converted to the Catholic Church in his early twenties. His best works of fiction, such as *The Power and the Glory* and *The Heart of the Matter*, explore struggling souls whose faith is challenged by the traps and temptations of the modern world. Williamson remembers Greene as an aged but vital man, cynical, lively, witty, warm and human, but despite these qualities, "a sad case." The seed had fallen on rock in Greene's case and as his Catholic faith weakened, his old attachment to communism reasserted itself. The man became, to quote the title of one of his works, "a burnt-out case," and sadly, so did his subsequent fiction.

The Marian pilgrimage continued with a visit to Lourdes and then Spain. He visited Loyola, the birthplace of St. Ignatius. He also made a special visit to a cave in Manresa in Catalonia. Here St. Ignatius retreated at the time of his spiritual awakening. His early days had been occupied seeking military honors and renown, but when recuperating from the crippling effects of a cannonball strike, he turned to a life of prayer and contemplation. From March 25, the Feast of the Annunciation, 1522, until mid-February 1523, he lived a solitary life of prayer in the cave, venturing out to assist at Mass. During these months, he sketched out the basics of what would become the *Spiritual Exercises*, one of his two great contributions to the Church during the time of the Counter-Reformation, the other being the founding of the Jesuit Order to combat the growing numbers of heresies and heretics in his day. The cave in Manresa became a pilgrimage site for Catholic souls and so the new convert made his journey there. Inside he found a typical device of the day set up for the advantage of the occasional visitor – a machine that gave basic information about the Saint, his life, his great works and his time at Manresa; however, before the instructive recorded presentation could be accessed, the pilgrim was obliged to drop a coin into the mechanism. When Williamson dropped in his offering, he was greeted with familiar musical notes – da-da-da-Dum, da-da-da-Dum, the opening of the Beethoven Fifth Symphony in C minor, those notes often referred to as "fate knocking at the door." In this case, as the Beethoven echoes carried the listener back to schooldays at Winchester and the beginnings of a long journey, they might be more aptly described as a proclamation of Providence.

He journeyed to Garabandal, in the northern mountains of Spain some 50 miles south of Santander, where Bob who first sparked his interest had visited. The apparitions of Garabandal, the sincerity and innocence of Conchita, one of the four young girls, and the stark vistas of the village made a lasting impression. He remains to this day a firm believer in the Garabandal message of the Warning, the Miracle and the possible Chastisement, even as many have abandoned any such trust.

From Seminary to Seminary

Then he traveled to Portugal and stayed for a time at Fatima. On a day of bad weather during this visit, a woman staying at the same hotel asked the pilgrim what he knew about the Sacred Heart. He admitted that he did not know much. She then gave him a copy of *The Way of Divine Love*, written by a nun, Sister Josefa Menendez, in Poitiers between 1920 and 1923. This seemingly insignificant Spanish nun, a Sister in the Society of the Sacred Heart of Jesus, became a victim soul, chosen by Our Lord to suffer for the salvation of many lost souls and to transmit to the world messages of Our Lord's love for sinners, calling on them to take refuge in His Sacred Heart:

> I know the very depths of souls, their passions, their attraction for the world and its pleasures; I have known from all eternity how many of them will fill My Heart with bitterness, and that for a great number both My sufferings and My blood will be in vain.... But having loved them, I love them still.... My Heart is not so much wounded by sin, as torn with grief that they will not take refuge with Me after it. I want to forgive. I want the world to know through my chosen ones that My Heart is overflowing with love and mercy and is waiting for sinners.

Sister Josefa Menendez, *The Way of Divine Mercy*, Rockford, Ill.: Tan Books, 1972, p. 186.

The book made a deep and lasting impression.

The pilgrim finished his continental journey and returned to England carrying books, pamphlets, folders, all replete with information on the Marian apparitions. Upon his return, he went to visit a priest he had met some time before, early in his spiritual expedition.

Counterpoint Exercise for English Horn and Trumpet

E.H.: "Come in. How are you?"

T: "Father, I've been received into the Church."

E.H.: "Great news. Congratulations. What have you been doing?"

T: "I've been on the Continent and I've made some tremendous discoveries."

E.H.: "Yes . . ."

T: "I've been following the apparitions of Our Lady and studying what she has to say about the modern world. And she has important messages for the whole Church."

E.H.: "Dear boy . . . how long ago were you received into the Church?"

T: "Three months ago, Father."

E.H.: "Yessss . . . yessss . . . That's it. Take it easy, dear boy, take it easy. Go your way and say your prayers."

Trumpet Solo

I knew the score of the modern world from my years of teaching the wild and crazy London boys with their deep devotion to the Beatles and little else. I knew the present situation. I knew from good priests and good books the truth of the ancient faith, given for all to see. Combining the rough, empty life of modern London with the enduring truths of the ancient faith made sense of Our Lady's words in her apparitions. 'Here is the situation in which the world exists and here is the solution.. Here is the truth.' Some good priests like Father Anselm knew all about the modern world but had forgotten the ancient truth, replacing it with a devotion to the modern "thought" of Teilhard de Chardin; other priests knew the ancient truth and stuck to it, but maintained themselves by refusing to learn about the horrors of the modern world. I found the complete and perfect combination of the two in the messages of Our Lady given in her apparitions: the full horror of the godless modern world and the full sufficiency of the ancient timeless truths to meet and overcome that horror. I did not find that combination complete in any one of the priests that I had got to know. Only our Lady of the Apparitions seemed to me to hold both ends of the chain as they need to be held. The priests were good men, pious men, kind men, and they all helped me, but there was something missing in them, something incomplete. I could not rest content with what they were telling me, with what they were giving me – it did not seem adequate. I respected and loved those men who had been so good to me, but I now had to judge them by the Apparitions and not the other way around.

And so providence led me to Archbishop Lefebvre. In him I found the serene urgency of the Madonna in a great man of God, embarking on his heroic defense of the old religion against a Church and world conspiring to get rid of it as a worn-out relic. In the Archbishop, I found her combination of faithfulness to the Truth and a deep concern for the modern world in all its modernity.

> Our Lady of the Apparitions, thank you for appearing and caring for all of us, your wayward modern children. Please keep me faithful, both to your Divine Son and to the stray souls for whom He died. I have only one wish, which is to do my best for Him and for you. Amen.
>
> —Bishop Richard Williamson's prayer

Hymn 1.

H -ve má-ris stélla, Dé-i Má-ter álma

The Voice of the Trumpet

> Happy is he who lives and dies under the protection of the Blessed Virgin.
>
> —St. John Vianney, the Curé d'Ars

◉

The knapsack kept filling with more books, the daily study of an article from the *Summa Theologiæ* continued, and notebooks overflowed with concise summaries of Thomistic rationality and objective truth. The tickets were now officially punched and, footloose and fired with the new-found faith, the recent convert, a touch dewy-eyed, hit the road again. The first destinations on the second rambling – the shrines in Germany and Austria. He visited the controversial site at Heroldsbach, which many believe to be the site of genuine Marian apparitions and others denounce as a fraud. It is reported that in 1967, a group of German pilgrims approaching the confessional of Padre Pio encountered the Saint who exclaimed, "What do you Germans want else! The Madonna has descended down to you! Heroldsbach is a place of grace." The controversy is ongoing.

The Bishop has never had any desire to visit Medjugore.

He rambled back to France, visiting Toulouse where he desired to meet Jacques Maritain. The noted writer resided at a religious house near Toulouse and dressed as a monk. He refused to meet with the younger man. Reflecting back, the Bishop now says, "There is no reason why he should have done so. I was interested in meeting those who might give me insight and understanding."

The wanderings continued for a year, but for all the many miles and countless kilometers, despite the great distances traversed, the pilgrim was going nowhere. The perambulations came to an end thanks to clear and di-

From Seminary to Seminary

rect comments from a pious Italian woman whose holiness had brought her special blessings. Williamson journeyed to San Damiano and met Mama Rosa.

◉

On the morning of September 29, 1961, Rosa Quattrini-Buzzini, a fifty-two year old widow, lay seriously ill and nearly dying when a woman wearing a blue shawl knocked on her door. Rosa's Aunt Adele who cared for her niece answered the door. The unknown lady requested money for Padre Pio. Rosa had only 1000 lire in the house but offered half of it for the holy man. The women prayed together and before the lady departed she touched Mama Rosa's wounds. Aunt Adele went to her room and prayed that the monetary gift would reach Padre Pio. A voice suddenly stated loudly and clearly, "Mama Rosa will be healed." Aunt Adele went to the kitchen and found Mama Rosa washing the dishes. The niece turned to her and said, "I have been healed." The two women were convinced that Our Lady had visited them.

Mama Rosa made a pilgrimage to San Giovanni Rotondo. The lady with the blue covering appeared to her again and said, "Do you recognize me?" Mama Rosa replied, "Yes, you are the Madonna and you healed me." The lady led her to Padre Pio who told her to return to San Damiano and to care for the sick, especially her Aunt Adele who was now ailing. And he told her to prepare herself as she would live through "a great event." Upon her return home, she experienced a series of apparitions and miracles that have made San Damiano a pilgrimage site, even though the Church authorities have never officially approved it.

Williamson stopped at the site on his way to Rome and spoke with Mama Rosa. He then traveled on and found Rome to be oppressive because of the weight of faithlessness evident in the clergy. The poison of Vatican II had spread quickly through the veins of the system, especially infecting the priesthood, driving clerics either out of the Church or into bizarre frenzies of apostate ideas. The only antidote, Catholic Truth, could not be allowed to flow freely. Greatly discouraged and burdened with the weight of what he saw, Williamson felt compelled to return to San Damiano. Once there, he asked to see Mama Rosa. The holy woman proved deserving of her maternal appellation by comforting, consoling and encouraging the dispirited man. When he admitted he did not know what to do, she asked if he had a spiritual director. He acknowledged that Father Flanagan was his spiritual director. She kindly but firmly said, "You must go and see him."

So in the spring of 1972, Williamson returned to where his journey had begun at the time of his conversion. He had fled in fear when Father Flanagan had suggested a religious vocation, but after his time of searching, he went back to Father Flanagan's office.

> And the end of all our exploring
> Will be to arrive where we started
> And know the place for the first time.

Father Flanagan in his wisdom, remembering the nervous reception of his earlier suggestion of a vocation, knew better than to sound the same chord at once. He knew that "success in circuit lies" and began by "indirection to [point] direction out."

From Seminary to Seminary

Duo 3 for Irish Harp and Trumpet

I.H.: "So what have you been doing, young man?"

T: "Well, Father, I've been traveling and . . . I've been reading . . . and . . . "

I.H.: "What're you *doing*?"

T: "Well, Father, I've been . . . I'm . . . "

I.H.: "What're you *doing*? You ought to be *doing* something. What *can* you do?"

T: "Well, Father, when I . . . "

I.H.: "What *did* you do?"

T: "Well, when I did do something . . . well, I was teaching . . . "

I.H.: "So you can teach?"

T: "Yes . . . "

I.H.: "Where were you teaching?"

T: "In a public school in London . . . "

I.H.: "What were you teaching?"

T: "Languages . . . "

I.H.: "Alright."

(Father Flanagan picks up the phone. Dials.)

"Have you got a vacancy for a young man who can teach languages? Good."

(Passes the phone to the discombobulated convert.)

"Young man."

T: "Hello. Yes, I taught languages at St. Paul's Boys School . . . You have a vacancy for the next term?"

I.H.: "Young man, you *take* the job."

T.: "I'll take the job."

The young man took the job.

So Williamson began teaching again at a school close to St. Joachim's Parish at Polegate in Sussex, where the priest could with a kind hawk-eye observe him, offer

The Voice of the Trumpet

him the sacraments and wait for the moment to swoop down and raise him up. The moment arrived; the priest struck.

Duettino 4 for Irish Harp and Trumpet

I.H.: "Alright, enough of that. Now you will try for the priesthood."
T: "If you say so, Father."
I.H.: "Yes. I say so. You're going to try for the local diocese."
T: "All right."

The diocese of Arundel and Brighton had a week-end long selection conference late in 1972 that lasted from Friday evening until Sunday afternoon. Thirty men attended the conference which was organized and run by a three-person "testing team" – one priest, one layman and one laywoman. Each candidate participated in a private interview with each of the three evaluators. The young man present through the auspices of Father Flanagan sustained a direct hit from a question from the laywoman.

Duettino for Snare Drum and Trumpet

Drum: "Can you endure celibacy?"
T.: [Silence.]

From Seminary to Seminary

Drum: (repeat): "Can you endure celibacy?"
T. (simple *pianissimo* toot): "I think so."

The three individual interviews were followed by a group session where one of the examiners threw questions at several candidates at once. This old technique often used in interviews in business and industry had a specific purpose: throw the unsuspecting interviewees a hunk of red meat and see what they do with it. Any simple polite answer could be seen as showing a lion's strength or a pussycat's docility, depending on the interpreter. Thus the candidate's future rested in the interpretation of the interrogator.

The probing then turned to questions of "peace and justice." When asked to offer his comments on the subject, the young man responded with the fearful prospect of souls being assigned to hell by God's justice and the need for so many modern men to do penance, prayer intentions laid out by the Blessed Mother through many of her recent apparitions.

End of interview.

A brief letter arrived on the desk of Father Flanagan with a direct message concerning the prospects of his recommended candidate: "Thank you – but no thank you." Father Flanagan's Irish temper flared and the flames crackled and burned in all directions. The candidate felt the heat for being "imprudent," an accusation that would hound the direct and forthright speaker for the rest of his days, sometimes even causing nuclear blasts. Father Flanagan flamed on, "I may have invited you to talk to the parish about the Marian apparitions but . . . but . . . . " The humbled candidate responded that the gleesome threesome had expected him to spout socialist claptrap and he was not about to do so; for obvious Catholic reasons he would not play their game according to their anti-Catholic wishes.

The Voice of the Trumpet

The Irish harp then became quite unstrung – "Take but degree away, untune that string/ And hark what discord follows." Father Flanagan directed his cacophonous roar at the local Bishop. He ripped off a letter, to be opened with asbestos gloves, raging against the totally inappropriate circumstance of having a laywoman as a member of a panel deciding potential vocations for the diocese. "How dare you have a laywoman judge candidates for the priesthood! How dare you have a laywoman ask candidates for the priesthood questions concerning celibacy!" The good Father's rage really took aim at the Conciliar Church that was growing rapidly into a predatory behemoth, crushing in its advance every young green shoot attempting to take root and grow.

A comrade priest and friend of Father Flanagan's from a nearby parish, Father Leonard Whatmore, suggested the problematic potential vocation might be sent to the London Oratory. The Oratory regularly received Oxbridge graduates who had means of their own and discovered their vocations a bit later in life. So in that same autumn of 1972, Richard Nelson Williamson entered the Oratory's postulancy. He submitted to an interview, conducted with two other candidates, then paid a day's visit that was succeeded by a week's visit and then by the postulancy. During this postulancy, a sweet old priest taught scripture to the young men, but taught exclusively out of a "new" Bible Commentary. The imprudent troublemaker piped up at one session and asked an outrageous question: "Father, why don't we read St. Augustine?" The old priest froze, looked over the top of his glasses and fixed his icy stare on the obstreperous troglodyte, seeking to leave him "pinned and wriggling on the wall." The inquisitive young man remained unmoved ; he thought he had asked a fair question. Shortly after the outrageous incident, the postulant had his regularly scheduled second-month evaluation with his superior who looked over his record and the comments of the Oratory priests and said, "Very interesting. Very impressive. Thank you but no thank you."

The uppity pup found himself back on the pavement and had to slink off to Father Flanagan again with his tail firmly planted between his legs; he scratched at the rectory door to be let in and whimpered like a whipped dog.

Duo 5 for Irish Harp and Trumpet

> I.H.: "Come in, young man, come in. So what is going on?"
> T: "The Oratory doesn't want me either."
> I.H.: "Well, young man, if you can't keep your big mouth shut, there's only one place for you and that's Écône."
> T: "But, Father, you don't agree with Archbishop Lefebvre."
> I.H.: "No. I don't."
> T: "Didn't you refuse to keep an appointment with him when he was in the area?"
> I.H.: "Yes. I did. But only when I learned he was standing in opposition to the Pope. The troubles in the Church are because of the terrible bishops. The Pope is a good man; the troubles are not his fault."
> T: "Well then, how? . . . Why? . . . "
> I.H.: [Silence.]
> [Silence.]

During his European grand tour, Williamson had stopped briefly at Écône. An American friend had recommended a visit there to meet an American priest, Father Urban Snyder, who was assisting in Écône, helping out Archbishop Lefebvre by teaching the seminarians. Williamson had been very impressed with Father Snyder, a genuine faithful priest, very intelligent, very quiet, an unassuming man who was no thunderer or world-shaker, but a good man of God. Williamson had stayed overnight in the area and had been introduced to Archbishop Lefebvre, himself a "troublemaker."

The Archbishop by that time in 1972 had ordained one English priest, Father Peter Morgan. Father Morgan agreed to visit Father Flanagan and the two men could discuss the suitability of Williamson going to Écône. The visit turned into a debate over canon law and though Father Morgan bravely defended the Society position, Father Flanagan, a proper Doctor of canon law, got the better of the argument. Father Morgan said he knew the priests at Écône well and suggested that Mr. Williamson ought to go to Écône and do the thirty-day Ignatian exercises.

Irish Harp Solo

Father Flanagan: "You ought to go to Écône...."

> Lord may we all have the courage like John
> Flanagan, Your priest, to speak out boldly in
> defense of Your Church and her teachings,
> no matter what the price may be.
> O God, teach us the lesson Your son and
> priest John Flanagan had learnt so well
> namely to suffer misunderstanding, frequently
> to bear calumny, and permanently contempt

From Seminary to Seminary

and division, and to be able manfully to unite it all with the sufferings of Your Divine Son.

Let us commend ourselves and the soul of John Flanagan to the maternal care of Mary, the Mother of God . . . Hail Mary, full of grace, the Lord is with thee. Blessed art thou amongst women and blessed is the fruit of thy womb, Jesus. Holy Mary, mother of God, pray for us sinners, now, and at the hour of our death.

> —Father Hugh Byron, at Requiem Mass of Father John Flanagan (1912–1977). *Requiescat in Pace.*

In 1975, Beatle Paul McCartney became a vegetarian. As he and his then "wife" Linda were dining on a meal of lamb, they saw lambs frolicking in a field. They stopped eating meat and became animal rights advocates.

"Little lamb, who [ate] thee? Dost thou know who [ate] thee?"

There is more than one way to eat a lamb.

The would-be priest, having faced rejection by the *novus ordo* establishment, made his way to Switzerland to begin the thirty day Spiritual Exercises of St. Ignatius among a band of outcasts and vilified reactionary counter-revolutionaries, led by a gentle, aging, detested and much beloved Archbishop. In November, 1972, Father Rivière began the Exercises, but had to go to Rome almost immediately. Father Barrielle took his place and that seemingly insignificant substitution in the long run "made all the difference."

Father Ludovic-Marie Barrielle had reached the age of 75 by the fall of 1972 and had devoted his life to the Spiritual Exercises. Born in the south of France, he had announced his own future vocation when in his mother's arms at the age of one-and-a-half. As a priest passed by in a procession with the Blessed Sacrament the babe in arms had uttered his first words, "Me pwiest," in French, of course. The words proved prophetic. Ordained in 1924, he began parish work in Marseilles. Fascinated by tales of soldiers from duty in World War II who told of the great spiritual benefits of the five-day retreats where Father Vallet offered the Exercises, Father Barrielle went to do the Exercises with the priest whose work was spreading the renewal of the practice. As a result, he entered into a small, new Congregation being formed by Father Vallet specifically to increase their promulgation.

For many years, Father Barrielle preached the Spiritual Exercises, but with the planned demolition team of Newchurch doing its best to gut the faith, tearing open traditional practices and draining souls dry, the Community came under attack. The strong brew of the Ignatian retreats had to be watered down to tepid "lite" beer. Father Barrielle refused to cooperate with the destroyers and so he was exiled to a small retreat house in the north of France where he could do less good and aid fewer souls.

And there he remained until the early 70's when Archbishop Lefebvre, having founded the seminary, sought out an older priest to provide spiritual direction to the young men beginning their training.

From Seminary to Seminary

The Archbishop thought of an old war-horse put out to grass in the north . . . he blew on his trumpet. The old horse, now in his seventy fourth year, pricked up his ears (yes it was the right trumpet again!), he snorted, he whinnied, he set off at a trot, soon the old legs were galloping to the aid of the Archbishop, and by the Archbishop's side he remained to the end of his days.

Letters from the Rector, No. 114.

The old priest proved a valuable addition to the seminary, a necessary and enlivening bonus to any institution of education, a large and unique personality to delight and challenge the young, giving their memories a treasure to sustain them in later, harder days. Father Barrielle possessed personality and radiated unforgettable character. The modern wasteland with its deracinated soil, a dry barren expanse, can rarely produce such figures, and the drought of grace not only threatens salvation but stunts souls, wrapping them in puny cocoons, preventing them from breaking forth in memorable flight as the colorful creatures God intended them to be. Father Barrielle: fully human; elderly; heavy and not handsome, but carrying a weight of wisdom; not intellectual but a master of discernment; boisterous and bullying; willing to bash, to cuff, to scold the seminarians, who loved him the more each time he laid on them the label of "blithering idiots." At the meal table when facing a special diet dish prepared to "make less [his] body hence," he would devour the meager fare and then help himself to the attractive provender on other plates, grazing on whatever he found most appealing. He was famous for his booming call of *Voce mea ad Dominum clamavi* at Friday Compline. One Friday when he did not appear, a smaller voice had begun articulating the words, when booming down the aisle came the familiar explosion of the late-arriving Father's prayer. *Voce mea,* indeed! When asked once if he would prefer instant coffee or filtered coffee, he announced, "Both!" The potential seminarian, now the Bishop, remembers the good Father as "intensely human and full of God."

At the end of his days, he would spend entire nights in devotion before the Blessed Sacrament, the same Body, Blood, Soul and Divinity of Our Lord that he had first encountered when held in his mother's arms and then, nodding in a chair during the day with a partially drained Coca-Cola can in his hand, he would, half-asleep but spiritually alert, deliver the Exercises to seminarians, so many of whom found their way to the priesthood, with stronger souls and vivid memories. In 1983, he departed to rest in other arms.

Bishop Williamson remembers him as "a model spiritual director." The good Father also passed to the seminarian an intense devotion to the Maria Valtorta *Poem of the Man-God,* a devotion the Bishop proclaims aloud to this day with the loud echo of Father Barrielle's booming voice. Father Barrielle understood the gift of this work to our time. In an age when good souls tend to drift into the clouds filled with the uplifting helium of piety, the gift of Our Lord was to remind them of the dust on His feet as He walked in a real world among real human beings, body and soul, with human failings, human passions, human good; the problem for us being the dangerous modern schizophrenia of angelism-bestialism so expertly defined by the remarkable Catholic writer Walker Percy in his masterwork, *Lost in the Cosmos.* The very human and very holy Father Barrielle understood this gift from the Man-God, for he was very human and very holy. Archbishop Lefebvre disagreed with Father Barrielle about the Valtorta work and they debated and disagreed, but they never cast each other into "outer darkness." *The Poem of the Man-God* is a matter of personal devotion, not dogma.

From Seminary to Seminary

It is no wonder that at the end of those first Thirty Day Exercises led by Father Barrielle, when asked by the Archbishop if he still wished to study for the priesthood at the seminary, Richard Williamson replied, "Yes, Your Excellency. I do."

> Then he that heareth the sound of the trumpet, whosoever he be, and do not look to himself, if the sword come, and cut him off: his blood shall be upon his own head. He heard the sound of the trumpet, and did not look to himself, his blood shall be upon him: but if he look to himself, he shall save his life.
>
> —Ezechiel 33: 4–5

Écône offered a refuge from the refuse of the wasteland of the modern world, an island of quiet tranquility in the turbulent wash of polluted waves flooding the outside. Archbishop Lefebvre did not brood like a mother hen over his seminarian chicks, but his presence permeated the halls, as he always watched and always prayed.

The Archbishop had contracted the time frame of usual seminary training from six years to five years because of the urgency of the conciliar crisis and the pleas of the faithful seeking traditional holy priests. That process accelerated even faster for the seminarian from England who officially entered in December of 1972. He took the cassock in February of 1973 and his years of study were reduced because of his academic preparation. His classical education followed by years of teaching languages allowed him to pass over the Latin courses, especially as the classical Latin he had studied and taught for years was more difficult and demanding than the Church Latin his

The Voice of the Trumpet

fellow seminarians were studying. His years in the company of St. Thomas Aquinas and the *Summa Theologiæ* and his self-imposed self-study course allowed him to sail over the first year of philosophy, landing him in the second year – metaphysics. The discipline acquired at Downsend and Winchester and Cambridge assured his competence in the coursework, compressing the five years of study into three and a half years.

Of course, the three and a half years of preparation had included spiritual training – prayer, meditation, penance, fasting – but they had also included special blessings. In April of 1973, fewer than six months after his admission to Écône, Father Barrielle had asked the newcomer to sacrifice his planned summer travel. He would become a retreat master and assist in giving the Spiritual Exercises. During the summer of 1973, Williamson helped Father Barrielle in three sessions offering the Exercises to receptive souls. The time he spent traveling through Europe with the older priest and the insights gained by working with the holy man proved a special grace.

In 1974, a French television crew requested permission to visit Écône and record the "strange goings on" of a traditional Catholic seminary. In fewer than ten years, the education of seminarians that had been standard practice for centuries had been transformed from the "normal" into the "odd." The Archbishop asked Williamson to be the "model seminarian" presented to the media investigators to prove that the seminarians at Écône were not peculiar pious misfits but men from the world who had decided after reasoned deliberation to become traditional Catholic priests. Williamson was thirty-four years old, a recent convert, who had studied at Winchester and Cambridge, had taught for several years and decided by his own choice to come to Écône. When shortly thereafter, a second French television crew arrived to do yet another mini-documentary, the Archbishop again put William-

From Seminary to Seminary

son forward as "the face of the seminary." In the interview he gave for the documentary, Williamson admitted that he could never rest content at the other institutions of learning he had attended, that his sense of the absence of an essential element in his education had provoked in him a strong urge to "smash the windows," but having arrived to study at Écône with its fullness of the riches of Catholic tradition, he felt no such impulse. All the windows remained in place and quite safe.

In the autumn of 1974, Rome, uneasy and frightened by the survival and success of "old Church ways" at Écône, sent two Belgian clerics to "investigate" what was transpiring there in the elevated Swiss countryside. Archbishop Lefebvre sent Williamson as the first seminarian to be grilled by the ecclesial detectives. During their visit, the two representatives of Rome scandalized the seminarians and enraged the usually placid Archbishop by openly and blithely questioning the Resurrection and Ascension of Christ, expressing doubts that Truth could ever be fixed and unchanging, stating their belief that the Catholic Church was not the sole possessor of Truth and looking forward to, in their view, the inevitable acceptance of married clergy. The visitors reported back to Rome with a generally positive report; the Archbishop reported back to Rome with the now famous November 1974 declaration.

Full Orchestra – *fortissimo*

We hold firmly with all our heart and with all our mind to Catholic Rome, Guardian of the Catholic Faith and of the traditions necessary to the maintenance of this faith, to the eternal Rome, mistress of wisdom and truth.

We refuse, on the other hand, and have always refused, to follow Rome of Neo-Modernist and neo-Protestant tendencies which became clearly manifest during the Second Vatican Council, and after the Council, in all the reforms which issued from it.

In effect, all these reforms have contributed and continue to contribute to the destruction of the Church, to the ruin of the priesthood, to the abolition of the Sacrifice of the Mass and the Sacraments, to the disappearance of the religious life, and to a naturalistic and Teilhardian education in the universities, in the seminaries, in catechetics: an education deriving from Liberalism and Protestantism which had been condemned many times by the solemn Magisterium of the Church.

No authority, not even the highest in the hierarchy, can compel us to abandon or to diminish our Catholic Faith, so clearly expressed and professed by the Church's Magisterium for nineteen centuries.

"Friends," said St. Paul, "though it were we ourselves, though it were an angel from heaven that should preach to you a gospel other than the gospel we have preached to you, a curse upon him" (Galations 1: 8).

Is it not this that the Holy Father is repeating to us today? And if there is a certain contradiction manifest in his words and deeds as well as in the acts of the dicasteries, then we cleave to what has always been taught and we turn a deaf ear to the novelties which destroy the Church.

It is impossible to profoundly modify the *Lex Orandi* without modifying the *Lex Credendi*: To the New Mass there corresponds the new catechism, the new priesthood, the new seminaries, the new universities, the 'Charismatic' Church, Pentecostalism – all of them opposed to orthodoxy and the never-changing Magisterium.

This reformation, deriving as it does from Liberalism and Modernism, is entirely corrupted; it derives from heresy and results in heresy, even if all its acts are not formally heretical. It is therefore impossible for any conscientious and faithful Catholic to espouse this reformation and to submit to it in any way whatsoever.

The only attitude of fidelity to the Church and to Catholic doctrine appropriate for our salvation is a categorical refusal to accept this reformation.

From Seminary to Seminary

That is why, without any rebellion, bitterness, or resentment, we pursue our work of priestly formation under the guidance of the never-changing Magisterium, convinced as we are that we cannot possibly render a greater service to the Holy Catholic Church, to the Sovereign Pontiff, and to posterity.

That is why we hold firmly to everything that has been consistently thought and practiced by the Church (and codified in books before the Modernist influence of the Council) concerning faith, morals, divine worship, catechetics, priestly formation, and the institution of the Church, until such time as the true light of tradition dissipates the gloom which obscures the sky of the eternal Rome.

Doing this, with the grace of God, the help of the Virgin Mary, St. Joseph, and St. Pius X, we are certain that we are being faithful to the Catholic and Roman Church, to all of Peter's successors, and of being the *Fideles Dispensatores Mysteriorum Domini Nostri Jesu Christ in Spiritu Sancto*."

+ Marcel Lefebvre

◉ ◉ ◉

I have often inquired earnestly and attentively of very many men eminent for sanctity and learning, how and by what rule I may be able to distinguish the truth of the Catholic faith from the falsehood of heretical depravity; and I have always and in almost every instance received an answer to this effect: That whether I or anyone else should wish to detect the frauds and avoid the snares of heretics as they arise, and to continue sound and complete in the Catholic faith, we must, the Lord helping, fortify our

The Voice of the Trumpet

belief in two ways: first, by the authority of Divine Law, and then, by the tradition of the Catholic Church.

—St. Vincent of Lerins

[W]e go along with about 95% of the Second Vatican Council....

—Bishop Bernard Fellay, Superior General SSPX, DICI, No. 6, May 18, 2001

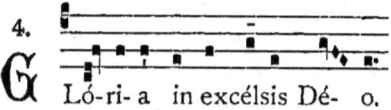

Layman Thomas Ashby.

—martyred at Tyburn, May 18, 1544

4. Gló-ri- a in excélsis Dé- o.

One serious gap remained in the Williamson education. He did have to be instructed toward a correct understanding of modern world events, the true face of which had been obscured or disfigured by "intellectuals" in ac-

From Seminary to Seminary

ademia and the media and government. He recalls with gratitude his fellow seminarian, Jean-Michel Faure calmly and clearly explaining to him the truth of recent French history, including the real agenda of Charles de Gaulle, who despite being a daily Mass attendee was one of the liberal destroyers. These new understandings led briefly to suspicions about much of transmitted history and resulted in one of the few reprimands he received during his Écône years. Writing an exam in a course on Church History that he had found to be less than illuminating, he wrote at the top of his exam paper in large letters: "*HISTOIRE FICTION.*" The Professor, understandably upset, sent the upstart student to the Archbishop. When the Archbishop queried as to the cause of the trouble, seminarian Williamson hid behind Jane Austen's skirts (the famous novelist never having worn pants) and referenced her opinion: "History, real solemn history, I cannot be interested in. I read it a little as a duty, but it tells me nothing that does not either vex or weary me." The Archbishop, with a hint of a twinkle in his eye, issued a slight reprimand, advising the student that he was occasionally "too fiery" and that he should attempt to "calm down."

He later developed a more serious attitude to the importance of and the truths evidenced by history.

Certain studies presented new fields for exploration: Metaphysics – pure philosophy, pure reason, being as being, the deepest analysis of natural reality; Apologetics – from the Greek word for "speaking in defense," in this case, defense of the Faith, the doctrines of the Church, the long-held beliefs; Moral Theology –the realm of ethics seen through the teachings of the Church, focused on the proper conduct of human actions (this in contrast to Dogmatic Theology that the seminarian had mastered through his lengthy and intense study of St. Thomas Aquinas); Scripture; Canon Law; Church History, and so forth.

Écône offered its seminarians a wide range of study, a thorough grounding in all aspects of the thought and teachings and life of the Roman Catholic Church. This preparation, once common, was now unique as one by one these courses of study were washed out of the Vatican II seminaries. They were replaced by studies in social justice, psychology, anthropology, sociology, the documents of Vatican II, modern Church history, and the exploration of the "modern" ideas of "pop" theologians : blondelism – subjectivism, heart over head; teilhardism – vital evolutionary progress, scripture as allegory; de lubacism – the supernatural as a necessary extension of the natural, grace being optional; rahnerism – ecumenism and indifferentism, many "saved" without knowledge and without the Catholic Church; von balthasarism: "Super Catholicism," the Church still developing, to be fulfilled in union with all other religions, submitting to the best of humanism. Before "global warming" and "climate change" became trendy, poor post-Vatican II seminarians had their brains overheated with such nonsense and eventually fried; the most deadly "climate change" came from the conflagration of false ideas propagated by the Conciliar Church. The preparation at Écône established a traditional sacred ground of thought and learning on which the life of a priest could be built.

The Traditional Latin Mass beat as the heart of the seminary, providing necessary graces and in its highest prayer grounding highest belief. Archbishop Lefebvre stated unequivocally, "If I have to change the Mass at the seminary, I may as well turn the key in the door and send everyone home." The Mass was the uranium at the core of the reactor; it fueled the seminary as it would fuel the lives of the future priests. The *Novus Ordo* mass

From Seminary to Seminary

at the progressive seminaries, man-centered rather than God-centered, might offer an occasional glowing ember of the Catholic faith but its rapidly cooling firebox could not provide any real spiritual combustion or generate profound warm charity. It is not surprising that so many seminaries became "pink palaces," invaded by troubled souls and turning out so many lavender narcissists. St. Paul had long ago issued the warning when he said, they "changed the truth of God into a lie and worshipped and served the creature rather than the Creator, who is blessed forever. Amen. For this cause, God delivered them up to shameful affections . . . " (Rom. 1: 25-26).

The Priest is for the Sacrifice and the Sacrifice is for the Priest. Abandon the Sacrifice and you abandon the reason for the priesthood.

Seminarian Richard Williamson had been led out of the modern land of liberal captivity, through the desert of the *Novus Ordo*, to the healing waters of Écône where he had fed on the milk and honey of objective timeless Catholic truth and where through the graces of the sacraments he came to the moment of ordination. He consulted his spiritual director and confessor Father Barrielle and asked, "Should I go ahead?" The wise old priest replied simply, "Yes."

He and thirteen other young men became priests, ordained to offer the great sacrifice and assist souls to heaven, on June 29, during the hot summer of 1976.

Deo gratias.

Glo- ri- a,   glo- ri- a

The newly-ordained Father Williamson at the beginning of his priesthood found himself in a familiar location –

The Voice of the Trumpet

at the front of a classroom. The location may have been familiar, but the teacher had greatly changed. The new priest with the grace of Holy Orders could hardly be compared with the lost soul of years before who had stood before students, he himself searching, studying, questioning, even as he tried to instruct and direct young souls. Now the new priest taught potential future priests God's truth so they might inspire, assist and lead souls to heaven.

His first teaching assignment for the SSPX found him in Weissbad in the Canton of Appenzell, eastern Switzerland, where he served as an assistant to Father Schmidberger. The minor seminary there had fewer than a dozen seminarians, but Father Williamson, uninterested in numbers, taught them philosophy, relying to a large degree on his own notes distilled from earlier years when he had explored St. Thomas's *Summa Theologiæ*. He possessed a special capacity, obviously a great gift from above and a huge help for any teacher, an ability to organize, condense and streamline complex ideas and arguments into clear, accessible and easily digested propositions. This special ability gave him his strength as a teacher and would prove invaluable in future years in his monthly *Letters from the Rector* and his weekly *Eleison Comments*, a series of observations and reflections that provide an unparalleled perspective into the lunacy of the modern world and the collapse of the Catholic Church and, sadly, of the SSPX itself. Future Church historians will unearth a trove of treasures when they begin excavating these missives.

The master American filmmaker John Ford transformed the western movie into great art and in his body of work

From Seminary to Seminary

gave America its only epic vision (with an epic hero named John Wayne). His last movie in the western genre is *The Man Who Shot Liberty Valance*. In that masterpiece, Ford presents the central event that gives the film its title as an action that is mysterious and misunderstood. The editor of the local newspaper faces a dilemma: how do you report an event that cannot be solidly verified by facts or credible eyewitnesses or precise history. The wise old editor states his solution: "Print the legend." Print what those who have handed down the report have come to believe – it as close as one can come to a truth.

LEGEND ONE

One wintry day snow fell on Écône, covering the seminary with the white purity of chilly flakes. The seminarians, called back to boyhood by the chance to frolic, gathered in the courtyard around the statue of Pope St. Pius X. Being young men, they did not just walk blissfully through "the new-fallen snow," but, rather, allowing deeper instincts to rule, they formed the crystalline flakes into weapons and, snowballs in hand, marched forward in two armies to a war-like confrontation.

Suddenly, the battle which had erupted halted. Fr. Williamson appeared in the courtyard on his way to take his daily constitutional. For a brief time, the wet wintry hostilities suspended, devotional calm returned to the courtyard. And then, just as the peacemaker prepared to exit the area, one snowball, hurled on a perfect track, smacked him squarely on the back of the neck. Turning around, he was surprised to see – and the seminarians stunned to see – Archbishop Marcel Lefebvre wiping his hands.

The Voice of the Trumpet

Let it snow! Let it snow! Let it snow!

His first teaching assignment lasted only one year as another "kerfuffle" had erupted in the lofty Swiss climes and the cool Swiss air in which the Écône seminary rested. A liberal revolt against the Archbishop's unyielding stance against modernism in the Church had rattled the seminary. Four professors and fifteen seminarians departed to found a new and more "accommodating" seminary in France (another liberal dream village that built on a "baseless fabric" would "dissolve/ And . . . /Leave not a wrack behind"). Forty-five seminarians remained but the Archbishop had an immediate need for teachers. Fr. Williamson returned to fill the "philosophy-theology" vacuum left by the departures. He remained to teach at Écône for five years.

The liberal revolt could not be viewed as a surprise. The streams of liberalism, laving every foundation of a submerging world, flowed into Écône not only from Rome. As the uprising made clear, the very faculty and seminarians who had been drawn to Écône were awash in it as well. The tranquility and order first encountered by Williamson upon his arrival could turn quickly into dispute and antagonism by the usual methods. One source of the turbulence arose from the exterior of the Archbishop himself. His outward manner remained consistently calm, always spiritual, harmonious and gentle. This encouraged some controversialists to push their ideas forward and attempt to increase their influence. The Archbishop, evidencing publicly the gentleness of the dove, would then display his own strong thoughts and crack down with the arm of authority. Explosions would result; order would eventually be re-

From Seminary to Seminary

stored, but at a cost. Some thought the Archbishop *too* conservative, some thought he himself *too* susceptible to liberal tendencies, some wished to revert to the already disappearing world of the 1950's (a tendency the seminarian then priest then rector then Bishop would confront for the rest of his days). Williamson recalls the Archbishop balancing "sweetness and toughness"; if the "sweetness" could sometimes be misread by individual crusaders, his subsequent "toughness" quashed any and all such forays. The balance in the Archbishop allowed the seminary to endure under pressures from without and within, the Archbishop spearheading a movement for tradition that provided a life raft for the Catholic souls drowning in the deluge of change, heresy and apostasy engulfing Rome and the world.

Another contributing factor to the occasional fracases could be understood through the application of an old aphorism: "Whatever is received is received in the manner of the receiver." Écône may have been a magnet, drawing the iron hearts of those who knew the Church whirled in crisis. They sought a unified message and a strong leader, but each viewed Écône in his own terms and drew a portrait of the Archbishop that corresponded to his own personal vision. The Archbishop challenged Rome and the solidity at Écône provided a counter force to oppose modernist Rome, but the problems rocking the Church were perceived through one's own set of eyes and the Archbishop's pronouncements were heard with individual ears. Many thus found the Archbishop too hard, others judged him to be an old softie and yet others contented themselves with the judgments and words of the Archbishop, reminiscent of the old tale of Goldilocks and the three bears – porridge too hot or too cold or just right, the chairs and beds too hard or too soft or just right. The bears at Écône, however, growled and demanded that *their* view of the future Society of St.

The Voice of the Trumpet

Pius X be adopted, hot and hard or cold and soft. Or in avian terms, the Archbishop found his nest in the higher atmosphere of the Swiss mountains to be filled with hawks on the right, doves on the left and some falcons in the middle. Feathers often flew.

Throughout all the turmoil, the Archbishop held his course and Fr. Williamson, his loyal son, stayed with him, teaching philosophy and theology to the remaining nestlings. The Archbishop understood and appreciated this loyalty and perseverance, seeing in the young priest a firm yet balanced mind combined with a solid and unyielding faith. He called on Fr. Williamson to take a journey in the summer of 1979. Fr. Williamson would travel from Écône to the United States, then to Japan, on to India, Australia, South Africa, and then return to Écône. He thus became the first SSPX priest to circle the globe on one trip, going around the world like Jules Verne's fictional British traveler Phileas Fogg, in about 80 days. The subsequent summers of 1980, 1981 and 1982 saw him again making extended trips at the Archbishop's behest. The missionary Archbishop perceived the same missionary spirit in Fr. Williamson, only these new missions would be to the priests, religious and laity who in the turbulent conciliar winds needed anchoring as surely as in former days pagans had needed conversion. So he traveled and would continue constant travel after the Archbishop had gone to his reward and the Society itself had begun to waver in the wind.

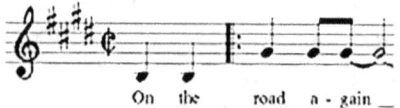

On the Feast of the Immaculate Conception, December 8, 1980, Mark David Chapman shot John Lennon out-

From Seminary to Seminary

side the Dakota Apartment House in New York City where Lennon lived as he returned from the Record Plant Studio where he had played lead guitar on a song for his then consort Yoko Ono's upcoming album. The number recorded that night was entitled "Walking on Thin Ice." Chapman held in one hand a copy of the adolescent-angst novel *The Catcher in the Rye*, and in the other hand the gun from which he fired four shots, all four striking their target. Rushed to St. Luke-Roosevelt Hospital, Lennon could not be revived by the attending physicians. At the moment they pronounced the world-renowned celebrity dead, the Beatles song "All My Loving" began to play over the hospital's public address system. Yoko Ono had Lennon's remains cremated. No funeral was held.

HAP-PI-NESS IS A WARM GUN

Tensions caused tremors that continued to shake the SSPX into the 1980's. Personal animosities made certain situations more serious. A contentious relation arose between Fathers Hector Bolduc and Clarence Kelly, both in America at the time and both later to leave the Society. The Archbishop, knowing he had to depend on the priests God had sent him to serve the faithful, sought to keep peace within the priestly order. Seeking to ease the tensions, the Archbishop divided the United States into two districts, giving each priest a sphere of influence. (Good priests are attacked with ferocity by the devil who knows if he can discombobulate them with his demonic wolvery, the sheep under their care become more accessible mutton.)

The Voice of the Trumpet

Fr. Williamson had visited the U.S. in 1979 and offered the Spiritual Exercises; in 1982, he traveled there again to scout out the situation and report to the Archbishop. Still "trailing clouds of glory," he did not recognize the severity of the problems developing in the United States. More serious rifts then personal tensions between individual priests would soon shake both the Society, many of its priests and threaten to topple many of its chapels. Fr. Williamson did not feel the ground shaking beneath his feet. One recommendation he did make to the Archbishop proved to be providential. Fr. Kelly hoped to bring St. Athanasius Church in Vienna, Virginia, into the SSPX fold. Fr. Williamson believed that as the laity had founded the parish and kept it running for a number of years, the church there should remain in the hands of the laity. The Archbishop agreed with the recommendation and thus St. Athanasius Church, soon coming under the leadership of Father Ronald Ringrose, remained an independent chapel, a chapel that would prove important to Williamson and the traditional movement in future years.

At this time, Fr. Williamson departed from the classrooms at Écône, being sent to be Sub-Rector at the American seminary in Ridgefield, Connecticut. ("Some people were glad to see my back at Écône. I don't always make everybody my friend . . . Can't think why . . . ") Not soon after his arrival at the Ridgefield Seminary, he realized how insufficient his evaluation of the problems besetting the SSPX in America had been. In fact, his naiveté had been such that on the flight across the Atlantic to assume the position of Rector, he had in all innocence said to fellow SSPX priests returning to the U.S. after a critical meeting in Écône, "This is going to be fun." It certainly turned out to be exciting. In April of 1983, nine of the eleven SSPX priests stationed in the United States openly rebelled against the Archbishop, believing he

From Seminary to Seminary

had become "too soft" and "too cold" in the struggle to preserve Catholic tradition. The issues that caused division focused on the status of the Pope and the use of the 1962 missal, among others. Their disagreements with the Archbishop and the SSPX had been voiced quite openly, but their plans had not. When the break came, the Nine, as they came to be identified, claimed the right to maintain their chapels and properties, and the right to begin determining their own agenda. Fr. Williamson, the Archbishop's most prominent representative as the Sub-Rector of the Ridgefield Seminary, found himself trying to manage rebels not without a cause, but who believed they had a very real cause. Of the five priests teaching at the Seminary, three quit, leaving only Father Williamson and Fr. Petit to continue teaching and trying to maintain some order. The Rector asked the Archbishop to send Fr. Bourmaud as reinforcement and the Archbishop complied. The situation, however, was dire. Chapels were divided; many faithful found themselves excluded from chapels they had long supported; suddenly they were no longer welcome or allowed to receive the sacraments. They cried out for help, but the few priests remaining with the Archbishop found it hard to answer so many calls.

Bishop Williamson still speaks of the great intelligence of then Fathers Cekada, Dolan, Jenkins, Kelly and Sanborn who had their own ideas of how to preserve tradition and help the wounded Catholic Church. He does level against them their secretive plans and their legal suits. Ownership of the chapels, the sacred spaces and all the properties became contested in civil courts and the lawsuits were stretched out Jarndyce-like for many years. The Bishop still views as unacceptable that the breakaway priests forced the Archbishop to come to America to be deposed in civil court matters by non-Catholic, combative lawyers.

The Voice of the Trumpet

The shepherd in Rome having been struck, the scattering of the sheep became inescapable. Combined with the deeply rooted American spirit of some of the rebel priests (1776-ers in clerical garb with a rootin', tootin', knock 'em down and drag 'em out wild west spirit?), the absence of an ultimate trusted authority in Rome made constant divisions and disputes a certainty. And the modern need for clear definitive solutions to all bewildering problems, even the mysteries and confusions of turmoil in the Church itself, God-permitted and eventually God resolved, would prove too great a temptation. The "simple answer" that had first tempted Luther and Calvin called to confused modern traditional Catholics. From the wound protestantism had inflicted on the Mystical Body in 1517 until the present day, divisions, antagonisms, individual judgments, solemn personal decrees could only multiply. Inevitably, the same zeal that had moved the Nine to revolt against their head afflicted the group as well. Soon after the split, the original Nine separated into two and one and one and one and one and one and one and one, just as the original rebellions of Luther and Calvin have resulted in something close to 27,000 protestant sects today, all challenging one another, anathematizing one another, bitterly disputing with one another. Having rejected the authority of Rome and that of Écône, but knowing authority remains essential, three of the Nine found means to have themselves consecrated bishops so they could be their own authorities with the intention of helping the faithful. Some years later Fr. Williamson, their adversary in the struggles of the early 80s, would be consecrated as a bishop. Archbishop Lefebvre chose him to be elevated to the episcopacy; he did not appoint himself.

From Seminary to Seminary

    But to me it is a very small thing to be judged by you or by man's day. But neither do I judge my own self. For I am not conscious to myself of anything. Yet am I not hereby justified; but he that judgeth me is the Lord. Therefore, judge not before the time: until the Lord come, who both will bring to light the hidden things of darkness and will make manifest the counsels of the hearts. And then shall every man have praise from God. But these things, brethren, I have in a figure transferred to myself and to Apollo for your sakes: that in us you may learn that one be not puffed up against the other for another, above that which is written. For who distinguisheth thee? Or what hast thou that thou hast not received? And if thou hast received, why dost thou glory, as if thou hadst not received it?

    —I Corinthians 4: 3–7

Verbal Music Interlude

O, when degree is shaked,
Which is the ladder of all high designs,
The enterprise is sick. How could communities,
Degrees in schools, and brotherhoods in cities,
Peaceful commerce from dividable shores,
The primogenity and due of birth,
Prerogative of age, crowns, scepters, laurels,
But by degree, stand in authentic place?
Take but degree away, untune that string,
And hark what discord follows. Each thing meets
In mere oppugnancy. The bounded waters

The Voice of the Trumpet

> Should lift their bosoms higher than the shores
> And make a sop of all this solid globe;
> Strength should be the lord of imbecility,
> And the rude son should strike his father dead;
> Force should be right, or rather right and wrong –
> Between whose endless jar justice resides –
> Should lose their names, and so should justice too.
> Then everything includes itself in power,
> Power into will, will into appetite,
> And appetite, an universal wolf,
> So doubly seconded with will and power,
> Must make perforce an universal prey
> And last eat up himself.
>
> —*Troilus and Cressida*, I, iii, 101–124

When Fr. Williamson had arrived in Ridgefield, Connecticut, in 1983, he came to a town nestled in the foothills of the Berkshires that had received some Englishmen many years before. The town had first sprung to life when a group of English colonists bought the land from an Indian chief of the Ramapo tribe, Chief Katonah. A royal charter was officially issued in 1709, one year after the original sale. In April, 1777, with the Revolutionary War rocking the colonies, the sole major encounter in Connecticut took place in Ridgefield, between the British forces led by General David Wooster and the Continental Army led by General Benedict Arnold. The British triumphed, General Wooster losing his life in the battle and General Arnold losing his horse, the animal

From Seminary to Seminary

being blown out from under him during the fight. ("A horse! A horse! My kingdom for a horse!") Despite their victory, the British forces never launched another inland drive into the state.

In 1781, a French army arrived, led by the Comte de Rochambeau. As they marched through the state, they paused at the town to celebrate Mass, Ridgefield thus becoming the site of the first Catholic Mass to be offered in the state of Connecticut. In 1969, the last traditional Catholic Mass was celebrated in Ridgefield until the 1980's when another French leader, an Archbishop, sent his priests to found a seminary in the town. Upon arriving to become Rector of the seminary, Fr. Williamson became yet another British leader fighting a rebellion taking place throughout the land. The conflict resulted, in October, 1987, in a second victory for a British commander as the courts ruled in favor of the SSPX.

After the first battle, a cannon ball remained lodged in the wall of a local tavern and rests there to this day; before, during and after the second battle, a line of seminarians received the Sacrament of Holy Orders, and the mark on their soul will remain there for eternity.

◉

Archbishop Lefebvre provided spiritual paternity to Richard Williamson; John Williamson provided the physical paternity, as well as a stable, moral, affection-filled home. The earthly father departed this earth on January 4, 1987.

Trumpet Solo

What a mystery, the life and death of a single man! One soul, one world, one eternity!

He died at the age of 83, quietly and peacefully, in a Catholic nursing home run by Irish Sisters where my mother could visit him every day, but he did not openly profess the Catholic Faith before dying....

Thank you for all your prayers which obtained for him at least a happy departure from this world, and, let us hope, a happy entrance into the next... God knows.

Visiting the funeral parlor on the eve of the funeral, my mother said, as her hand gently caressed the last thing she could touch of him, the simple tablet bearing his name on the closed coffin: "He was a good man. He looked after me for fifty years. That is something." Youngsters, hold your marriages together, because there is no substitute for staying together, until death do you part.

—*Letters from the Rector*, No. 45

Father Thomas Plumtree.

—martyred at Durham, January 4, 1570

In early June of 1988, the phone rang on the Rector's desk at the Ridgefield seminary. On the line – Archbishop Marcel Lefebvre; the message – later that month the Archbishop wished to consecrate Father Richard Williamson a bishop in the One, Holy, Apostolic, Roman Catholic Church.

The Archbishop had struggled for some time with the question of possible episcopal consecrations. Many tra-

From Seminary to Seminary

ditional Catholics demanded of him that he "do something" and ensure the continuance of tradition; others warned him against such "precipitous action" that would be seen by many as an act of schism. The Archbishop wrestled with the potential act, knowing the possibility of seeming disobedience on the one hand, versus the unlikelihood any other bishop would undertake such a consecration. And age came on him. For some time he had prayed and asked God for a sign, stating at one point that "Very respectfully, I wish the Mother of God would appear to me and tell me to consecrate bishops." No such vision materialized; but as the situation in Rome deteriorated, two signs were given. The first came in a refusal by the Roman authorities to respond to a sincere and polite request by the Archbishop for an explanation as to how the new Conciliar Church teaching on religious liberty could be squared with the traditional teachings of the Church. Unable to hammer their round liberal peg into the four-square Catholic hole, the "guardians of the faith" refused to answer. Ironically, twenty-five years later, one of the four bishops consecrated in 1988 would boldly go where even Rome hadn't dared to go before. The then Superior General of the SSPX, Bishop Bernard Fellay, in an interview in May of 2012, offered the following explanation during an interview with the Catholic News Service: "The Council is presenting a religious liberty which is in fact a very limited one. Very limited . . . [in] our talks with Rome, they clearly said that to mean that there would be a right to error or right to choose each religion is false." And a stern voice from beyond the grave would still demand, "Why have they not said anything like this in public? How do they reconcile such words in private with their actions in public? How do they explain and justify this in light of their actions. A very limited amount of strychnine in the lemonade still poisons the whole pitcher." No explanations are necessary for the inhabitants of CloudCuckooLand.

The second sign given to the Archbishop invaded the church in Assisi in a parade of heresy and heterodoxy never before seen in a public pontifically-sponsored event. Such gatherings had been condemned by countless earlier pontiffs who understood why the First Commandment came first, earlier shepherds who guarded the flock, not seeking the applause of the world. The Archbishop expressed shock at how few traditionalists seemed dismayed or outraged by the public encouragement and support of false religions. "All are marinated in liberalism," he sadly observed. He often spoke of the fact that the bishops make the people, not the people the bishops. The conciliar bishops catered to the whims of the world, submitted to the flesh and ignored the Father of Lies who chuckled at their puppet master . . . "Take but degree away, untune that string . . . " The Archbishop, realizing the impossibility of ever mixing the healing waters of the faith with the oily sludge in Rome, decided he had an obligation to act.

The Bishop-elect Father Richard Williamson reacted with appropriate English phlegm and an unmoved upper lip. His calm reaction reflected the sense of this as one more step in a series that had raised him one degree at a time from a lost soul in the modern world, to an uneasy soul in the modern world, to an explorer of the Catholic

From Seminary to Seminary

religion, to a member of the Mystical Body, to a seminarian at Écône, to an ordinand to the priesthood, to a teacher following and transmitting traditional doctrine under the guidance and governance of a saintly Archbishop and now to a bishop. At no stage had it ever appeared to him to be unreasonable not to move on to the next rung of the ladder, especially now, called to duty by the Archbishop. If the Archbishop had made this choice, then Father Williamson would continue the climb.

Summoned to a two to three day retreat at a private home in Sierre in the Valais, the four Bishops-elect received a series of conferences from the Archbishop to prepare them for the upcoming consecrations. In retrospect, Bishop Williamson remembers the principal themes of those conferences – the necessity of Christian charity in the increasingly dark and destructive modern world and the practical problems the four would soon face. These words and insights delivered by the Archbishop are remembered now by one of the auditors as "spot on."

The Archbishop moved forward to the day in late June with complete calm. Believing sincerely that providence had compelled him, he fared quietly on. The four chosen by him followed. A few Nicodemuses from Rome contacted him privately, but no public support came from any official quarter. The eventual reinforcement from Bishop Antonio de Castro Mayer of Campos, Brazil, who against the advice of his physicians came to Écône as co-consecrator, offered sufficient proof to the Archbishop that his action had a special blessing. The Archbishop had stated that if in the early 1970's he had found five or six fellow bishops to work with him, they could have thrown a monkey wrench into the despotic grinding machinery of the revolution in the Church. These men could not be found. The forthright and public support of this Brazilian Bishop therefore meant that much more to Archbishop Lefebvre.

The Voice of the Trumpet

The Conciliar Church reacted with predictable rage against the action; the media spat venom.

Journalists and broadcasters are now the high priests of the revolution; newspapers and newscasts the instruments of so-called "democracy." For centuries the Catholic Church defied the revolution and exposed its evils. Modernism however spread its virus and many churchmen became infected. The "old Church" seemed to have passed away after the scourging it took at the Second Vatican Council and the modernists had celebrated nonstop since that time, convinced their old nemesis had been euthanized and buried. And then one old French Archbishop dared to crawl out of the seeming grave, stand upright and speak once again with the voice of the Church of All Time. And now he dared to take action in public to protect and secure its permanence.

Small wonder then that on June 29, 1988, when the faithful gathered to celebrate this monumental moment dubbed "Operation Survival," small wonder that the media, fenced in an enclosure a distance from the sacred rite, spat venom. To their credit, these high priests of modernism had a deeper and truer sense of the enormity of the action in maintaining the Catholic Church, their old nemesis, than did many of the Catholic hierarchy and the Catholic faithful. The media mavens boiled with the rage and powerlessness of a vampire confronted with a crucifix. In the face of such an epochal sacred act, they were powerless to stop the sacrament; the four traditional Bishops were consecrated.

The Episcopal coat of arms for the newly-consecrated Bishop Richard Williamson (see page facing the Table

From Seminary to Seminary

of Contents) represents an English heraldic lion brandishing a sword over its head like the Lion of Venice in the coat of arms of Pope St. Pius X. The background is blue, in honour of the Blessed Virgin. Beneath the lion is a cross with an English rose, the flower of England. The motto reads *Fidelis Inveniatur*, words taken from St. Paul's First Letter to the Corinthians, "Here now it is required among the dispensers that a man be found faithful." (4.2.) The words make clear that the Bishop intends to be "found faithful," which is "required" "here now" because so many "dispensers," i.e., those who have been consecrated in the line of the apostles to teach and to provide the sacraments, have *not* been "found faithful."

His Excellency neglected to recall that the Rosicrucians, early ancestors of the Freemasons, also place a rose on the cross, leading in later years to the accusation that he is an infiltrator from that secret society. He is used to such accusations, as his friendship with Malcolm Muggeridege has been used as proof of his Fabian Socialist allegiances and his connection with certain priests and his ordaining of certain seminarians has been taken as proof that he is "light in the loafers." His response to such allegations is a simple one: "Let the dogs bark."

He is an Eng-lish-man

Trumpet Solo

If asked what was the Archbishop's greatest quality – his charity? his humility? his spirituality? – I would answer – his objectivity. In a world drowning in subjectivity, he believed in objectivity, truth, faith, the Catholic Church – and he believed all that had to be preserved. He knew that the Ecclesia Dei Commission was a trap for fools. If you put your little finger in the *novus ordo* system, it will eat your finger; if you put your hand in, it will eat your hand; it will eat your elbow, your shoulder, it will eat the rest of you. Now the SSPX wants to put its finger in. They have become liberals, crusaders, dreamers, hoping for a "nice" world. The minute you step in with Rome, you have to stop criticizing Vatican II and the new mass. Sooner or later, if you're a priest, you're going to be willing to celebrate the new mass. It may take ten years, fifteen years, but there is a logic involved. It is unbelievable. It seems fated for this cause to be abandoned and abandoned and abandoned – all liberals, all dreamers, all crusaders, all hoping for a "nice" world. There are two standards – the standard of Christ and the standard of Satan. And all the hundreds and hundreds of other standards are standards of Satan because you cannot compromise with Our Lord. No compromise is possible.

So speaks the true son of Archbishop Marcel Lefebvre.

The Ridgefield seminary began to swell with seminarians; clearly, a larger home would be necessary. Word arrived one day that a property in Winona, Minnesota, was for sale, a former Dominican monastery euthanized by the potent drug of Vatican II, but where many departed religious who died natural deaths rested in a cemetery on the property. It had briefly been used as a rehabilitation site for addicts, poor drug-enslaved teens of Minnesota, who, not surprisingly in acting out their rage against the world in which they had been deformed, had left the structure in worse repair than had the devout souls when they in their time had exited the property.

From Seminary to Seminary

The Rector visited the spiritually and physically distressed place and scouted the surrounding territory, especially the smallish, solid if sleepy town at the foot of the high hill that the monastery/ rehab center crowned. He liked what he saw. He asked the then Superior General of the SSPX, Father Schmidberger, to come and do his own inspection. Approval granted, the SSPX purchased the property at reasonable cost and without massive mortgage debt. Peter Sardegna, a faithful traditionalist with construction and engineering expertise, moved into the small cottage on the property and with the support and sweat and prayers of many faithful Catholic souls, repaired and prepared the new home of St. Thomas Aquinas Seminary. Father Williamson had visited the property in 1987 and in 1988 Bishop Williamson oversaw the move to Winona.

If Winona, Minnesota, had been settled on a sand bar in the Mississippi River, that "strong brown god" was not its only natural attraction. The bluffs that tower majestically above the flowing waters below give the city a gentle distinction similar to those grander locations where sea and mountain meet – western Ireland, northern California, the French and Italian Rivieras, the Latin American coastlines east and west. In early days, the Moewakanton band of the eastern Sioux tribe had made their home on the banks of the river and called their village Keoxa. The current appellation "Winona" derives from the name of a daughter of Chief Wapasha III, Princess We-Noh-Nah.

On August 9, 1805, twenty-six year old Army Lieutenant Zebulon Pike, stationed at Fort Bellefontaine near St. Louis, received an order from General James Wilkinson to travel north into the upper reaches of the Louisiana Territory, newly purchased from Spain, to locate the source of the Mississippi River. After a five week journey up "ol' man river," Pike with his four ships and many

The Voice of the Trumpet

sailors arrived at "island number 72" (so named on his map) in the Mississippi Valley, a location that would one day be the home of the city of Winona. Unlike his failed attempt on his second expedition to reach the summit of the peak in Colorado that now bears his name, Pike did make it to the summit of the bluffs and set down his reactions in his log, September 15, 1805.

> Mr. Frazer, Bradley, Sparks and myself, went out to hunt. We crossed first a dry flat prairie; when we arrived at the hills we ascended them from which we had a most sublime and beautiful prospect. On the right, we saw the mountains which we passed in the morning and the prairie in the rear; like distant clouds, the mountains at the Prairie Le Cross; on our left and under our feet, the valley between the two barren hills through which the Mississippi wound itself by numerous channels, forming many beautiful islands, as far as the eye could embrace the same; and our four boats under full sail, their flags streaming before the wind. It was altogether so variegated and romantic that a man may scarcely expect to enjoy such a one but twice or thrice in the course of his life.

The Expeditions of Zebulon Pike, Volume 1, New York: Frances P. Harper, 1895, pp. 54–55.

On October 15, 1851, riverboat Captain Orrin Smith, recognizing that new treaties would create new reservations in the interior of Minnesota, founded the new town on the river and looked forward to commercial success in the future. In 1855, Kashubian Polish families fleeing the Prussian *Kulturkampf* began arriving in large numbers, making Winona the center of the Kashubian diaspora in the United States. In the 1860's when southern Minnesota became the largest wheat producer in the country, the grain was shipped out from Winona as its main port. Lumbering and lumber mills brought more

From Seminary to Seminary

prosperity and in 1968 a Winona native, J. R. Watkins, came up with the eponymous American business promise – the "money back guarantee."

Today Winona has both a summer Beethoven Festival and a Shakespeare Festival and is the stained glass capital of the United States. St. Thomas Aquinas Seminary, created for faithful young men to flee from modern liberal persecution as had the Catholic Poles more than a century earlier, established itself in Winona in 1988. It remained there until 2017.

LEGEND TWO

When St. Thomas Aquinas Seminary transferred its operations from Ridgefield, Connecticut, to Winona, Minnesota, not only many fond memories were left behind. There remained many good Catholic souls from the area who had supported the Seminary for many years in a variety of jobs, some salaried, some volunteer. Those good souls had to be replaced by Minnesotans from the Winona area and such folks appeared, all working together to make the new building habitable and well-run. No position demanded more special skills and special dedication than the new secretary who would "man" the front office. Anyone who has worked in any capacity for any business or establishment, school or office, clinic or community, knows the central role a good secretary plays in organizing, assisting, working, supporting, managing, and, yes, mothering. Being a secretary is one of the three occupations in which women have always worked because they are essential, essential because of their special God-given attributes. The secretary, the grade school teacher (including the librarian) and the nurse, by radiating femininity and the loving motherly spirit transform any institution into a human community with the air of a home. Many remarkable women over the years remained unmarried and devoted their lives to becoming helpmates and mothers in public schools and hospitals and offices.

The Rector set about finding a woman to fill this essential position. Having interviewed a few, he found a young woman who had all the necessary qualifications, but, unfortunately, one serious impediment; she was tall, she was beautiful and she was, as the Germans say, "zaftig." The Rector realized it would be a mistake to hire her. Being a modern woman, she bristled when politely informed of the problem, not appreciating what temptation could ensue from allowing one lovely heifer into a pen of young bulls, even good-hearted bulls. No lawsuit was filed.

Fact: the Rector hired a devoted, charming, hard-working and good humored married lady who would be his support and a kind maternal friend to the seminarians for decades to come. God bless Mrs. Sherry Mehren.

A sec - re - tar - y is not a toy

The episcopal consecrations of 1988 resulted in a number of priests and faithful breaking their ties with the SSPX. There was not a purge, nor a massive revolt, but a stream of departures based on conscience. Most joined with the newly-formed Fraternity of St. Peter, an organization flowering into life thanks to the action of Archbishop Lefebvre. Some seminarians departed as well, but at the start of the 1988–1989 year in the new Seminary at the top of the road leading to the heights of the Ossa-like piled bluffs above the Old Muddy, the number of young

From Seminary to Seminary

men remained close to the number of seminarians who had departed Ridgefield, that edifice itself changing from a seminary to a retreat house. The numbers remained steady from 1988 until Bishop Williamson's departure for Argentina in 2003. The majority of the seminarians had their roots in the American landscape.

The traditional Catholic faith slowly withered away in much of Europe as the Conciliar Church could no more bring forth new growth than the fig tree blasted by Our Lord could produce fresh figs. In America, surprisingly, a land founded on masonic principles, tradition showed continued slow growth and new green shoots. The influx of Catholic immigrants in the latter part of the nineteenth and the early years of the twentieth centuries had found refuge in the new country. The Irish and Germans and Italians and Poles, though encouraged by a compromised Catholic-American hierarchy to keep their faith a private matter and adhere devoutly to the American ideal so as to maintain their chairs at the ecumenical table, nevertheless had the faith rooted deep at the core of their Catholic hearts. The anti-Catholic prejudice they often encountered tested their faith; for good or ill, in pride or shame, they had to decide what their Catholic heritage meant to them. When assaults on their faith came from the Eternal City itself, many simply abandoned the Church, but others would not be shaken and persevered with renewed iron wills.

A major problem did however accompany their fervor. The Catholic hierarchy that for years had proclaimed "life, liberty and the pursuit of happiness" at the same time as it promoted Catholic truth could only result in a kind of schizophrenia for American Catholics; were they Americans who loved liberty and attended Mass on Sunday or were they Catholics who built their lives on Catholic Truth and walked guardedly through the temptations of free democratic America?

Trumpet Solo

Liberty has got to rest on Truth. If you rest Truth on liberty, you've got the cart before the horse. It is best when liberty is measured by Truth for liberty must rest on it, whereas if you rest Truth on liberty, then liberty becomes your real religion; any other religion becomes secondary. So for Americans, liberty is the real religion, an unconscious religion, a deceptive religion for it seems to open its doors for Catholics. And the Catholic immigrants brought to the shores of America generosity, vitality, innocence. They never ratted on their Catholic heritage as the Europeans did. But Americans have liberalism in their bloodstream. America, founded on liberty, has a bad foundation.

Such comments aroused anger among many traditional America-first traditional Catholics, and they accused the Bishop of "anti-Americanism." Nevertheless, young American Catholics kept arriving at the Seminary and they were generally and genuinely good young men. They did not come out of ambition nor did they seek worldly preferment, or, as His Excellency puts it, ambition "for a few red buttons to draw them forward." Many arrived from traditional families; others came after courageously going against the wishes or express commands of their *Novus Ordo* families; others walked up the hill having turned their backs on the alluring, seductive, glistening tinsel promises of the midway of the modern world's crass carnival. They possessed genuine virtues – humility, simplicity, innocence. They seldom demonstrated pompous pride or seethed with the anger that troubled so many adolescents of the time.

Even in the 1970's at Écône, however, the Archbishop had noticed a different sort of difficulty that often arrived with American seminarians. Bright-eyed and bushy-tailed, youthful and eager, they were ready to drink in all

From Seminary to Seminary

the seminary had to offer, to work with sweat and sincerity to advance to the priesthood. The problem came from notions of that liberty that they had imbibed with their mother's American milk, nourishment that gave them strength but had grown strong in them with their brains, hearts and souls. Liberty had given them emotional ground on which they rested, but under the ground shifted unstable tectonic plates; as those plates slow-slipped, the liberal soul in all sincerity imperceptibly moved with them; thus the media, following "slow-slip" events with earth-shaking tremors, could shape the opinions of whole generations to accept blithely many horrors – contraception, abortion, cohabitation, gay "marriage," transgender surgery – that would have outraged and disgusted their ancestors. The American seminarians obviously rejected such outright abominations, but underneath them lay instability. The Bishop explains: "It is difficult with a liberal to hit bedrock. The foundation of a liberal is like plastic and it can change. The foundation of Faith is bedrock, so to build a priest you must have bedrock. Bedrock you cannot change; it is the enemy of false liberty."

The Rector and the professors sought to install the bedrock necessary for the priesthood or, at least, to help the young men understand the problem of liberty, kissing cousin of liberalism. Small seeds of understanding could shoot up green tendrils of recognition, but they could also be too easily washed away. Liberty is a hard, wasting downpour of acid rain, and in the land of *E pluribus unum*, "the rain it raineth every day."

Perhaps this sad reality explains why so many priests, many years later, proved quite susceptible to the rejection of what the Archbishop stood strong for and what the Bishop had tried to hammer into them, choosing rather to follow an appealing will-o'-the wisp down a muddy path toward what was evidently and clearly a washed out gully.

The Voice of the Trumpet

St. John Vianney had but begun his seminary studies in 1809 when he was drafted into Napoleon's armies. Falling ill, he spent time in a hospital and during that time his company marched without him. He hid out as a deserter until 1810 when an amnesty was declared and he returned to study at Ecully. In 1812, he went to the minor seminary in Verrières-en-Forez and then in 1813 to the seminary at Lyons. Lacking the gifts for deep study, he had no knowledge of philosophy and found Latin nearly impossible to learn. Returned to Ecully and the supervision of a good Abbe, he persevered. The Abbe persuaded the Church authorities that the young man's Catholic faith and intense piety more than compensated for his inability to learn. So despite having twice failed his examinations before ordination, he became a priest on August 12, 1815. The great saint was unlearned, but certainly not ignorant.

Father Charles Mahony.

—martyred at Ruthin, North Wales,
August 12, 1679

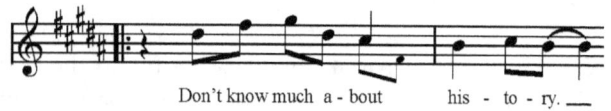

The Archbishop encountered a second obstacle exhibited by the American seminarians who came to Écône – they had contracted "American education" disease. The

From Seminary to Seminary

earliest American colonists, having not yet lost their common sense or their European, i.e. Catholic, inertia, realized that basic education, the rudiments of reading and writing and mathematics, needed to be taught to children in the home by the family, those who could best provide the most basic essentials for teaching – individual attention paid to each student and individual love directed to each pupil. But by the mid-nineteenth century, the love and attention that provided discipline and motivation passed from the family to schools where from the earliest days the affection and oversight of parents got scuttled and replaced by the theories and experiments of "education experts." That which began as common sense practice morphed into compulsory education engineering. The theorists sought from their first machinations to turn out "model citizens," not wise and independent human beings. Dr. Andrew Bell and Joseph Lancaster, two British theorists, devised an educational "system" where teachers are assisted by their brighter pupils whose own education is interrupted so they may become mini-teachers and help educate their peers. In the early years of the nineteenth century, these theories spread like a spider's web across the globe, ensnaring teachers and pupils alike, and soon came to capture the innocent, well-meaning Americans who adopted the practices from their one-room schools to their larger public institutions. The British may have lost the war but they seized the revolutionary reins and triumphantly guided American education out of the home and into formal educational institutions.

The Prussians then took control from the Brits as Massachusetts Secretary of Education Horace Mann (1796–1856) adopted and promoted the model of what were called "common schools," a system that proposed basic educational content be taught to every student. (The "common core" has a long ancestry in the United

States.) This universal program of study was to be free, open to one and all alike, without religious or philosophical constraints, and the outcome-based result would be the model citizen, upright and virtuous, who would help create a model, i.e. efficient, practical, non-doctrinaire, social order. Age became a way of compartmentalizing students who would all be placed in the same grade determined by their years, and would progress in lock step through their education, linked to their fellows like prisoners in a chain gang. Natural abilities, special talents, individual aptitudes, all God-given gifts, assigned with divine order and purpose to compose the Mystical Body in the world, would be suppressed for the sake of uniformity (just as "diversity" today means everyone thinking, speaking and behaving exactly alike, distinguished only by an array of pigmentation, private parts and proper perversion).

Education became compulsory in most states and by 1918 every state required children to complete at least an elementary education – the mandatory sentence slowly creeping forward to mandatory middle school and then high school and now the "*de rigueur*" college years, even though more and more of those college students can barely perform on a middle school level. By the time of the mandatory education fever, most states had already adopted the Blaine Amendments, first proposed by President Ulysses S. Grant and formulated by Congressman James G. Blaine, Congressman from Maine who became Speaker of the House, then a Senator from Maine, then Secretary of State and, in 1884, the Republican candidate for President, being defeated in the election by Grover Cleveland. The Amendment prohibited the use of public funds for parochial schools, under the obsessive "separation of church and state" claim, an idea which most Americans still erroneously believe appears in the Constitution; it actually appears in a letter writ-

From Seminary to Seminary

ten by Thomas Jefferson to the Danbury Baptist Association in 1802 – but then the study of American history is but one of the casualties of American education. The Amendment was passed by thirty-seven States, failing to receive the necessary two-thirds majority; nevertheless, over time most States adopted the amendment on their own. Catholic schools sat in the bulls-eye of the Blaine Amendment target. "Separation of church and state" zinged like an arrow into the heart of the citizenry; religion should be private, not public, especially the Catholic religion, which dared to assert it alone possessed the embodiment of Truth. The religion of atheism thus flourished in the schools, driving out all vertical, spiritual dimension of study.

And then came "Progressive Education," the monster created by John Dewey, a professor at the University of Chicago and later Columbia University in the Big Apple (the civic core of conceited temptation). Dewey promoted his belief that the purpose of education was to prepare the student for the future life, giving him command of himself, training him so he will have full and ready use of all his capabilities. Dewey believed that education should be the vehicle for social change, creating citizens sharing in the "social consciousness . . . the only sure method of social reconstruction." Education as social engineering became fully established.

"Progressive Education" carried additional baggage for the student, who like an over-burdened and overwrought porter cannot figure out how many bags he is carrying, whom they belong to, or where he is to take them. The new ideas formulated by these new experts focused on ideas and skills that would define "progress," ideas and skills that inevitably centered more and more on social action, social improvement and material prosperity. As Pope Leo XIII noted in his encyclical *Testem Benevolentiae Nostrae*, the heretical notion of separation of church and state must lead to the primacy of "personal" beliefs, rejection of Catholic doctrine and the disparagement of contemplative orders. Action would triumph over meditation; the inner man could not be bound by dogma; the old traditions could not restrain new advances.

In education, over time, this meant the enthronement of Science and Mathematics and Technology, an obsession with politics, and the triumph of training over learning. Philosophy and literature, music and art, became, like grandma's old quilts in the attic trunk, lovely relics of a bygone era, but when the day arrived when the attic space was needed to build a bigger machine, those old patchwork coverlets, the work of human hands and much love, had to be jettisoned. All education budget cutters felled their excising axes on those humanities courses and the accompanying "extra-curricular activities." With the fixation on action and the body, sport became untouchable; the school could no longer afford the band because the football field needed new turf. Or as Groucho Marx said as Quincy Adams Wagstaff, President of Huxley College: "[W]e can't support both [the stadium and the college]. Tomorrow we start tearing down the college." Out went the courses and studies and pursuits that gave life-blood to the interior life, the natural nourishment of the heart and soul.

In the 1930's a diocesan Bishop invited one Father Castellani in Argentina to open a seminary in the northern reaches of the country. The good priest replied,

> Your Excellency, you don't need a seminary, you need a seminary school so there will be in the future something to build on – the Greek classics, Virgil, the other Latin classics. All that has gone by the board, the humanities, the ABCs of human life. Twenty five years

From Seminary to Seminary

later they brought into Argentina "American education" which means math and science. The humanities went by the board. Youngsters knowing nothing but physics and chemistry, know nothing of the sublime.

Trumpet Solo

Without the natural foundation created by the humanities, the seminary years only drop six years of St. Thomas Aquinas, the spiritual writers, the Church Fathers, parachuting all that on a football player. God bless them for their good qualities, but there is a great gap. That's why I instituted a year of humanities, trying to catch them up in one year on what they should have spent the last ten or fifteen years learning. That is why I introduced them to classical music and literature and history. Between the rock music in their blood and the Gregorian chant they learn with the best of good will and the best of results, there is a schizophrenia. There is nothing to join the two together. The danger then is a crack-up. They go through six or seven years of seminary training. They do very well, they are very pious, they step off the conveyer belt a shiny new priest, but underneath is a little rock-and-roller crying for oxygen. Then something happens in their priesthood... and *voom*... the whole thing collapses. A priesthood cannot rest on rock-and-roll but rock-and-roll is what they have in their entrails. Grace requires a solid natural mind; grace will push and heal and lift, correct and form nature, but that means learning the basics of nature in themselves, basics which may not have anything to do with the higher faith, but *basics* because they are absolutely necessary for grace to build on. Today those basics are missing more and more, and one wonders how tomorrow there are going to be any Catholic priests at all.

Or as he would often say in later years, "You cannot make bricks without straw."

The Voice of the Trumpet

A Greek Orthodox Tale

Not too many years ago, a young monastic aspirant went to Mount Athos. In talking with the venerable Abbot of the monastery where he wished to stay, he told him, "Holy Father! My heart burns for the spiritual life, for asceticism, for unceasing communion with God, for obedience to an Elder. Instruct me, please, Holy Father, that I may attain to spiritual advancement." Going to the bookshelf, the Abbot pulled down a copy of *David Copperfield* by Charles Dickens. "Read this, son," he said. "But Father!" objected the disturbed aspirant, "This is heterodox Victorian sentimentality, a product of the Western captivity! This isn't spiritual; it's not even Orthodox! I need writings which will teach me spirituality!" The Abbot smiled, saying, "Unless you first develop normal human Christian feeling, and learn life as little David did – with simplicity, kindness, warmth, and forgiveness – then all the Orthodox 'spirituality' and Patristic writings will not only be of no help to you – they will turn you into a 'spiritual' monster and destroy your soul."

Nature is the first consideration of any object.

—St. Thomas Aquinas, *Summa Theologiæ* I-II, Q. 49, Art. 2

From Seminary to Seminary

Englishman though he was, the Bishop responded to the stream of Scottish blood that ran through his veins. Part of that heritage included the stereotype of the Scotsman as parsimonious. As with all stereotypes, the various accusations and the accompanying humor are rooted in some reality (as the garrulous joking Irishman Bernard Shaw once observed – at the core of every good jest is a truth). If the Scots were known to be penny pinchers, the Bishop could squeeze the copper coin between his fingers until it cried, "Ouch!" Sometimes the pressure became so intense poor Honest Abe screamed for mercy. Correspondents became accustomed to receiving missives from Winona written on the back of old scrap paper; every piece of string could find a new use; plastic utensils would be washed and carefully stored as if they were the finest family silver. The recycling crowd could have crowned the Bishop as their patron saint, or at least their poster boy, had they not as green earth-worshippers been put off by his belief in and devotion to God, the doctrines of the Catholic Church and his assertion of objective reality as the guide to objective truth.

Just as he had been exceedingly careful in finding a suitable property at a reasonable price and paying for the Winona seminary as soon as possible, he ran the establishment on a tight budget. The choice of Winona itself leaned toward economy. The former Dominican house stood apart from any megalopolis, in a rural setting, surrounded by farmland and benevolent nature (excepting the winters that could be less than kind, but that offered material for meditation on coldness, desolation and death).

The Voice of the Trumpet

Let a former seminarian describe his memory of the management of the Seminary by the Rector.

[T]he seminary was in a . . . "survivalist friendly" location. Away from large population centers, cozily tucked into the middle of "flyover country."

In 2001 or 2002, Bishop Williamson was getting a natural gas tank and generator installed. The seminary already had quite the farm setup – garden, orchard, pigs, chickens, cows, and much of our food came from there. 100% of our fruit preserves (for daily breakfast) was produced from the land and the volunteer work of the canning ladies. He infused reality into our daily life, trying to re-form the minds of the seminarians who lived there. It worked on me; I don't know about the others. Even small things like having the chef bake bread rather than buying the ridiculous stuff that passes for bread at the store. Everything was "real." Very down to earth and connected with reality. The seminarians did all the chores, the maintenance work, and even chopped wood that provided half of our heat every winter. And let's not forget +W's famous guideline for when the heat came on every winter – let's just say he made us wait a bit.

He was trying to make real men out of us. And even though the minimum age was 18, there were plenty of "boys" entering the seminary.

And I believe he succeeded with many of us. Remember the saying *"nemo dat quod non habet"* ["no one gives what he doesn't have"]? So I'm not surprised that +W was able to teach us how to be men. He's a man himself.

As many people know, he also expects a chastisement in the near future. He also had a speaker come in and give a talk to the seminarians about biological, chemical, and nuclear warfare survival. He is very friendly to the survivalist movement. He would never have wanted to move the seminary anywhere near the East Coast . . . .

The seminary gave up its auxiliary farm. The cows and pigs, the chickens, the gardens, the orchard departed

From Seminary to Seminary

before the priests and seminarians and staff did. The blackberries and raspberries rested unpicked by religious hands. And the fruit jam . . . .

The spanking new and imposingly large seminary opened in Virginia in the fall of 2016, at a very great cost.

Gon-na build a moun-tain

LEGEND THREE

In the early 1990's, a meeting of the USCCB, the United States Conference of Catholic Bishops took place at St. Mary's College in Winona, Minnesota, located at the foot of the high hill topped by the seminary. Needless to say, the Bishop who resided at the top of the hill did not receive an invitation to the gathering. His fellow bishops, however, who would never have requested his participation at the Conference, could not restrain their curiosity about the "goings on" looming above them. One morning during the Conference, a seminarian came around the corner outside the Chapel to discover a small gaggle of ecclesiastics peering through the doors at the Mass being celebrated, a Mass they had abandoned many years before. He politely greeted them and invited them to come with him as he was sure that the Rector, Bishop Richard Williamson, would be happy to meet them and talk with them.

Without so much as a word, the small flock of prelates took wing and flew with alacrity down the driveway, heading for the more comfortable collegial aviary below.

The Voice of the Trumpet

When the French film crews arrived at Écône in the 1970's, Archbishop Lefebvre chose seminarian Williamson to accompany them and be interviewed by them; shortly thereafter when the three "visitors" came from Rome to evaluate the seminary, the Archbishop chose the same seminarian to escort them; in the middle of the 1980's during his negotiations with Cardinal Ratzinger in Rome over the status of the Society and the role of tradition in the Church, the Archbishop when told he could put forward one name to be elevated to the episcopacy forthrightly named Father Richard Williamson. The media folk and the three not-so-wise men from the Vatican in the 70's, and then Cardinal Ratzinger in the 80's, had to be unsettled by the man presented to them by Archbishop Lefebvre to guide, to explain, and then to be raised to the rank of Bishop, for Father Williamson differed from other men of his day. Rome especially must have been unnerved and as a result kept delaying the date when a new traditional Bishop could be consecrated, a delay that eventually made manifest to the Archbishop the Vatican's real intentions – delay and disingenuousness. How could such men be trusted?

Why did Father Richard Williamson so upset those who encountered or learned about him? Because he was unlike them; he had little in him of modernism. To the imprecision and sentimentality of the media, he presented calm reason and thoughtful logic; to the subjectivity and contradictions of Vatican II, he asserted objectivity, Thomistic logic and theological clarity, and, most unsettling, a deep knowledge of tradition, especially as delineated in the Encyclicals of the great recent Popes. In a "new church" turning dogma into doggerel, he held firmly to hard, unchanging and unchangeable doctrine. They knew he would not likely yield, bend, compromise or equivocate. How could you deal with such intransi-

From Seminary to Seminary

gence? Modern Rome wanted nothing to do with such a churchman.

In his years as Rector of the St. Thomas Aquinas Seminary, Father Williamson in Ridgefield and then Bishop Williamson in Winona had irritated countless flag-waving, blue-white-and red blooded good American traditionalists with his criticism of America's masonic roots, lessons learned on his arrival in the country by reading Solange Hertz's "Big Rock Papers" and her classic book *Star Spangled Heresy*. He would remind Americans that being founded in revolution as a masonic-protestant Nation, they had never betrayed Our Lord and His Church as profoundly as the European countries had when they abandoned their Catholic roots and Catholic civilization, but he warned that democracy could be manipulated to enslave the people as pawns, turning them into "customers" rather than citizens. He had even dared to criticize the ladies' choice of *habillement* and attacked sweet Hollywood "Catholic" confections. Many American traditionalists had had their fill of him and his outspokenness. Certain areas, particularly Post Falls, Idaho, and chapels in California, would not be putting out welcome mats for his visits. This Bishop believed in Truth and he insisted on trumpeting it.

And then came GREC.

Let Bishop Tomas Aquino, OSB of the Santa Cruz Monastery in Nova Friburgo, Brazil, give the history.

> In 1995, shortly before his death, the former French ambassador to the Vatican, Gilbert Pérol, wrote an article of "good offices" with the intent to promote a friendly rapprochement between the Society and the official Church. In this project, his widow, Mrs. Huguette Pérol, continued after his death.
>
> Shortly after, this group took the name . . . GREC [*Groupe de Réflection Entre Catholiques*, i.e. Inter-cath-

olic Think Tank], and it reunited members of the SSPX with the progressive clergy. Over the years this group attracted the attention of the French episcopate, no less than that of Rome. The objective of GREC, as one of its founders, Father Michel Lelong, explains "is the necessary reconciliation between Tradition and Rome." An objective mistake, because as Archbishop Lefebvre stated: "Rome has lost the faith . . . Rome is in apostasy." [Conference to priests in Écône during the retreat for priests on September 1, 1987]. However, for GREC these words of Archbishop Lefebvre do not deserve attention. They are words spoken in a "time of distress" as one of the defenders of Bishop Fellay [says]. The members of GREC believe they see events from a higher standpoint, with more serenity, thus targeting an "impossible reconciliation," as Fr. Rioult says very well, reconciliation between two opposing realities: between the true Church, eternal Rome, and the official church, modernist Rome. The truth is that here we see all the drama of the Society because Menzigen has continued since then to seek this reconciliation advocated by GREC, using its authority to stop criticism of the Holy See, i.e., the modernists that occupy it. This is the reason [behind] Bishop Fellay [asking] Bishop Williamson to cease his 'Eleison Comments' [weekly public letters to the faithful] and to stop making strong criticisms of the last ecumenical meeting at Assisi.

When Bishop Fellay became Superior General of the SSPX in 1994, a position that Archbishop Lefebvre explicitly stated should *not* be held by any of the four Bishops he had consecrated in 1988, the new head of the Society faced the "Williamson problem." How could he hope to assist GREC in their plans for a smooth ride to reconciliation with Rome when this huge and unyielding roadblock loomed implacably in the middle of the motorway? A high Vatican official would one day in the future precisely state to an SSPX priest scouting in the Vatican,

From Seminary to Seminary

"Rome knows – it is Williamson or Fellay." Bishop Fellay from the start of his long tenure knew the reality of this alternative – who was to determine the future course of the SSPX – Williamson or himself? The Archbishop had made his choice many years before, but he was now dead and buried. Soon the Society he had founded would begin a painful slow descent into its own grave.

Bishop Fellay began his quiet campaign against Bishop Williamson with a tactic he would use against any future opposition in order to insure his rebuilding of the Society according to his wishes – exile. In sending Williamson to a more obscure corner of the globe, he could please many annoyed American faithful, prove his own *bona fides* with Rome, lay significant groundwork for the triumph of GREC and forcefully establish himself as the undisputed leader of the SSPX. In the spring of 1999, Bishop Fellay relayed to Bishop Williamson his intention to remove the Rector from St. Thomas Aquinas Seminary and relocate him in the Philippines where he would become Asian District Superior.

The Intractable Prelate said, "No." He protested the move on the grounds that his proposed successor did not yet possess the necessary experience and knowledge to hold the position. (Bishop Fellay would also in years to come use this tactic to consolidate his power – put greenhorns in elevated positions where they could be easily manipulated from the Superior General's pinnacle of power.) Bishop Fellay backed down and the Rector remained in his position on the bluffs above the river.

In December of 1999, George Harrison, former Beatles' guitarist and then Hindu disciple faced a knife attack at his home in Friar Park, Oxfordshire. The assailant, 36-year-old Michael Abram, used a kitchen knife in the vicious attack. Harrison's then "wife," Olivia, finally stopped the onslaught by pummeling the attacker with a poker and a lamp. Harrison was hospitalized with more than forty stab wounds.

The 1999 mini-confrontation only confirmed to the Superior General the extent of the problem he faced. In 2003, he made a second attempt. He proposed yet another relocation, i.e., removal. Bishop Williamson would become Rector of the Seminary in La Reja, Argentina. Williamson viewed this as a reasonable request and thought his new replacement at Winona to be better qualified to run the Seminary than the previously named replacement. He agreed to the move.

So saying farewell to Winona and packing his bags for the journey, Bishop Williamson prepared his departure from the United States. He headed for the Latin American Seminary outside of Buenos Aires, where an Archbishop named Bergoglio had already begun to pollute the "good air."

Nearly forty years had passed since Sgt. Pepper's Lonely Hearts Club Band had paraded through the world, attracting more souls to follow the misleading tune than the Pied Piper of Hamelin's tunes had drawn rats. The very different drummer being marched to was not the

From Seminary to Seminary

band's own Ringo Starr, but the "father of lies" who *conduit le bal*. The Beatle-y horde had flown through Argentina as well, depositing its larvae on the rolling pampas. Insect hoards had hatched from the soil, dancing to the music and creating their own, one of the few outlets for identity for the spiritually impoverished young. The "liberation theologians" had also helped to misshape and harden them; these misnamed false pastors knew little theology and enslaved rather than liberated.

Despite the swarming of many motley musical wannabees and atheistic collared Marxists, some young Argentinians had through the grace of God made their way to the Seminary in La Reja. The Bishop had first visited Latin America during the early years of his priesthood accompanying Archbishop Lefebvre on one of the prelate's mission visits. Between his own consecration in 1988 and his arrival in 2003, Bishop Williamson had made a few visits, providing the Sacrament of Confirmation and teaching the faithful. On his arrival at the Seminary Nuestra Señora Corredentora, Our Lady Co-Redemptrix, he encountered a very fine staff. Two Argentinian and two Spanish priests had been instructing and guiding the future priests for a dozen years. His Excellency remembers them as "the Four Pillars of the House." He delighted in becoming the head of already well-established and dedicated workers in the vineyard on whom he could depend. Their expertise and solid management of the Seminary freed him from certain administrative burdens and allowed him to focus on his accustomed role of teacher, as well as giving him time to provide spiritual direction to the young men.

There were very real differences between the run of life in the northern and southern hemispheres. Broadly speaking, the Bishop describes North Americans as excellent in getting the small details of life right but many big things wrong. The streets in the United States are clean and the lawns mowed; the planes and trains and buses run on time; life is organized and efficient with a friendly and generous populace. But scratch below the surface and you will find English principles – liberal, protestant, democratic, and a citizenry whose true religion is politics. The Latins are laid back, not particularly well-organized, with scruffy lawns and bumpy roads; inefficient means of travel; a people accepting, unhurried, content. But scratch a South American and you find Catholic principles built on a Catholic foundation, their basic heritage. They cannot take their politics or their politicians very seriously, knowing that the coming and going of the potentates of power is a sham, the pursuit of political ends mostly a waste of time. They accept with ease right-wing dictatorships that are closer to basic Catholic ideas. Liberalism has continued its slow creep into the various countries from the founding of independent masonic states in the 1800's up to the radical Marxism of the 1950's and 1960's, but life goes on. Regimes, like the tides, come and go.

The Argentinians have their own special character. In many ways the country is the most European of the Latin American nations. As the influx of French into Louisiana turned that State into the State with the most European atmosphere, so an influx of Italians in the 1900's (Bergoglio?) mixed with the Spanish heritage and gave Argentina a unique and distinct European aura. For this reason Archbishop Lefebvre decided to open a Latin American seminary in Argentina, outside of Buenos Aires.

This special mixture had its influence on the Argentinian character as well. There is a certain pride in the people, a more complex temperament, a sense of superiority. The Mexicans say, "If an Argentinian wants to commit suicide, he climbs up on his ego and jumps off." Or they state in more mundane commercial terms, "If

From Seminary to Seminary

you wish to deal with an Argentinian, buy from him for what he is really worth; and sell to him for what he thinks he is worth."

The Argentinian seminarians carried within them their Catholic heritage, but they too, as with all the young, had been bitten by the liberal ticks and lost some of their blood. His Excellency discovered that for the two decades preceding his arrival, the Argentinian educational system had been infested with the crazy-cootie-American idea of the supremacy of studies in mathematics and the sciences at the expense of the humanities. When students are programmed robotically with figures, formulas, equations, hypotheses, and technology, they become easier to monitor and command. Engineers fixated on their screens can be more easily socially engineered; abundant integrals will make humans less whole. The youngsters' minds were filled with numbers and their feet tapped to the prevailing beat, but they lacked the humanity and warmth of heart that had been at the core of their parents' school days.

Having already confronted the same problem at Winona and having some degree of success in his attempted fix, Bishop Williamson launched a Humanities program at La Reja. Over the Christmas holidays when most boys headed to the soccer field for sport, the Bishop invited them to game on the seminary grounds and also spend some time with some music, some literature, some history, not to mention the highest good of all, close access to the sacraments. The Christmas soccer-music-sacrament celebration became immediately successful and was extended to a summer session as well. All young men, not just seminarians, were invited and welcome to attend and many came, seventy, eighty, ninety, each year. Rockers and rowdies with the extra-musically mandated long locks for whom music meant guitars playing a predictable pattern of chords to a prescribed thunka-thunka beat had their ears shocked with two violins, one viola and one cello playing new melodies, odd harmonies and startling rhythms in a quartet created long ago by the Bishop's deaf, dead, distant beloved Beethoven. Or they heard his first violin sonata played on a real violin by a flesh and blood violinist with an actual human pianist accompanying on eighty eight real piano keys. Or they witnessed the keyboard artist test his digits by tackling real revolutionary music – Beethoven's "Appassionata" Sonata. Conferences were given explaining and exploring what they were about to hear or what they had heard, the live performers bringing the music to audible aural life, sometimes more than once. What effect could the ethereally painful and achingly beautiful music of the dying thirty-one year old Franz Schubert in his last composition, the String Quintet in C Major, have on a ragtag assortment of modern Argentinian youth? They know and God knows, and therein lies the mystery of the arts, for the arts possess the potential for humanizing the heart and soul.

Maybe half a dozen each year would respond to the experience and the special graces of the sacraments and enter the Seminary where they would be given a full year of such study. Most others would wander back into the modern world but carrying with them a private gift they never before had been given, a gift that truly would keep on giving. For those who continued at La Reja, the week became a summer, and the summer became a full year, and the full year perhaps became many years; some departed as priest, having moved from the humanity of great art to the true religion of the Man-God and the Glory of the Three-in-One.

From Seminary to Seminary

Communication with the outside world could be difficult as pranksters would occasionally cut the telephone lines and thieves would steal the copper wires. Buenos Aires, thanks to a modern road, lay a mere forty-five minutes to the east. But the distance between the Bishop at the Seminary in La Reja and the Cardinal at the Cathedral in Buenos Aires could not be measured in miles. No meeting ever occurred, as between the two lay "a great gulf fixed" and no modern gauge could calculate it; the gap could only be grasped in the light of eternity.

And then in fall of 2008, the Bishop during one of his episcopal visits agreed to be interviewed on German soil by a reporter for Swedish television. And that, as the poet says, "has made all the difference."

India, August, 2008.

The teacher in Ghana.

Le Moulin du
Pin, July 6, 1990.

The Voice of the Trumpet

Rowing at Cambridge.

The Voice of the Trumpet

The young Williamson at Winchester.

The Voice of the Trumpet

With the gym class.

Visiting Bekkanschaft in San Damiano.

The Voice of the Trumpet

Lecturing at Winona, Summer, 1997.

A talk at St. Vincent's,
Kansas City, Mo., Oct. 7, 1990.

The Voice of the Trumpet

Ceylon, 1996.

Écône, 1997, with Msgr. Fellay.

Pittsburgh, 1984, with Archbishop Lefebvre.

Écône, June, 2002.

Fr. Schmidberger and the bishops,
Rickenbach, Switzerland, April 26, 1990.

The Voice of the Trumpet

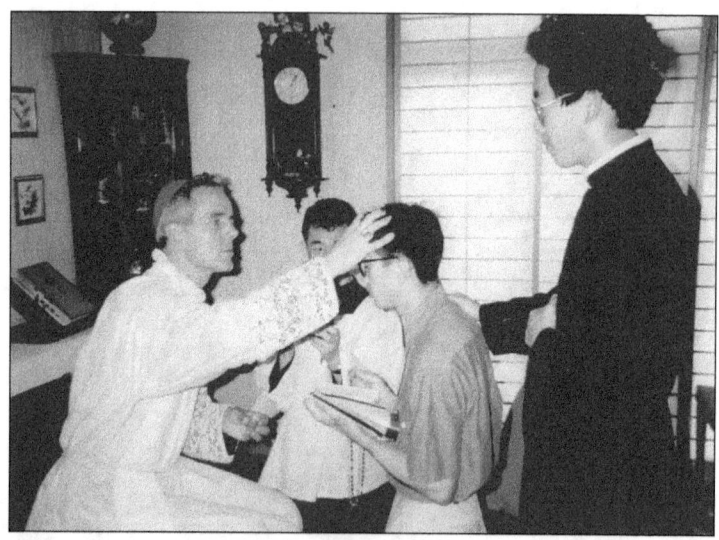

Confirmations in Tokyo.

Sydney, Australia, March, 1995.

The Voice of the Trumpet

The priestly blessing.

Ss. Joseph and Padarn, London, 1992.

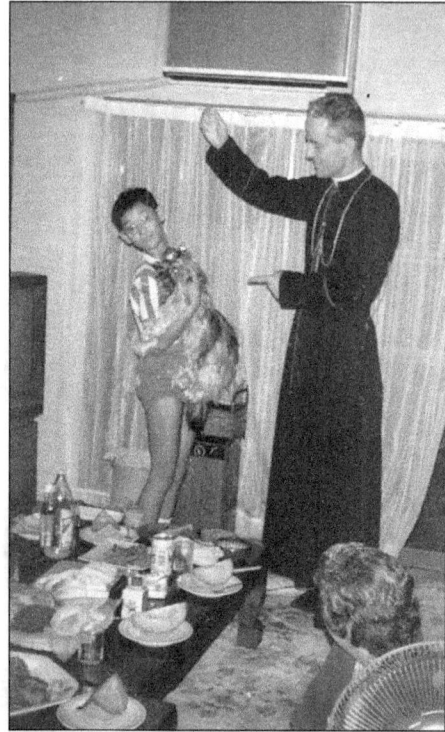

Fun with a dog during the Osaka/Tokyo visit.

Seoul, July 30, 1989.

Seoul, July 30, 1989.

With parents upon graduation from Cambridge.

Near Tokyo with Sister Sasagawa of Akita, July 12, 2002.

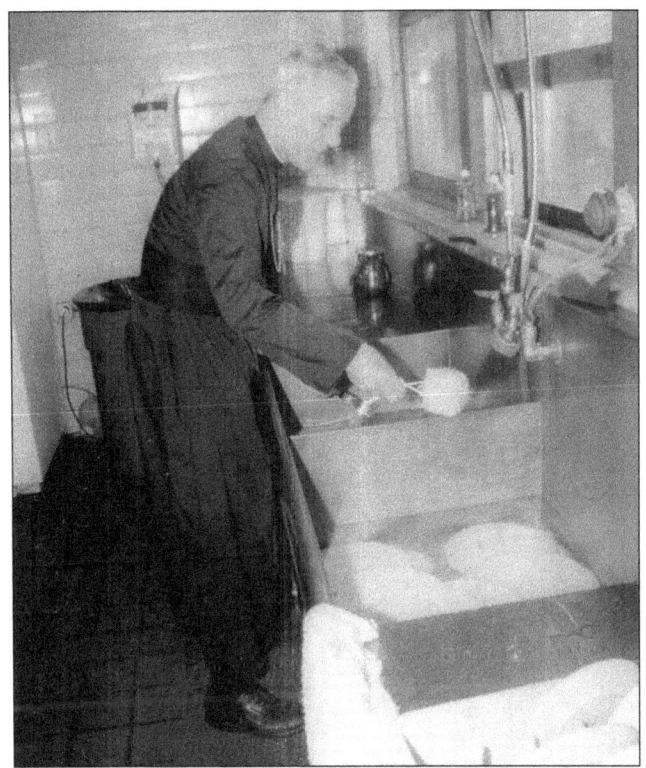

A bishop's work is never done!

At the (American) family gravesite, McConnellsburg, Penn., October 1992.

The Voice of the Trumpet

With faithful in Japan.

Durban, 1994.

The Voice of the Trumpet

Gabon,
April, 1997.

PART THREE

Explosive Missives

"Music goes very deep. Tell me your music and I'll tell who you are."

—Bishop Richard Williamson

"And the Lord God made for Adam and his wife garments of skins, and clothed them."

—Genesis 3: 21.

Scherzo

THE ORIGINS ARE NOT PRECISE OR HISTORically clear. Some say the source can be found in the New Harmony utopian community founded in Indiana in 1825. Others contend the innovation started as an appeal in 1849 published in the *Water-Cure Journal*, an early health-body physically-obsessed publication, that called on women to find an alternative to the corset-petticoat-long-waisted skirts that squeezed and discombobulated their insides, turning their inner parts into squashed, displaced organs of potential disaster, disease and death. What can be stated with certainty is that the new ladies' apparel took its name and its subsequent explosive growth from the many articles that appeared in the women's newspaper and temperance journal *The Lily* penned by demure schoolteacher Amelia Jenks Bloomer. An abolitionist, temperance advocate, and fervent supporter of women's and children's rights, Miss Bloomer promoted the new and revolutionary fashion creation so vehemently that the garment, a loose bodice and a knee-length skirt worn over pantaloons, forever after carried her name – "bloomers."

Ridicule that began to be heaped on the new creation with its visual echo of Turkish dress came from the pulpit, politicians, newspapers and social gatherings. So effective was the championing of the new garment that the catcalls and condemnations had little effect. The progressive raiment offered more "freedom" than mere ease of movement; bloomers became a symbol for greater "freedom" for women to break the bonds that had held them captive for too long. The most prominent suffragettes who demanded women's right to vote, Susan B. Anthony, Lucy Stone, Elizabeth Stanton, began sporting the revolutionary garb, until they realized crowds gathered not to hear their transformational oratory, but to gape at them, just as circus patrons delight in seeing peculiarly outfitted bears and monkeys. The sisters in reform reverted to their traditional attire to better cover their subversive message.

Bloomer hysteria swept the nation. Societies for the advancement of dress reform became popular; another health guru Mary Gove Nichols put forward a "Declaration of Independence from the Despotism of Parisian Fashion;" across the fruited plain, the bloomer boom resounded. Like mushrooms on a damp dark forest floor, bloomer picnics, bloomer festivals, bloomer societies, bloomer clubs, bloomer parties sprang up everywhere. Factory owners encouraged their female employees to adopt the "safer dress" and the textile mills in Lowell, Massachusetts, hosted a celebratory banquet for those

Explosive Missives

lady laborers who "don[ned] the gay apparel" before Independence Day, 1851. Bloomers meant independence, specifically and unspokenly, "freedom" from male authority.

I am wom-an, hear me roar.

These early "bloomers" blossomed in that late nineteenth and early twentieth centuries into the full flower of the fair sex outfitted in masculine togs. Athletic bloomers brought the girls out of the salons and kitchens onto the fields of play and the courts of competition to bounce and shoot and and kick and run; secular nurses treated patients unencumbered by the garments that once linked them to sisterhood and motherhood; full-trousered women wranglers and hands joined the men in the field and the barn and on the ranch; and when, in the 1930's, the silver screen goddesses Katherine Hepburn and Marlene Dietrich paraded in panted glory before celebrity-dazzled and screen-hypnotized fans, the set-up was complete. The one final decisive blow to the flowing skirts of femininity came with one of the devil's favorite tools – war.

> Fredonia's going to war . . . !
> —Groucho Marx as Rufus T. Firefly in
> *Duck Soup* (1933)

When God chose in our time to warn the world of its impending punishment for sin, He sent His Mother. The message to the peasant children of Fatima (at least those words which the Church, in opposition to Our Lady's clear command, has condescended to make public) speak of war. The bloody war that still blazed in 1917 would end, the children were told. The beautiful lady dressed in soft white garments and shining in purity warned that if mankind did not repent, a second and greater war would flame up as just retribution.

World War II was not a noble confrontation between the gleaming sword of righteousness against the wicked powers of darkness; it was not the "greatest generation" going forth to crush the minions of iniquity; it was not the triumph of civilization over barbaric savages. The Virgin Mother of God, Mary Most Holy, told the world in advance what the war would be and what it turned out to be – a punishment for sin. Few saw clearly the horrible nature of the clash. Evelyn Waugh, who wrote the greatest of all World War II novels, *Sword of Honour*, quite rightly defined it as "a tug of war between two groups of indistinguishable louts." Atheistic materialists from around the world pounded on each other until some of the combatants had worn down, devastated and crushed some others; millions died in the conflagration. Individual stories of sacrifice and courage, devotion and loyalty were all genuine, and many souls must have turned to God imploring His pardon as they were pulverized, but even the best souls who fought and died did so for what? Those who survived returned home to what? The further expansion of atheistic communism into eastern Europe, into the far East, into Latin America; the explosion of already enervated democracy and unrestrained materialism in the "victor" nations in the 1950's that led to the bursting of the boil in the turmoil of the 1960's. Good men fought and good men died so the Kingdom of anti-Christ could firmly establish birth control, abortion, lawlessness, anti-authoritarianism, upheaval, violence, drugs, divorce, Vatican II, ecumenism, religious liberty, dumbed-down "education," rock music, punk music, rap music, hip hop, filthy cinema, unreadable books,

Explosive Missives

televised stupidity, day care, nursing homes, euthanasia, gay marriage, transsexual surgery and women in pants. Forcing women into the factories and the political sphere to "aid the war effort" sealed the deal, zipped up the alterations, pulled up the sweats. Rosie the Riveter had a big, manly muscle and displayed it with pride. Rosie and her off-spring (if she produced any) learned they no longer needed male guidance or husbands or fathers. The old saw may have said that "clothes make the man" but clothes had now made the woman the faux-man.

Throughout his twenty years as Rector of the St. Thomas Aquinas Seminary in the United States, first in Ridgefield and then in Winona, Father Williamson in Connecticut and then Bishop Williamson in Minnesota consistently taught the faithful through a series of monthly letters. Among the nearly two hundred and fifty letters which he penned, two in particular, "like eagle[s] in a dovecote/ Fluttered" the faithful, causing feathers to fly, with accompanying cacophony of angry cooing and pecking and squawking. The first appeared in September, 1991, when his observations concerning women in slacks set off a feminist fire-storm.

His comments merely echoed traditional Catholic teaching on the subject. The Blessed Mother herself taught the children at Fatima that "certain fashions will be introduced that will offend Our Lord very much." She did not delve into dress specifics, but anyone with eyes to see and a brain with which to ponder can easily draw up a list. A Cardinal Vicar, not named, during the reign of Pope Pius XI, drew up a list of "The Mary-like Standards for Modesty in Dress (as set down by the Vatican)." His sensible guidelines pertain only to dresses and skirts, the good Cardinal's thought in his day not being able to predict what loomed in the denim-days ahead.

The Bishop's 1991 letter sets forth such profound insights that it deserves to be recalled in full:

Trumpet Clarion Call

Summer's end may not seem to be the cleverest moment to choose to write about women's dress. Surely the arrival rather than the departure of warm weather would be the time to inveigh against immodest clothing. However, several ladies happen to have raised with me this summer the question of women wearing trousers or shorts (pants), and the problem is broader and deeper than just immodesty, grave though immodesty is.

For instance, Bishop de Castro Mayer used to say that trousers on a woman are worse than a mini-skirt, because while a mini-skirt is sensual and attacks the senses, the trousers are ideological and attack the mind. For indeed women's trousers, as worn today, short or long, modest or immodest, tight or loose, open or disguised (like the "culottes"), are an assault upon woman's womanhood and so they represent a deep-lying revolt against the order willed by God. This may be least true of the long "culottes," trousers most closely resembling a skirt, and at best mistakable for a skirt, but insofar as "culottes" establish the principle of dividing woman's outward apparel from the waist down, they merely disguise the grave disorder. What disorder? ("Excellency, this time you really have flipped your lid!")

In the beginning, God created man and woman, both human but quite different, firstly man, secondly woman (Gen 1: 27, 2: 22); woman to be man's help-mate like unto himself (Gen. 2: 18). Woman for man, not man for woman (I Cor. 11: 9) for: "the man is not of the woman but the woman is of the man" (I Cor. 11: 8). Thus even before original sin happened,

God ordered between man and woman distinction, inequality, and the headship of man over woman for purposes of living in society and in the family upon this earth.

Original sin, whereby Eve made Adam sin and not the other way round (I Tim. 2: 14), entailed Eve's being punished, amongst other things turning of her natural and painless subordination to Adam into a punishing subordination of him over her, for she had shown by seducing him that she needed to be controlled . . . " thou shalt be under thy husband's power, and he shall have dominion over thee" (Gen. 3: 17). Thenceforth with the transmission of original sin to all the children of Adam passes to all the daughters of Adam (except, of course, the Blessed Virgin Mary) this punitive subordination.

As with all problems of sin, the only true solution is the grace of Our Lord Jesus Christ. For instance in a Catholic marriage the painful control of man over woman, evident in all non-Christian cultures and re-emerging in our own anti-Christian culture, becomes by supernatural grace more and more that subordination of woman to man which is in accordance with their nature and which is profitable to both, which Eve had before she and Adam fell.

But away with Eden by grace! The modern world will have none of Jesus Christ's solutions to Adam's and Eve's problems. Making idols of liberty and equality, to refuse any inequality or subordination of woman to man, it will deny any distinction between them, as it denies of course any order of God in His creation, any need for Redemption and it will deny if necessary God's very existence. Today's feminism is intimately connected to witchcraft and Satanism.

These considerations have taken us a long way from the question of women's trousers, and of course not every woman putting on a pair of shorts is consciously thinking of defying God or of defying her menfolk. She is, however, conscious of something. She is clearly aware that divided shorts are not like an undivided skirt, and the difference is that abandoning the skirt gives her a vague feeling – surely of unease, or emancipation, or both . . . . What is that feeling based on?

Clothing divided for the legs obviously liberates the mobile lower half of the body for a number of activities for which clothing undivided like a skirt is relatively cumbersome. Adam then having to earn his family's bread by the sweat of all kinds of activities outside the home, it is entirely normal for the man to wear trousers, and if a girl gets into her head to join him in these activities, obviously trousers likewise emancipate her to do so. Shorts are the outward and visible sign of her liberation from the restricted range of home-making activities.

However, she is uneasy because trousers are not the natural wear of a woman. However it be with other species, in the human species the female is designed to attract the eye of the male much more than the reverse – compare the number of male and of female beauty magazines on the market. Now original sin wounds human nature with concupiscence (unlawful desire) particularly in the senses of sight, touch and imagination. It follows for questions of clothing that what might arouse concupiscence needs more to be disguised in woman from man's eye than in man from woman's eye. Hence as trousers benefit the activity of man, so skirts disguisingly loose fit the dignity and honor of woman. Hence while donning his emancipatory trousers, she feels uneasy (at least until her conscience is dulled) as she is moving away from her identity and role and dignity as a woman. In her conscience is resounding the voice of the Lord her God pronouncing in the Mosaic Law: A woman shall not be clothed with man's apparel, neither shall a man use woman's apparel: for he that doeth these things is abominable before God (Deut. 22: 5). And trousers are normally man's apparel, for reasons given above.

Of course if one denies the original sin which inflamed man's concupiscence (Gen. 3: 7) and sharpened women's subordination (Gen. 3: 16), women's trousers are not so unreasonable, but see all around you the absurd consequences of denying original sin! – sweet Pollyanna goes to the office dressed fit to inflame a stone, but woe unto the poor male colleague in the office who fails to react like a stone, because with recent laws (in the USA) she will attack him in court! Insanity! Places of work will soon have to extract in advance from women sworn declarations whether or not they do, or do not, want to have advances made to them. But what was to be expected when women were pulled out of their home? It all serves liberal men right, for so misleading their women ....

For the true womanliness of woman, its importance cannot be exaggerated. It all turns on women being essentially designed by God for motherhood; for the bringing of children into this world, and for their rearing; for the giving of life, warmth, love, nursing and nourishment, everything represented by mother's milk. For this men are not designed, of it they are intrinsically incapable, yet upon it they are wholly dependent if they are to become human, as opposed to inhuman beings. In a valuable book, *The Flight from Woman*, a cultivated Jewish psychiatrist [later a Catholic convert], Karl Stern, tells how he could discern in countless ills of the big city patients coming through his Toronto practice after World War II a pattern of womanlessness with which he was familiar from the works of famous modern writers such as Goethe, Descartes, Tolstoy, Ibsen; not a lack of women, but a lack of truly womanly women, because modern men and women alike are trampling upon the womanly qualities and virtues. Shakespeare distilled this spirit in Lady Macbeth, the proto-feminist and Satanist:

> Come you spirits
> That tend on mortal thoughts, unsex me here,
> And fill me from the crown to the toe top-full
> Of direst cruelty .... Come to my woman's breast
> And take my milk for gall, you murdering ministers ....

(*Macbeth*, Act I, scene v).

Heaven help us! The womanliness of our women is being rooted out and the result is a way of life doomed to self-destruction, doomed to abort.

Girls, be mothers, and in order to be mothers, let not wild horses drag you into shorts or trousers. When activities are proposed to you requiring trousers, if it is something your great-grandmother did, then find a way of doing it, like her, in a skirt. And if your great-grandmother did not do it, then forget it! Her generation created your country; your generation is destroying it. Of course not all women who wear trousers abort the fruit of their womb, but all of them help to create

The Voice of the Trumpet

the abortive society. Old-fashioned is good, modern is suicidal. You wish to stop abortion? Do it by example. Never wear trousers or shorts. Bishop de Castro Mayer was right."

—Letters from the Rector, No. 97

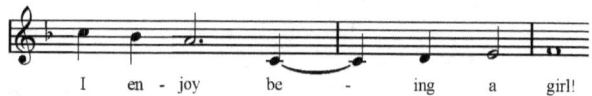

I en - joy be - ing a girl!

Letters of protest marched in on loud hobnail boots defending the "right" to wear whatever apparel the writer saw fit. Fashion bonded the women together – what many wore, most willed to wear. Having freed themselves over the centuries from the chastity belt and the corset and the skirt, they would wear what they would wear "And there's no doing anything about it!" Traditional Catholics they may be, but having put on new garments for comfort and now racing about in less restrictive raiment, no Bishop was going to suggest to them that they return to freedom-inhibiting frocks. The catawampus hissing echoed from chapel to chapel; the catcalls came scratched on stationery; day by day the objections and outrage arrived on pretty cards and note leafs and legal pad pages, brought to His Excellency's office by the postalperson.

Dozens of daughters of Eve demanded to be removed from the mailing list. Their requests were honored. To be fair, half the letters supported the Bishop (how many of those favorable responses came from delighted husbands awaits future federally-funded scientific study). Many of the letters defending women in pants "confined themselves to saying, some politely, some less politely, that His Excellency had indeed 'flipped his lid'."

Explosive Missives

In his response, "Slacks II," sent out as the monthly letter of November, 1991, the Bishop proved himself prophetic. In defending his logical, obvious Traditional Catholic position, he pointed to two potential dangers arising from the garb conflation. He referenced the then current Senate hearings on Clarence Thomas's appointment to the Supreme Court, hearings that turned into a media circus focusing on an accusation of "sexual harassment." "[B]efore the hearings there was a hysterical uprising amongst women across the land to insist her [the accuser's] fantasizing be heard, during the hearings it received an inordinate amount of attention and after the hearings there has been a spate of lawsuits being filed by her imitators who feel themselves similarly victims." The media, he recognizes, "played no doubt a large part in inflating the issue out of all proportion," but he also notes "a deep sense of grievance on the part of many women – like a feeling they have been betrayed. Something is going profoundly wrong in man-woman relations."

Nearly a quarter-century later as women have more and more abandoned the home where babies are born, children are raised and nurtured, hearts are formed, and manners and civility are taught, "sexual harassment" is now epidemic and the source of endless civic strife. No amount of mandatory and endless "sexual harassment training" (non-stop blathering seeking to quell nature and overturn God's order) seems to stop the plague. In the military, in the schools, in business, in finance, in government, in the media itself, gawking and groping and lewdness and lust seem to be everywhere and seem to be unconquerable, like the moles in the carnival game who pop up from inside the gameboard, and no amount of mallet-whacking can vanquish them. No conditioning or cajoling or criminal filings seem able to stop the pestilence. The men who no longer have any strong masculine moral models ("[John Wayne], thou shouldst be living at this hour!/ [America] hath need of thee . . . ") and denied the civilizing influence of loving mothers in their youth for which the finest day-care worker can never provide an adequate substitute, have indeed become, with their concupiscence unleashed and confronting constant temptation in the workplace, little better than goats; their aggressive, violent, brutish behavior reveals the pervasiveness of the catastrophe. The only possible liberal utopian solution to this intractable social mayhem can only cause greater upheaval. If women insist on taking over the public sphere by taking over the roles of men, then the men, to be prevented from behaving like loutish beasts in public, must be refashioned into women, staying at home in the private sphere, becoming sweet, soft and feminine.

And here the Bishop in 1991 again correctly foresaw the logical and demonic outcome of the sexual identity conflagration: "[A]nother example of this grave disruption of nature in the USA today: the invasion of public life by gays and lesbians, men and women being 'delivered up to shameful affections . . . changing the natural use into that which is against nature' (Rom. 1: 26, 27), then flaunting their unnatural vice in public and being rewarded by the vile media with a blaze of publicity. And decent citizens seem unable to do much about it . . . . "

He goes on to state the hard truth that the so-called "alternative life-style" is in fact one of the four sins that the Catholic Church has always taught as being so offensive as to cry to Heaven for vengeance. (In the first "Slacks" letter, he had already pointed out how sexual confusion had led to the self-destructive and murderous act of abortion, another of the four grave sins.) He lays the fault at the feet of the men, who have by their liberalism and moral cowardice allowed the catastrophe to occur.

Explosive Missives

So now, a quarter century later, endless lawsuits clog the courts (presided over more and more by female judges); the battle of the sexes has gone nuclear; the number of murdered children from the abortuaries approaches sixty million; the "marriages" of gays and lesbians have become common and have been approved by the highest court in the land (and woe to the baker who will not bake the cake or the photographer who chooses not to memorialize the abomination); transsexuals in their mental and spiritual malaise have become the new cause *du jour* as they insist on serving in the military, and their "reconstructive surgery" is now paid for by taxpayer dollars. With all this hellish lunacy destroying any social stability, the Bishop's warning is more pertinent than ever. And fewer ears, even Traditional Catholic ears, are able or willing to hear.

The Amazons, those strong, tough, armoured, manly women warriors, currently enjoy their greatest popularity. As women rise to the top of the ranks throughout the military, the Amazons become recruiting posters for equality in the armed forces. In mythological terms, these "warring Amazons, man-haters," as Aeschylus labeled them, were in reality distant minor figures. They play no major role in the great literary catalogue of the Greek myths or the epic poems of Homer. The Amazons march onto the expanse of the Greek stage of myth rather late in the action and seem to have been born in another sphere, arriving through "charmed magic casements" from "faery lands forlorn."

The Voice of the Trumpet

"Forlorn" appropriately describes their eventual end, not their late beginning. Legend says the martial troop had unlikely parentage, sired by Ares (Mars), the god of war on the sweetest of nymphs "Harmony, heavenly Harmony." The daughters decided to model their behavior and their actions on their father, taking on his bellicose nature, rejecting completely the calm, gentle, feminine beauty of their mother.

Living in the Caucasus, in their chief city Themiscryra, they had sufficient Greek good reason not to try to integrate themselves with male armies. When Shakespeare's Cleopatra protests her exclusion from Antony's army, Enobarbus, Antony's right hand man, in an aside states the obvious reason: "If we should serve with horse and mares together,/ The horse were merely [utterly] lost, the mares would bear/ A soldier and his horse." (3. 7. 7-9.) The Amazons avoided the concupiscent-created chaos of the modern "integrated" military by keeping their units single sex. No male members allowed.

Unfortunately for them, the result meant defeat. In the bits of different stories that mention them, they fall before the forces of Achilles, Bellerophon, and Theseus. In a humiliating defeat, they are overcome by a single man. The ninth labor of Hercules takes him to carry off the girdle of their Queen, Hippolyta. When the Amazons charge his ship, Hercules vanquishes them, kills their Queen and leaves with her girdle (not her bloomers).

The Amazons do not have an impressive military record; however, the "female of the species" manages to revenge her sex on Hercules in a humiliating way. Hercules having in a fit of anger committed a savage murder, some versions say several murders, is ordered by Zeus through the Oracle at Delphi to suffer punishment by becoming a slave to Queen Omphale in Lydia for a year, some versions say three years. The Queen, seeing an op-

Explosive Missives

portunity to humiliate the great hero-warrior even further, dresses him in women's clothing and forces him to do women's work. This greatest hero of all Greek legend must abandon his sword and take up the spindle, stop making war and start weaving cloth, all the while garbed like one of the fairer sex and doing domestic chores. Such reversal of sexual roles and appropriate dress brought shame. The Greeks grasped essentials and knew, as St. Thomas would state many centuries later, "nature is the first consideration of any object," *Summa Theologiæ* I-II, Q. 49, Art. 2. Surely an individual's sexual identity in physical, social and fashion terms is the first consideration of any created being. "Male and female He created them . . . ."

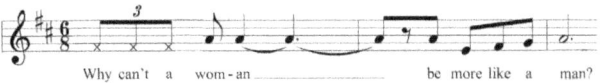
Why can't a wom-an be more like a man?

The teaching of Bishop Williamson on this subject follows in Catholic order and tradition with the consistent Catholic thought up to the time when the cataclysm of Vatican II devastated not only the Church but also the dress shops. The revolution invaded the stores where cotton dresses and silk gowns and velvet robes once were displayed and even blasted away ribbons and lace and buttons and sashes, all feminine adornments that ladies loved and that delighted men's eyes. Not even hats survived; sweat bands supplanted them; skirts vanished as denim triumphed. The Bishop's voice rang out nevertheless with unbending Catholic sense.

On June 12, 1960, Giuseppe, Cardinal Siri, sent a notification from his archepiscopal seat in Genoa to his clergy, his teaching sisters, his "beloved sons of catholic action," and "educators intending truly to follow Christian doctrine."

Solo of the Raganella (i.e., a watchman's rattle, used to summon worshippers and to give a warning)

The wearing of man's dress by women affects firstly the woman herself, by changing the feminine psychology proper to women; secondly it affects the woman as wife of her husband by tending to vitiate relationships between the sexes; thirdly it affects the woman as mother of her children by harming her dignity in her children's eyes. Each of these points is to be carefully considered in turn: –

A. Male Dress Changes the Psychology of Woman.

In truth, the motive compelling women to wear men's dress is always that of imitating, nay, of competing with the man who is considered stronger, less tied down, more independent. This motivation shows clearly that male dress is the visible aid to bringing about a mental attitude of being "like a man." Secondly, ever since men have been men, the clothing a person wears, demands, imposes and modifies that person's gestures, attitudes and behavior, such that from merely being worn outside, clothing comes to impose a particular frame of mind inside.

Then let us add that woman wearing man's dress always more or less indicates her reacting to her femininity as though it is inferiority when in fact it is only diversity . . . .

B. Male Dress Tends to Vitiate Relationships Between Men and Women

In truth, when relationships between the two sexes unfold with the coming of age, an instinct of mutual attraction is predominant. The essential basis of this attraction is a diversity between the two sexes which is made possible only by their complementing or completing one another. If then this "diversity" becomes less obvious because one of its external signs is eliminated and because the normal psychological structure is weakened, what results is the alteration of a fundamental factor in the relationship.

The problem goes further still. Mutual attraction between the sexes is preceded both naturally, and in order of time, by that sense of shame which holds the rising instincts in check, imposes respect upon them, and tends to lift to a higher level of mutual esteem and healthy fear everything that these instincts would push onwards to uncontrolled acts. To change that clothing which by its diversity reveals and upholds nature's limits and defense-works, is to flatten out the distinctions and to help pull down the vital defense-works of the sense of shame.

It is at least to hinder that sense. And when the sense of shame is hindered from putting on the brakes, then relationships between men and women sink degradingly down to pure sensuality, devoid of all mutual respect and esteem.

Experience is there to tell us that when woman is de-feminised, then defenses are undermined and weakness increases.

C. Male Dress Harms the Dignity of the Mother in Her Children's Eyes

All children have an instinct for the sense of dignity and decorum of their mother. Analysis of the first inner crisis of children when they awaken to life around them even before they enter upon adolescence, shows how much the sense of their mother counts. Children are as sensitive as they can be on this point. Adults have usually left all that behind them and think no more of it. But we would do well to recall to mind the severe demands that children instinctively make of their own mother, and the deep and even terrible reactions roused in them by observation of their mother's misbehavior. Many lines of later life are here traced out – and not for good – in these early inner dramas of infancy and childhood.

The child may not know the definition of exposure, frivolity or infidelity, but he possesses an instinctive sixth sense to recognize them when they occur, to suffer from them, and be bitterly wounded by them in his soul.

Let us think seriously on the import of everything said so far, even if woman appearing in man's dress does not immediately give rise to all the upset caused by grave immodesty.

The changing of feminine psychology does fundamental and, in the long run, irreparable damage to the family, to conjugal fidelity, to human affections and to human society. True, the effects of wearing unsuitable dress are not to be seen within a short time. But one must think of what is being slowly and insidiously worn down, torn apart, perverted.

Is any satisfying reciprocity between husband and wife imaginable, if female psychology be changed? Or is any true education of children imaginable, which is so delicate in its procedure, so woven of imponderable factors in which the mother's intuition and instinct play the decisive role in those tender years? What will these women be able to give their children when they have so long worn trousers that their self-esteem goes more by competing with the men than by their functioning as women?

Why, we ask, ever since men have been men, or rather since they became civilized – why have men in all times and places been irresistibly borne to make a differentiated division between the functions of the two sexes? Do we not have strict testimony by all mankind of a truth and a law above man?

To sum up, wherever women wear men's dress, it is to be considered a factor in the long run tearing apart human order.

The logical consequence of everything presented so far is that anyone in a position of responsibility should be possessed by a SENSE OF ALARM in the true and proper meaning of the word, a severe and decisive ALARM....

Men may come and men may go, because God has left plenty of room for the to and fro of their free-will; but the substantial lines of nature and the not less substantial lines of Eternal Law have never changed, are not changing and never will change. There are bounds beyond which one may stray as one sees fit, but to do so ends in death; there are limits which empty philosophical fantasizing may have one mock or not take seriously, but they put together an alliance of hard facts and nature to chastise anybody who steps over them. And history has sufficiently taught, with the frightening proof of the life and death of nations, that the reply to all the violators of the outline of 'humanity" is always, sooner or later, catastrophe.

From the dialectic of Hegel onwards, we have had dinned in our ears what are nothing but fables and by dint of hearing them so often, many people end up by getting used to them,

Explosive Missives

if only passively. But the truth of the matter is that Nature and Truth, and the Law bound up in both, go their imperturbable way, and they cut to pieces the simpletons who upon no grounds whatsoever believe in radical and far-reaching changes in the very structure of man.

The consequences of such violations are not a new outline of man, but disorders, hurtful instability of all kinds, the frightening dryness of human souls, the shattering increase in the number of human castaways, driven long since out of people's sight and mind to live out their decline in boredom, sadness and rejection. Aligned on the wrecking of the eternal norms and to be found in broken families, lives cut short before their time, hearths and homes gone cold, old people cast to one side, youngsters will fully degenerate and – at the end of the line – souls in despair will take their own lives. All of which human wreckage gives witness to the fact that the "line of God" does not give way, nor does it admit of any adaptation to the delirious dreams of the so-called philosophers!

—Giuseppe Cardinal Siri

Cardinal Siri's warning alarm rattle of 1960 proved prophetic and accurate; Bishop Williamson's warning trumpet call of 1991 proved prophetic and accurate. The bubbling poison cauldron of social decay boiled over from religious indifferentism to all of the disorder leading to violence against oneself or other souls or whole nations. The devil shrieks with glee at his temporary triumph; Our Lady will crush his head . . . soon. "Watch and pray, watch and pray. Fifteen mysteries every day."

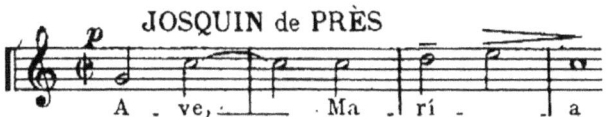

The Voice of the Trumpet

Alpine Trio – *anime giocoso*

> Kitsch causes two tears to flow in quick succession. The first tear says: "How nice to see children running on the grass!" The second tear says: "How nice to be moved, together with all mankind, by children running on the grass!"
>
> —Milan Kundera

The criticism was harsh, the words severe and the angry responses came marching in on mountain-climbing boots, crushing the edelweiss. Here are a few of the remarks that set off the avalanche of outrage:

> What is it that makes millions of people buy and like *The Sound of Music* – a tribute to "freshness" that is so mechanically engineered, so shrewdly calculated that the background music rises, the already soft focus blurs and melts, and, upon the instant, you can hear all the noses blowing in the theatre? Of course, it's well done for what it is: that is to say, those who made it are experts at manipulating responses. They're the Pavlovs of movie-making: they turn us into dogs that salivate on signal. When the cruel father sees the light and says, "You've brought music back into the house," who can resist the pull at the emotions? It's the same tug at the heartstrings we feel when Lassie comes home or when the blind heroine sees for the first time; it is a simple variant of the surge of warmth we feel when a child is reunited with his parents. It's basic and there are probably few of us who don't respond. But it is the easiest and perhaps most primitive kind of emotion we are made to feel. The worst despots in history, the most cynical purveyors of mass culture respond at *this* level and may feel pleased at how tender-hearted they *really*

Explosive Missives

are because they do . . . .

Whom could it offend? Only those of us who, *despite the fact we may respond*, loathe being manipulated in this way and are aware of how self-indulgent and cheap and ready-made are the responses we are made to feel. And we may become even more aware of the way we have been *used* and turned into emotional and aesthetic imbeciles when we hear ourselves humming those sickly goody-goody songs. The audience for a movie of this kind becomes the lowest common denominator of feeling: a sponge. The heroine leaves the nuns at the fence as she enters the cathedral to be married. Squeezed again, and the moisture comes out of thousands – millions – of eyes and noses . . . .

"High on a hill sat a [candid bishop]," but he did not pen these words at his desk above the city of Winona. The hard-headed denunciation appeared in *McCall's Magazine*, one of the many journals for home-makers that were popular in America; ironically, their greatest popularity came on the eve of the wives and mothers leaving their homes, igniting their undergarments and slogging off into Caliban's swamp while chanting "freedom, heyday, freedom." The criticism reflects a female sensibility as they focus on feelings and skewer the contrived emotions that lured audiences to shell out shekels for the studio which piled up mounds of money greener than the Austrian hills. Not for nothing did the industry moguls come to refer cynically to the blockbuster entertainment as *The Sound of Money*. The review by liberal film critic Pauline Kael resulted in her being cashiered by the magazine. She moved to *The New Yorker* where her tart opinions and verbal wit made her one of the most influential movie critics of the day; one wag referred to her as "the Beatles of film criticism."

The Bishop upon experiencing the soggy wiener schnitzel examined it, not surprisingly, with his Thomistic analytical skill, and picked the phony sacher torte to pieces, exposing the poison in the pretty cake:

Trumpet Solo – *forte*

Firstly, Julie Andrews is nice (of course), but she is too high-spirited to be a nun (of course), waving her arms around and singing (presumably to the grass) that "The hills are alive with the sound of music." The hills seem very unmoved but they do look beautiful, as does Julie Andrews (of course. We know she would wear perfume and make-up to go jogging).

Fortunately, the Mother Superior is also nice (of course, at least in 1965. Today she would be a child-abuser), so she and the other nuns are very understanding and let Julie Andrews go, to try out being a governess of a tyrannical widower's unruly children who have (of course) chased away several governesses before her. What shall she do? Have no fear! The Power of Positive Thinking (of course) – she sings a gutsy little number along the lines, "I have confidence in sunshine, I have confidence in rain . . . besides which, you see, I have confidence in me." Bravo.

Sure enough, once inside the door she gives a dazzling demonstration of the superiority of liberty and equality over stuffy old Austrian ways! Immediately undermining – in front of the children – the Captain's tyrannical discipline over them, she proceeds to win their hearts (of course) by a combination of being their friend, taking their side, making them sing and have fun, all this without a trace of motherliness and all the time looking as cute as a kitten. She even looks cute when she prays, in fact who would not pray when it makes you look so specially cute?

Explosive Missives

Of course the stern Captain is soon won over by his domain being turned into a gigantic playpen, so he breaks out in that favorite Austrian number "Edelweiss" [composed for the musical], whereupon they all burst into song because the family has been rebuilt on the liberty-equality model. By now Julie Andrews is looking goofy around the Captain (of course), so there is a ball, and they dance (of course), and dancing reveals more of her charms (of course), whereupon the Captain also looks goofy around her (of course).

But enter now the villains! Firstly, a glamorous Baroness previously engaged to be married to the Captain, who schemes to get Julie Andrews out of the way, back to the convent (but didn't you know, : "The path of true love never did run smooth"?) Secondly, villain of villains, a – a – a NAZI! (Original sin? – never heard of it! Isn't all sin Nazi sin?)

Pan back to the Convent for a heart-warming feminine dialogue: Mother: "You're unhappy." J. A. "I'm confused." Mother: "Go back to him." Him of course is delighted when she returns, so there is a duet of swooning, spooning and crooning by – guess what! – moonlight! "But will the children approve of our marrying?" (Of course!) Shiny white wedding dress (of course), wedding bells all over the place and a lovely ceremony (of course), to be spoiled only by the brutal reappearance of the nasty Nazi – the Captain must report for duty to the Third Reich!

The family try to sneak away. The nasty Nazi spots them, so now they all break out into singing "Edelweiss." The nasty Nazi is foiled when the family escape to the convent (where else?) but drama rolls as the nasty Nazis close in one the convent. (But didn't you know, "Life is not just a bed of roses?") The Captain is heroic (of course), but the dastardly villains are only foiled for good when their car is incapacitated by the nuns turned into mechanics (of course), and the last shots show the "family" climbing a mountain path to get out of the Third Reich, amidst hills which are once more – go on, don't tell me you couldn't guess! – "alive with the sound of music." How truly heart-warming!

Dear friends, please excuse this long excursion into the audio-visual scenery of an average modern Christmas, but no less may be necessary to rub noses in the falsity of the soul-rotting slush. Clean family edification? Nothing of the kind!

As for cleanness, many films may be worse than *The Sound of Music*, but stop and think – are youth, physical attractiveness and being in love the essence of marriage? Can you imagine this Julie Andrews staying with the Captain if "the romance went out of their marriage"? Would she not divorce him and grab his children from him to be her toys? Such romance is not actually pornographic but it is virtually so, in other words all the elements of pornography are there, just waiting to break out. One remembers the media sensation when a few years later Julie Andrews appeared topless in another film. That was no sensation, just a natural development for one canine female on a roll.

As for being a family film, by glorifying the romance which is essentially self-centered, *The Sound of Music* puts selfishness in the place of selflessness between husband and wife, and by putting friendliness and fun in place of authority and rules, it invites disorder between parents and children. This is a new model family which in short order will be no family at all, its liberated members flying off in all directions.

Finally as for edification, in *The Sound of Music* the Lord God is mere decoration. True, His Austrian mountains are beautiful (beautiful decoration), but His nuns are valued only for their sweetness towards the world and their understanding of its ways, while His ex-nun is wholly oriented toward the world.

Dear friends, any supposed Catholicism in *The Sound of Music* is a Hollywood fraud corresponding to the real-life fraud of that "Catholicism" of the 1950's and 1960's, all appearance and no substance, which was just waiting to break out into Vatican II and the Newchurch. Right here is the sweet compassion for homosexuals and the bitter grief for Princess Di, the sympathy for priests quitting the SSPX for the *Novus Ordo*. Everything is man-centered and meant to feel good, the apostasy of our times.

But, somebody may object, *The Sound of Music* is only entertainment. Reply, is the world in a mess, or not? Now, has the world got to where it is by people listening to sermons in church? They do less and less of that. Then what do they drink into their hearts and souls and minds? Is it not their "entertainment," *The Sound of Music* in season and countless films like it out of season? Then if the world around us is corrupt, it sure fits these films being corrupt, whereas if someone can see no problem with *The Sound of Music* (1965), how can he see no problem with Vatican II (1962–1965)? The simultaneity in time is no coincidence.

Dear friends, "entertainment" requires serious attention....

—*Letters from the Rector*, No. 168

Unlike Miss Kael, the Bishop could not be fired from his position because of a tsunami of angry letters from those devoted to the devious mush. Many readers remained rankled for years to come, but thanks to His Excellency's response to the harsh criticism of his remarks, taken as always by him on light shoulders, the very name of the movie became in future years a subject for future mirth.

Sentimentality is the bank holiday of cynicism.

—Oscar Wilde

The Sound of Music opened on Broadway in 1959, the last of the Richard Rodgers – Oscar Hammerstein musicals.

The Voice of the Trumpet

Oscar Hammerstein died of cancer in 1960. The last lyrics he penned were for the faux-folk song "Edelweiss." The theatre critics wrote stringent reviews, but the public could not get enough of the music-kugel. The musical won six Tony Awards and ran for 1,443 performances. The original cast album stayed at the top of the Billboard charts for sixteen weeks and remained on the charts for 276 weeks. The stage musical has received over 20,000 productions and to this day more than 500 productions are staged each year in American theatres, professional, semi-professional, community, and schools.

The film rights were sold in 1960 for $1,250,000, an all-time high for such a sale. Preview screenings were held in February, 1965, in Minneapolis, Minnesota, and Tulsa, Oklahoma ("Oklahoma – O.K.!"). The audience responded ecstatically. When the "evaluation responses" were tabulated, the results were Fair – 0, Good – 5, Excellent – 460. The reviews were again, as with the Broadway production, mixed, but by 2014, the film ranked as the fifth highest grossing movie of all time, having earned in inflation adjusted dollars $2.366 billion world-wide. In Hong Kong, the title appeared as *Fairy Music Blow Fragrant Place, Place Hear*, and in many Latin American countries it screened under the appropriate moniker *The Rebellious Novice*. The film bombed in Germany and flickered on Austrian screens for a brief three weeks. The movie nevertheless had a lasting effect on Austrian tourism as a third of a million fans trek to Salzburg every year.

The soundtrack album spent 70 weeks at the top of the Billboard charts and for the year ranked second only to *Sergeant Pepper's Lonely Hearts Club Band* in total sales. In 2001, the Library of Congress selected the movie for preservation in the National Film Register, an honor reserved for those films which are "culturally, historically or aesthetically significant."

Explosive Missives

With God's help we will always have control over our emotions.

—St. John Vianney

Carousel, the second Rodgers and Hammerstein musical which followed *Oklahoma*, began to wobble down the path of sentimentality. The ending, a particularly egregious tear-jerking construct, has the deceased robber-hero return from "the beyond" to be present at his daughter's high school graduation to inspire her and to inform her mother that his love has not died. As this transpires, the assembled chorus sings the musical's "Climb Every Mountain"-inspirational-tune-of-uplift, "You'll Never Walk Alone." Hearts are buoyed and warmed as tears cascade downward.

In a summer theatre production in northern Illinois in the 1970's, a director overseeing a production of the *Carousel* decided all this calculated emotional flap-doodle could be pushed further to squeeze a few additional drops from sobbing eyes. He decided that as the chorus hit the climactic note at the close of the number "You'll NE-ver walk alone," doves would be released from the stage to wing their pure white way over the heads of the weepers. To that end he assembled the prop crew and directed them before opening night to purchase a score of birds, construct netting above the stage and rig a release system. Troopers that they were, they obeyed.

Opening night arrived, the show proceeded to its end, the chorus lifted its voice in touching song and as the tuneful sentiments hit their high note, the stage manager gave the signal and the nets were opened, releasing the birds. Unfortunately, no one had taken into account the scientific fact that birds held in nets for many hours next to extremely hot lighting instruments would not fly because they had been baked. Fricasseed doves began to drop from above directly on the startled cast. Many of the birds were already dead, some gave final pathetic wing-flutterings before they perished. The music stopped, the actors stood frozen in shock, the audience gasped in horror. Hard facts of nature will always trump cheap sentimentality.

Such excessive gestures of phony bathos do not occur only in small Midwestern playhouses. They can also be found in ancient reverent marble halls. The Vatican II popes have an addiction to dove exploitation that also results in avian trauma.

Pope John Paul II established the practice of releasing, with the enforced assistance of children, two white doves from the window of his Vatican apartments on his "Day of Peace," the last Sunday of January each year. Bernard de Cottignies, a Vatican Radio journalist and a man who has raised champion doves in his private dovecote, realized that the birds end up homeless and starving. For five years in succession, he would find the stray birds, half-starved and lost in and around St. Peter's Square, and take them to a friend's house in the country.

In 2012, Pope Benedict XVI aided by two children released two doves in observance of World Leprosy Day. One perched on the railing next to the Pontiff and refused to move; the other retreated at once back into

Explosive Missives

the papal apartments. The Pope spontaneously cried, "Mamma mia!"

In 2013, Pope Benedict XVI aided by two children staged a ceremonial release of a dove to honor the victims of the "holocaust." He had just concluded his prayer for the victims and said to the children by his side, "That was successful," when a large gull attacked the dove, pinning it against a window pane. The flying "holocaust" memorial disappeared in a cloud of feathers.

On January 26, 2014, Pope France aided by two children appeared on the Apostolic Palace balcony and appealing for "peace in Ukraine" released two "doves of peace." They were promptly attacked by two larger birds, a seagull and a black crow. The tens of thousands of pious observers below witnessed in horror "nature red in tooth and claw." Following this latest episode of dove abuse, the Animal Protection Agency called on the Vatican to stop these dove-destructive symbolic displays.

Pure white doves do not exist in nature. The birds are specially bred in captivity to be completely white so they can be used at weddings or funerals or sentimental musicals or "holocaust" remembrances or leper recognition. Thrown into the air of "great created nature," they become obvious prey for predator birds because of their unnatural artificial whiteness.

> At the end of the storm is a golden sky
> And the sweet silver song of a lark . . . .

Or the death-induced squawks of a dove . . . .

Verbal Music Interlude

> The dove descending breaks the air
> With flame of incandescent terror
> Of which the tongues declare
> The one discharge from sin and error.
> The only hope or else despair
> Lies in the choice of pyre or pyre
> To be redeemed from fire by fire.
>
> Who then devised the torment? Love.
> Love is the unfamiliar name
> Behind the hands that wove
> The intolerable shirt of flame
> Which human power cannot remove.
> We only live, only suspire
> Consumed by either fire or fire.
>
> —T. S. Eliot, "Little Gidding"

◘

In her job-terminating review of *The Sound of Music* for *McCall's Magazine,* Pauline Kael made the following observation: "Wasn't there perhaps one little von Trapp who didn't want to sing his head off . . . or who got nervous and threw up if he had to go out on stage?" But sentimental art cannot allow the realities of nature or original sin or lived life to intrude into its artificial construct of fakery. In reality, Maria von Trapp was prone to violent outbursts in which she yelled, threw things and slammed doors. The family did not escape by climbing every mountain hauling their luggage but rather took a comfortable train to Italy in 1938 on their way to America in 1939.

Explosive Missives

Reality had certainly existed during the filming. The famous opening sequence of Julie Andrews crossing the fields in ecstatic freedom proved nearly impossible to shoot. She would begin her movement as a helicopter with an intrepid cameraman hanging out its side would approach from the opposite side of the field. As the two got closer, the whirlybird would produce such a strong downdraft that just as our heroine opened her lips to sing that "The hills are alive . . ." she would be flattened to the ground by the air-burst. The weather in Salzburg during the filming proved particularly miserable – cloudy, rainy, cold. In the month-long filming of the "Do Re Mi" number, the children huddled together wrapped in blankets between takes. Some scenes had to be filmed in the rain under tarpaulins and the cinematographer had to use everything in his photographic bag of tricks to conceal the bad weather. In one scene a boat overturned and the actress playing Gretel nearly drowned; the actress playing Liesl crashed through a piece of plate glass when filming one of her dances. And Christopher Plummer playing Baron von Trapp brooded about the set, refusing to "cast [his] nighted color off," seemingly preparing for his next performance as the melancholy Prince of Denmark. Pauline Kael would honor his performance by calling it "the spider on the valentine."

Sentimental art is dishonest because it refuses to allow or face any hard truths. Even the greatest fairy tales, those beautiful children's stories of moral order that move inexorably to a happy ending, acknowledge pain and sorrow and blood and loss. Honest sentiment in art is earned; sentimental art cheats and steals. And when it sets itself up as a vision of life, in its phony fabrications it opens itself up to mockery.

The mocking of *The Sound of Music* followed a string of successful "sing along" screenings of the film from England to Europe and Australia and America. The fans

The Voice of the Trumpet

would sing with the music on the screen, hiss the unpleasant characters, boo the Nazis and often shout inappropriate comments. They would buy packets of phony edelweiss, cough drops and foam-rubber nun puppets. Soon they began arriving at the special showings wearing costumes:

> The costumes worn by the audience members get more and more baroque with every new city the *Sing-a-Long* conquers. In addition to the obvious girls in white dresses with blue satin sashes or the fellow who dressed all in bright yellow as Ray, a drop of golden sun, there have been costumes that have strained credulity and taste – the gentleman wearing overalls and brandishing a plunger as "Chris the Plumber" or the young lady festooned with a bevy of brown balloons who came as "The Lonely Goat Turd." At the Hollywood Bowl showing in 2005, the winner of the best costume competition was given quite a run for his money: a pair of drapes . . . , a quartet of very buxom ladies whose "hills" were quite lively, a little girl with a pale pink coat, and the inevitable bright copper kettles and warm woolen mittens. But the gentleman who received first prize . . . was dressed as an eight-foot carburetor – as in the one that the nuns remove from the Nazis' car at the end of the picture.

Lawrence Maslon, *The Sound of Music Companion*, London: Pavilion Books, 2007, p. 158.

> Dear friends, "entertainment" requires serious attention.
>
> —Bishop Richard Williamson

Explosive Missives

that's en - ter - tain - ment!

Man is a maker. Whether he be Michelangelo under papal mandate painting the Sistine Chapel ceiling or an amateur carpenter in his garage building a pair of end tables or a mother-to-be knitting booties for the baby she carries in her womb, man creates. The order given by God to Adam and Eve in post-lapsarian Paradise, "Go forth and multiply," constituted a mandate to make more men, to extend God's own creation by populating it with new bodies, each of which contains a soul that is destined, if it observes God's laws and cooperates with God's grace, for heaven and eternal happiness. Thus the greatest creative act is the conjugal union of husband and wife for the proliferation of mankind. "The world must be peopled!"

To insure the participation of man in the creative act and to endow the act with the fullness of its great purpose and high end, God gives a special thrill in its consummation. This gift may be abused. To grab for mere personal pleasure or to block the creative end of the act is to commit grave sin; it is thieving man robbing from God, "thou shalt not steal" on a higher plane. Shakespeare concludes his stark, frank and brutally honest Sonnet 129 on "lust in action" with the words:

> All this the world well knows, yet none knows well
> To shun the Heaven that leads men to this Hell.

Modern man, consumed with lust like the complete animal into which he is rapidly descending, deliberately occludes the natural consequences of the act reserved for the marriage bed. Through denying new life by means of contraception or by murdering it before birth by means of abortion (1.34 billion dead children world-wide in worship of Satan at the time of this writing), he seeks pleasure without responsibility and in the process creates a horrifying alternative. He may still be unknowingly seeking the divine joy that is woven inextricably by God into the creative act. In liberal phony utopian fashion, modern man is seeking heaven here on earth, but the only creation being realized is an extension of the infernal realm. As Malcolm Muggeridge so aptly stated, "Sex is the mysticism of materialism."

$$\text{\texthalfnote.} + \text{\texthalfnote.} = \text{\textquarternote}\text{\textquarternote}\text{\textquarternote}$$

Man also creates on a more mundane but still essential level. These efforts, the bringing into existence of new objects that never before existed, a pie, a poem, a chair, a chorale, are all the extensions of the baker, the poet, the carpenter, the composer. Each newly created object may reflect the Creator Himself through the True, the Good and the Beautiful, to a more or less degree. A pastry chef or a mother in her kitchen who bakes a lemon meringue pie may achieve success in that venture or be a failure. The crust may be soggy, the lemon filling too sweet, the meringue runny, but the product is still a pie that never before existed. Or the same chef or home-maker may be inspired, gifted by hard work and blessed by circumstances, to pull from the oven a "true" lemon meringue pie (one approaching the Platonic ideal of a perfect pie), a "good" lemon meringue pie ("that's absolutely delicious!"), a "beautiful" lemon meringue pie ("that looks too good to eat!"). If a carpenter's chair collapses under you, it cannot be called a "true" chair, for chairs by definition are furniture pieces on which one may sit, nor could it be called a "good" chair if you try to sit on the wreckage on the floor, and certainly the ruins could not be labeled "beautiful." On the other hand . . . Chippendale!

The higher arts must be judged by the same test. Whether painting or poem, sculpture or symphony, drama or decorative frame, the work must be True: that is, honestly reflective of the highest possible ideal and uncompromising in its presentation; Good: that is, approaching the highest perfection of its kind by genuinely reflecting the moral order of the First Creator; Beautiful: that is, balanced and harmonious in its parts, pleasing to the senses in accordance with its aims (*Macbeth* is *meant* to terrify us); through the combination of these three ideals, the work should both delight and instruct the observer. The continuum of delight on one end and instruction on the other provides the yardstick on which a work of art will fall. Whatever its ultimate aim, the work of art must still reflect to a degree all three high ideals, whether it fall toward the end of delight (Charles Schulz always provided some "instruction" in his *Peanuts* comic strip, "I'll tell you what Christmas is about, Charlie Brown") or the end of instruction (the medieval morality play *Everyman* shines with a precious beauty when the weak "Good Deeds" rises from the ground, agreeing to accompany Everyman on his journey to the grave and to the Great Judge). Beauty, it is true, may be "in the eye of the beholder" as the old saw has it, but it is also in the beholder's mind, heart, knowledge and experience. Some critical evaluations carry more weight and should evoke more interest than others; the man who knows well all of Beethoven has more credit in his comment on "I Want to Hold Your Hand" being dull and predictable than does the fourteen-year-old who says, "Well, I like it."

Too many traditional Catholics have a tendency to judge instantly a work of art by asking of the artist, "Is he Catholic? Was he Catholic?" If the answer is "no," they then dismiss the work. St. Thomas Aquinas gives a very sensible and thoughtful rebuttal to such narrow and impulsive judgment in Pt. I-II, Q. 57. Art. 5, of the *Summa Theologiæ*:

> The good of an art is to be found, not in the craftsman, but in the product of the art, since art is right reason about things to be made: for since the making of a thing passes into external matter, it is a perfection not of the maker, but of the thing made, even as movement is the act of the thing moved . . . . Consequently art does not require of the craftsman that his act be a good act, but that his work be good.

Non-Catholics may produce good work, for God has not given his many gifts only to Catholics. And by extension, even a man reprehensible in his personal life may produce great art. A Christopher Marlowe could write *Doctor Faustus*, Caravaggio could paint *"The Beheading of John the Baptist,"* Richard Wagner could compose *Der Ring des Niebelungen*. Catholics do not ask before buying a pair of well-crafted shoes, "Is the shoemaker Catholic?"; they do not ask before driving across a bridge, "Was the construction engineer Catholic?"; they should not ask such a question about art, but rather ask, "Is it True? Is it Good? Is it Beautiful?" And when God gives his greatest gifts to a Palestrina and a Giotto and a Dante and a Shakespeare and a Mozart, who have a Catholic belief system on which to construct their new creations, then the world can delight in the truly sublime!

Explosive Missives

The modern artist faces special challenges in, as Hamlet says, "hold[ing] the mirror up to nature." Artists are naturally obligated to explore and explain the age in which they live and only by immersion in the here and now, the local, the specifically personal, can they ever hope to convey eternal truths. The time in which we live is a refuse heap of lies and ugliness, blood and horror, madness and apostasy. Earlier artists may have dared to delve into the darkest recesses of sin, the *Inferno, Macbeth, Crime and Punishment*, but the artists themselves did not live in a barbaric century. The greatest literary artist of our age, Alexander Solzhenitsyn, faced with courage and honesty the unendurable nightmare of his own totalitarian, demonic world, experienced in the Gulag and the Soviet state. He reflected in his great art both the hellish world in which he found himself and the beauty and goodness and truth that can never be destroyed. Here first the horror:

> ["Mamka" is a "disparaging, diminutive suffix" in Gulag slang; not a "mother" but a degenerate woman.]
>
> In 1954 at the Tashkent Station I happened to be spending the night not far from a group of zeks [prisoners] who were on their way from camp and who had been released on the basis of some special order. There were about three dozen of them, and they took up a whole corner of the hall, behaving very noisily, with a semi-underworld insolence, like genuine children of Gulag, knowing what life was worth and holding in contempt all the free people there. The men played cards and the "mamki" argued loudly about something. And all of a sudden one mother screamed something more shrilly than the rest, jumped up, swung her child by the legs and audibly banged his head on the cement floor. The hall of *free* people gasped: A mother! How could a *mother* do that! . . .

The Voice of the Trumpet

They just didn't understand that it was not a mother – but a *mamka*.

The Gulag Archipelago, Volume 2, p. 246.

Here the eternal:

Plundered of everything that fulfills female life and indeed human life in general – of family, motherhood, the company of friends and perhaps even interesting work, in some cases in art or among books, and crushed by fear, hunger, abandonment, and savagery – what else could the women camp inmates turn to except love? With God's blessing the love which came might also be not of the flesh . . . . But from its unfleshly character, as the women remember today, the spirituality of camp love became even more profound. And it was particularly because of the absence of the flesh that this love became more poignant than out in freedom! Women who were already elderly could not sleep nights because of a chance smile, because of some fleeting mark of attention they had received. So sharply did the light of love stand out against the dirty, murky camp existence! . . .

Lithuanian women were married across the wall to Lithuanian men whom they had never seen or met; and the Lithuanian Roman Catholic priest (also, of course, a prisoner in the standard pea jacket) would provide written documentation that so-and-so and so-and-so had been joined for eternity in holy matrimony in the eyes of God. In this marriage with an unknown prisoner on the other side of a wall – and for Roman Catholic men such a marriage was irreversible and sacred – I hear a choir of angels. It is like the unselfish, pure contemplation of the heavenly bodies. It is too lofty for this age of self-interested calculation and hopping up-and-down jazz.

The Gulag Archipelago, Volume 2, pp. 239, 249.

Explosive Missives

This is great art. One sign of the decadence of the age is the modernist reader or viewer or listener turns away, rejecting it because *The Gulag Archipelago* or *The Waste Land* or *The Collected Stories of Flannery O'Connor* are "dark" and "disturbing," not "upbeat" and "pious." Cozy comfort is sought where the "hills are alive," though they are really dead and dishonest.

What relation does the sentimental, feminized, delicate, milk-white Christ in nineteenth and early-twentieth century painting have to the bloody, masculine, wounded imprint on the Shroud of Turin? There is a work of Supreme Art given to us at a crucial moment in time by the Greatest Creator that contains in its ensanguined weave all of Eternity.

1. O CA- PUT CRU- ENTA- TUM *Spi- ná-rum á-ci- e

And so a young man putting a 78rpm vinyl recording of Beethoven's "Eroica" Symphony on a turntable could be led to the moral complexities of Shakespeare's tragedies and end up reading St. Thomas Aquinas's *Summa Theologiæ*. We call it God's Providential Design and art plays its part.

Scherzo Reprise

> Martha (to her weak husband George): "I'm loud and I'm vulgar, and I wear the pants in this house because somebody's got to...."
> —Edward Albee, *Who's Afraid of Virginia Woolf?*, Act 2

The Voice of the Trumpet

The Captain (dying mad, when his wife deceives him by claiming their daughter is not his child): "Put my tunic over me. Ah, my tough lion's skin that you would take from me! Omphale! Omphale! You cunning woman, lover of peace and contriver of disarmament. Wake, Hercules, before they take away your club! You would trick us out of our armour, calling it tinsel. It was iron, I tell you, before it became tinsel. In the old days the smith forged the soldier's coat, now it is made by the needle woman. Omphale! Omphale! Rude strength has fallen before treacherous weakness . . . . "

> —August Strindberg, *The Father*, Act 3 (trans. Elizabeth Sprigge)

Mistress Ford: "Are you not ashamed? Let the clothes alone."

> —William Shakespeare, *The Merry Wives of Windsor*, Act 4. Scene 2

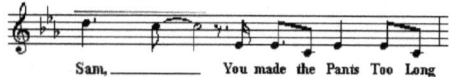

Padre Pio's attitude towards modesty of wearing apparel on women and girls (also on men and boys) was well known, documented, and always enforced at least in his physical presence. He was especially adamant on the wearing of slacks (and shorts) by women. I

Explosive Missives

had occasion in April of 1963, to interview, in San Giovanni Rotondo, a Catholic lady, Italian by descent, and fluid in the language of her forbears, who had been refused absolution in confession, by Padre Pio, because she sold pants and pant-suits in her dress shop in Vancouver.

 He commanded her to return home to Canada, and dispose of *all* this stock, and not to give any of the items to people who might wear them, and if she wanted absolution, she could come back to Italy and receive it, only after she had ruthlessly carried out his orders. The alternative was, she could seek the absolution in another confession, back in Canada, but he, Padre Pio, would know whether she had done what she'd been told.

   —Anne Cillis, *Arrivederci Padre Pio*
   pp. 191–192

Bishop Williamson teaches the same Catholic truth taught by Cardinal Siri, Bishop de Castro Mayer and Padre Pio. This is what arouses the ire of the Conciliar Church and puts him out of step with those in the hierarchy marching determinedly to the abyss.

But the shrill, willful voices still cry, "What about Joan of Arc?" So out of love for the ladies and with all due respect, the gentlemen reply, "Very well. When God calls on you through the voices of His Saints to take the sword, mount your steed and charge into battle (because the men have shirked their duty and failed to muster and mobilize and maintain the moral order), then, my dears, hoist up your trousers, put on your faulds, your chausses and poleyns, your schynbalds and greaves and cuisses, your sabatons and tassets, and wrapping lovely scarves around your necks, ride forth. Until then, fight the foe as the Blessed Mother teaches by example – as the heart of the home, loving and sewing, praying and cooking, nurturing and washing, nursing and sweeping, inspiring and cleaning.

Tell your beads and bake a beautiful lemon meringue pie, prayer and pastry, for your family, for your friends and neighbors, and all the poor lost souls orphaned in the modern whirlwind.

And wear a pretty skirt!

Gabon, April, 1997.

PART FOUR

Veritas *Variations*

"Music is a gift of God to the world He created, an expression of the harmony which He planted at the centre of His universe, to which all living members of that universe respond."

—Bishop Richard Williamson

Theme & Variations

THEME: "Thou sayest that I am a King. For this was I born and for this came I into the world; that I should give testimony to the truth. Everyone that is of the truth heareth my voice."

Counter-theme: "Pilate saith to him: What is truth?" (John 18: 37–38).

First Variation – *Reality*

Chorale

At the age of twenty-eight, Bishop Richard Williamson had handed to him a gift worth more than bags of gold and sacks of silver. After the inquiring young man had dabbled briefly in modern pseudo-Catholic theology and philosophy, the intellectual equivalent of phony fiat paper currency, he sought knowledge more solid and more satisfying, wisdom of worth. The good Father Lovell had suggested that he take up Augustine or Aquinas. Picking up Fr. Gilbey's *Philosophical Texts of Aquinas*, he found the bedrock of unyielding solid theology and clear doctrine that would underlie the remainder of his days, his thought, his life.

So in the summer of 1969 he made his first excursions into the treasure vaults of Thomistic thought, depositories of riches both natural and supernatural. When he faced the young Beatles' disciples in his language classes at St. Paul's School and shared this wealth with them, that the solution to the problems of the modern world could be found in the Catholic faith, the teacher spoke from conviction. The boys' logical demand "Are you Catholic?" received a negative response so they followed with another sensible query – "Then why are you telling us this?" Williamson in all honesty and with complete sincerity responded, "Because it's true."

The teacher taught well. He could do so because he stood on the rock of Peter. In the Encyclical Letter of Pope Leo XIII, *Aeterni patris*, "On the Restoration of Christian Philosophy," August 4, 1879, the Holy Pontiff had, near the conclusion, made the following exhortation:

> Let, then, teachers carefully chosen by you do their best to instill the doctrine of Thomas Aquinas into the minds of their hearers; and let them clearly point out its solidity and excellence above all other teaching. Let this doctrine be the light of all places of learning which you may have already opened, or may hereafter open. Let it be used for the refutation of errors that are gaining ground.

Summa Theologiæ, Westminster, Md.: Christian Classics, p. xviii.

Veritas *Variations*

The future Bishop before his formal conversion unknowingly complied with the pontifical command. Already in the core of his soul and in the quest of his mind and heart, providence had placed the eternal fact: "[T]ruth is truth. To the end of reckoning."

◉

Father Edmund Brindholm, lay-brother William Horne, and laymen Giles Heron and Clement Philpot.

—martyred at Tyburn, August 4, 1540

━

What drove the teacher seeking to be taught into the vast universe of the *Summa Theologiæ*? The encyclical of Pope Leo XIII makes telescopically clear the gravitational pull of that great star and the subsequent perfectly patterned orbit of the satellite mind attracted to it:

> Now far above all other Scholastic Doctors towers Thomas Aquinas, their master and prince. Cajetan says truly of him: 'So great was his veneration for the ancient and sacred Doctors that he may be said to have gained a perfect understanding of them all.' Thomas gathered together their doctrines like the scattered limbs of a body, and moulded them into a whole. He arranged them in so wonderful an order, and increased them with such great additions, that rightly and deservedly he is reckoned a singular safeguard and glory of the Catholic Church. His intellect was docile and subtle; his memory was ready and tenacious; his life was most holy; and he loved the truth alone. Greatly enriched as he was with the science of God and the science of man, he is likened to the sun; for he warmed the whole earth

with the fire of his holiness, and filled the whole earth with the splendor of his teaching....

[T]he Angelic Doctor, in his speculations, drew certain philosophical conclusions as to the reasons and principles of created things. These conclusions have the very widest reach and contain, as it were, in their bosom the seeds of truths well nigh infinite in number. These have to be unfolded with most abundant fruits in their own time by the teachers who come after him. As he used his method of philosophizing, not only in teaching the truth, but also in refuting error, he has gained this prerogative for himself. With his own hand he vanquished all errors of ancient times; and still he supplies an armory of weapons which brings us certain victory in the conflict with falsehoods ever springing up in the course of years.

Moreover, carefully distinguishing reason from Faith, as is right, and yet joining them together in harmony of friendship, he so guarded the rights of each, and so watched over the dignity of each, that, as far as man is concerned, reason can hardly rise higher then she rose, borne up in the flight of Thomas; and Faith can hardly gain more helps and greater helps from reason than those which Thomas gave her.

Ibid., pp. xiv–xv.

In Canto X of the *Paradiso*, Dante the Pilgrim enters the heavenly Sphere where the theologians dwell forever in transcendent bliss and the light of God's Triune Glory. Appropriately, the great theologians spend their eternity in the realm of the Sun, and perhaps this suggested to Pope Leo his simile. The first voice to proceed from the whirling dance of perpetual lights appropriately identifies himself: "I am Thomas of Aquino." In Canto XI, he explains:

> Cosí com'io del suo raggio resplendo,
> sí, riguardando ne la luce etterna,

Veritas *Variations*

li tuoi pensieri onde cagioni apprendo . . . .

La provedenza, che govern ail mondo
con quell consiglio nel quale ogne aspetto
creato è vinto pria che vada al fondo,

pero che andasse ver'lo suo diletto
la sposa di colui ch'ad alte grida
disposo lei col sangue Benedetto,

in se sicura e anche a lui piu fida,
due principi ordinò in suo favore,
che quinci e quindi le fosser per guida.

L'un fu tutto serafico in ardore;
l'altro per sapienza in terra fue
di cherubica luce uno splendore.

Just as I shine reflecting His own rays
So, as I gaze into the endless light,
I understand the reason for your thoughts . . . .

The Providence that governs all the world
With wisdom so profound none of His creatures
Can ever hope to see into Its depths,

In order that the Bride [the Church] of that sweet Groom [Christ],
Who crying loud espoused her with His blood,
Might go to her Beloved [God] made more secure

Within herself, more faithful to her Spouse,
Ordained two noble princes to assist her
On either side, each serving as a guide.

One of the two shone with seraphic love [St. Francis],
The other through his wisdom was on earth
A splendor of cherubic radiance [St. Dominic].

The Voice of the Trumpet

Dante's Divine Comedy: Paradiso, tr. Mark Musa, Bloomington, In.: Indiana University Press, 2004, pp. 102–105.

Thomas of Aquino, the Dominican, goes on to tell the life story and sing the praises of St. Francis. In Canto XII, Bonaventura, the Franciscan, will do likewise in speaking of St. Dominic, Dante thus proving the unity of "Heavenly Harmony." Dante penned these words near the end of his life in 1321; the Bride of Christ awarded Thomas of Aquino sainthood in 1323.

But now we come to the greatest glory of Thomas – a glory which is altogether his own, and shared with no other Catholic Doctor. In the midst of the Council of Trent, the assembled Fathers so willing it, the *Summa* of Thomas Aquinas lay open on the altar, with the Holy Scriptures and the decrees of the Supreme Pontiffs, that from it might be sought counsel and reasons and answers.

Pope Leo XIII *op. cit.*, p. xvi.

In his extended study, subsequent teaching and life-long devotion to the *Summa* of St. Thomas Aquinas, Richard Williamson found "counsels and reasons and answers," all leading to ultimate truths. His continual and uncompromising adherence to those truths and his perpetual voicing of them would make him an outcast and the most reviled Bishop of his time.

What basic truths did the seeker Williamson find in the philosophy of Aquinas, essentials pared down to their basic core that he then wished to pass on to his students, the seminarians and the sheep entrusted to his care? Given our dull nature and our suburban-created sloth, we sheep cannot grasp much high thought, nor do we necessarily wish to seek it. "Humankind cannot bear very much reality." So here, in clear and assimilable words are two principles from Aquinas that Bishop Williamson believes to be essential for modern Catholics:

One. "Nature" comes from the Latin root of "nat-," or "natus," meaning "Having been born." As we come into life through nature, so that with which we have arrived in life governs what we *are* for as long as we *are*. Nature, our nature, makes us, or any *thing*, what we *are* or what it *is*. Nature, as source of all being, gives us our *essence* and our own nature. Our essence, our nature, defines *how we act* in our lived lives. A cat will behave and act as cats behave because of its "catty" nature; a dog will act and behave as dogs behave because of its "doggy" nature; a human being will act and behave as he does because of his "human" nature. The Bishop states that this fundamental tenet of Aquinas's comprehensive system is a "lost concept." The proud and twisted, God-denying modern mind, awash in the polluted waters of the mire of phony evolutionary "religion," insists that cats do not have a "catty" nature, nor dogs a "doggy" nature, nor humans a basic "human" nature; rather, all nature is moving and fluid, flowing progressively from one form to another – from microbes that became plankton that became fish that grew legs and walked out of the water becoming birds that gained size and substance, transforming themselves into dinosaurs. Such a foolish idea, denying the essence of created nature, will one day be as extinct as the giant behemoths that once crushed the earth as they lumbered about.

(NOTE: The day these words were written, a news report proved their accuracy. A woman with a pet service-dog, one that in its "doggy" loyalty to his master helped her move about in nature, decided to attend a

Broadway musical. Her dog accompanied her. Unfortunately, she chose the musical CATS. Her dog, asserting his "dogginess" and seeing before him what he took for a panoply of felines reveling in their "cattiness," broke loose and attacked the actors on stage. Fortunately, given their "human" nature, they subdued the angry canine and no one was hurt.)

Two. Aquinas works from the self-evident axioms, principles and concepts that are solid common sense. "Common sense" through the Middle Ages counted as one of the "five wits." Those sensible and ordered minds knew we had five senses – sight, hearing, smell, taste and touch, known as the five outer senses. They also knew we had five wits – common sense, fantasy or fancy, imagination, judgment or estimation, and memory – known as the five inner senses. In that spiritual age, men recognized that they could know the real physical world through their outer senses, but also realized they could know something of the real spiritual world through inner senses. With the loss of the awareness of the interior life, our knowledge and trust in our inner senses or five wits slowly eroded and disappeared, leaving us mere organisms in an environment.

Thomism relies on common sense and raised it to a technique. It is no accident that with the denial of the essence of human-ness, common sense, a defining element of the human, has all but vanished. Its replacement by un-common non-sense has been instrumental in transforming the world into the modernist lunatic asylum in which we are confined. All things follow their nature and action follows being. A square pencil and a round pencil are placed on a table. The table is then tilted. The square pencil may slide, but the round pencil will certainly roll. The round pencil cannot merely slide because its nature includes its "round-ness"; the square pencil cannot roll because its nature includes its "square-ness." Each thing

Veritas *Variations*

acts in accordance with its nature. Its essential nature, the basic concept behind each thing, is that by which it is. The spectrum of being runs thus:

Uncreated being	Created being	No being
GOD	MAN	NOTHING
Pure Act	*Act limited by potency*	*Neither act nor potency*
All-powerful	With some power to act	Wholly powerless to act

Man stands between God and Nothingness – given the divine spark but facing the void of nihilism. He is given the freedom to choose his actions through his will. He is dependent on grace to choose wisely but he is also capable of choosing nothingness. Christ is Man with Pure Act and Omnipotence; Satan seeks to lure man toward emptiness, hopelessness and the paralyzing, powerless darkness of his infernal kingdom. Modern man in his denial of God and rejection of Christ still exhibits his potential to act and his freedom to choose. As Dante insists throughout the *Inferno*, man *chooses* hell.

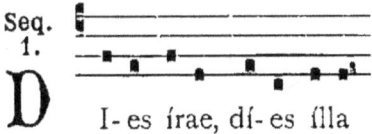

The very notion of creation comes from faith. By pure rational philosophy alone, one cannot prove that the world began nor can one prove that it did not. We know in what we observe around us and what we know inside us that existence is real. The most famous action meant to prove the reality of existence comes from an episode sometimes called "the Kick of Refutation." James Boswell in his classic biography *Life of Samuel Johnson* recounts this incident involving the brilliant critic, poet, journalist, eccentric and all-around genius:

> After we came out of the church, we stood talking for some time together of Bishop Berkeley's ingenious sophistry to prove the nonexistence of matter, and that everything in the universe is merely ideal. I observed that though we are satisfied his doctrine is not true, it is impossible to refute it. I shall never forget the alacrity with which Johnson answered, striking his foot with mighty force against a large stone, till he rebounded from it – "I refute it *thus*."

James Boswell, *Life of Samuel Johnson*, London: Oxford University Press, 1957, p. 333.

This is Pure Thomistic common sense advising us to trust the authority of our senses, outward and inward.

Essence defines the "what-ness" of a thing; existence defines the "that-ness" of a thing. A fly that is squashed on a fly-swatter is still a fly in that the "fly-ness" of the creature still is evident; however, it no longer possesses existence – it was *that* fly which lived but it no longer lives. It possesses no existence.

Shoo fly, don't bo - ther me

As philosophy began to be twisted out of shape by arrogant but clever wordsmiths and self-indulgent sophists, the solid realistic grip of the great Greek philosophers began to be ignored and their masterful insights were dropped along the path in the roadside shrubbery. The remarkable work of the ancients exhibited the highest truths conceivable by man without the assistance of Divine Revelation. They were tossed aside as were the mysteries of grace, all the accumulated wisdom dismissed as "old" and "dated" and "outmoded." " Essence" itself came under attack as a relic of the past and the enduring insights into "being" were washed away by an impermanent but constant flow of "becoming." The new philosophy, assembled from scraps and shards of random philosophical thought, created a new philosophical monster, not unlike the monster assembled by Doctor Victor Frankenstein from purloined body parts. Kant and Hegel and crew transformed the solidity of God's creation into an evolving, unstable flow that freed modern man from God's order, God's created universe and eventually from God Himself. This constant change afforded "man, proud man" the superiority to be what he himself desires to be, not a creature formed by God and no longer limited according to His design. Thanks to our own free will, our own fallen nature, we would become whatever we wished to be. The rushing waters of constant "becoming" swept away original sin along with essence. All nature morphed into a playground for "progress" that allows us to "re-create" creation as we want to dream of it in our imaginations, rather than to recognize our particular place in a pre-existing and clearly defined order that we may "rough hew" as we will, but that is ultimately overseen by a "divinity that shapes our ends." Darwin merely provided the phony "scientific" support for deranged philosophical thought that had already infected men's minds.

The Voice of the Trumpet

> Let me take you down 'cos I'm going to Strawberry Fields,
> Nothing is real, and there's nothing to get hung about,
> Strawberry Fields forever . . . .

> The Pope began his discourse by painting a portrait of the Society. That it is not a "still life" but a multi-faceted framework and in motion. The Society itself – he said – is *"in progress,"* in *"becoming."*
>
> —Antonio Spadaro, S.J., "A Historic Event: Francis at the General Congregation [of the Society of Jesus]," www.gc36.org (emphasis added)

A parishioner after one Sunday Mass asked, "Who is this Hegel that Father mentioned in his sermon?" On being told of the Hegelian notion of constant change, historic inevitability and the thesis – antithesis – synthesis paradigm, he sensibly responded, "I never did care much for synthetics."

St. Thomas had himself "synthesized" in a way, but not to create a new "thesis" perpetuating endless change and continuing an evolutionary piper's parade; rather, he had taken the truth found in the writings of Aristotle, whom he refers to throughout the *Summa* as "the Philosopher," a high compliment indeed, and united it with the highest truths found in the writings of the early Church Fathers. This union would give birth to a "coherent philosophical system" of Truth unequaled before or since.

The keystone of that system of thought and thus the basis of Bishop Williamson's world view is the primacy

Veritas *Variations*

of objective reality. If the modern suburban-dweller demands fantasy to re-create all things into his personal vision, the Bishop, relying on the teachings of St. Thomas, insists that objective reality exists, that it exists outside of our own minds, that it is knowable and it *must* be known. Before one can grasp truth, one must comprehend the reality of all things. To reach the truth, man must establish a clear and precise correspondence between the reality that exists outside his mind, and then accept and comprehend that reality within his mind. A Kant who would pronounce objective reality as fundamentally unknowable; a Descartes who would posit "being" within one's own mind; a Hegel who would insist the order outside of us is in constant flux; these men cannot, according to Thomistic common sense, ever know Truth; nevertheless, they churned out tome after tome of consequent imprecision, doubt and error, all mixed in a stew of self-conceit and pseudo-intellectualism. And modern man licked it up as a kitten in its "cat-ness" laps up cream.

The Catholic Church well understood what a great gift St. Thomas had bequeathed it. His amalgamated truths of the reasoning Greeks and the inspired Catholic Fathers proved a precious treasure trove of insight, sanity and clarity. Any human mind and soul seeking truth need only open the treasure chest to be rewarded with the greatest wealth of supernatural and natural gold. Modernists seek to "feel" truth and to "feel" it with sustained intensity. For them, truth must be constantly changing, providing them with novelty and surprise. Only new ideas will get their sap rising (sap indeed).

Our Lord told us "the Truth shall set you free." That is the only true liberty. Modern "liberty" is opposed to such truth because the dictates of God's truth, unchangeable and unchanging, seem to modern men to be a prison. For them, the Thomistic system of thought is

The Voice of the Trumpet

too logical, its constraining view of reality too confining and too permanent. As a Boeing 747 is "imprisoned" by the rules of flight, so man is necessarily restrained by God's law and the Church's teachings. The Boeing 747 that denies its essence and the restraints of aerodynamic law in seeking freedom of flight will crash and burn. The modern world and the modern Church have followed phony "freedom" and have crashed; they will soon burn.

Born free,

[A]ll of us who are faithful sons and daughters of the Church can and must be Thomas's disciples, *at least to some extent*.

—Pope Paul VI, September 14, 1974, speaking on the square at Aquino, Italy (emphasis added)

St. Thomas has pointed out a path that can and should be followed *and updated* without betraying its spirit and fundamental principles while also keeping in mind *modern scientific conquests. Science's true progress* can never contradict philosophy just as philosophy can never contradict faith. The new scientific contributions can have a *cleansing and liberating function* in the face of the limits imposed on philosophical research by *medieval backwardness*, not to speak of the *non-existence of a science such as we possess today* ....

I urge you to continue, with great

Veritas *Variations*

commitment and seriousness, to accomplish the goals of your Academy so that it can be a *living, pulsing, modern centre* in which the method and doctrine of St. Thomas [thesis] can be put into constant contact and serene dialogue with the *complete leavens of contemporary culture* in which we live and are immersed [anti-thesis].
["I never did care much for synthetics."]

> —Pope John Paul II, September 13, 1988, addressing the Eighth International Thomistic Congress (emphasis added)

I had difficulty penetrating the thought of Thomas Aquinas, whose crystal-clear logic *seemed to me too closed in on itself, too impersonal and ready-made . . . a rigid, neo-classical Thomism that was simply too far afield from my own questions.*

> —Joseph Cardiinal Ratzinger, Milestones: Memoirs 1927–1977, San Francisco: Ignatius Press, 2005, p. 38 (emphasis added)

Discussing [his] apostolic exhortation . . . , Pope Francis said that "the morality of *Amoris laetitia* is Thomist." He said that critics of the document miss its message because of their "purely casuistic" approach. The Pope said that the Thomism of the document is not the *dry approach of the neo-scholastic manuals that, he said, prevailed when he was educated.* He said: "But today it is a matter of *how you express God, how you*

— 251 —

tell who God is, how you show the Spirit...."
—*Civilta Cattolica*, catholicculture.org, September 28, 2017 (emphasis added)

> The Eucharist, although it is the fullness of sacramental life, is not a prize for the perfect but a powerful medicine and nourishment for the weak.
>
> —Pope Francis, Apostolic Exhortation *The Joy of the Gospel*, November 24, 2013, No. 24

Pope Francis claims that *Amoris laetitia*, in allowing adulterers to receive the Eucharist, is providing "medicine and nourishment" for sinners who are *not* in a state of grace when they receive.

But St. Thomas writes as follows (*Summa Theologiæ* III, Q. 40, Art. 4, "On the contrary"):

> The Apostle says (1 Cor. 11: 29): "He that eateth and drinketh unworthily, eateth and drinketh judgment to himself." Now the gloss says on this passage: "He eats and drinks unworthily who is in sin or handles it irreverently." Therefore, if anyone, while in mortal sin, receives this sacrament, he purchases damnation, by sinning mortally.

The morality of *Amoris laetitia* is Thomist?

The first intervention Archbishop Lefebvre made at the Second Vatican Council expressed the need for all the documents of the Council to be written in Latin, the traditional language for Church pronouncements because of its precision and clarity. The Council rejected the appeal, making clear their knowledge that imprecision and obfuscation as hallmarks of modernism would ease their destruction of Catholicism and their imposition of Conciliarism. It is not surprising, therefore, that the Vatican II Popes have been critical of and uncomfortable with the writings of St. Thomas. Thomistic philosophy and the expression of it in the great Saint's work rests on reason, objectivity, directness and lucidity; the Conciliarists need vagueness, ambiguity, subjectivity and obscurity to do their work. The conciseness of St. Thomas stands as a rebuke to the verbosity of the modern "theologians." St. Thomas wrote much, but each sentence shines with jewel-like light; the modernists write more and more and more, only to increase the "darkness visible." How better to attack the Word Incarnate than by desecrating and degrading language itself?

The example constantly set forth by Bishop Williamson of Absolute Truth, the Objective Reality of which cannot be questioned and to which our mind must submit is the mathematical proposition: 2 + 2 = 4

> Freedom is the freedom to say two plus two make four. If that is granted, all else follows.
> —George Orwell, *1984*, Chapter 7

> And Bertrand Russell's little improbable son/ said to his teacher, a friend of ours at Princeton,/ when they came to "two plus two equals four,"/ piped up, "My *father* isn't sure of that...."
> —John Berryman, *Love and Fame*, "I Know"

The Voice of the Trumpet

> Theology is not Mathematics. 2 + 2 in Theology can make 5. Because it has to do with God and real life of people....
>
> —Father Antonio Spadaro, papal confidant, *Catholic World News,* January 6, 2017

Second Variation – *History*

Courante

From the first blow of the revolutionary hammer into the first nail driven into the church door to the forceps crushing the skulls of infants in the mother's womb, man has busted his collective buttons with demonic pride. "Most ignorant of what he's most assured," man in his disdain for God's created order has come to despise God, Christ, God's laws, the Catholic Church, western civilization, reason, nature, order, truth, beauty and goodness. The sooty lightless dawn of the en-darken-ment extended in its phony "glorious" strides forward to the looming dark that now envelops almost all of humanity. The lies still hold sway, even if all evidence points to their destructive power. The old dirt path became a road, then a street, then a highway, then an interstate super-highway and then a race track; the vehicles pile up like crushed tinfoil and the pavement is littered with bloody corpses, but man's heavy foot still pushes down more forcefully and with mad resolve on the accelerator.

The catechism of bogus beliefs is mouthed emptily but repeatedly by ill-educated boobies, trained like barking seals to make loud repetitive honks to gain their fishy rewards:

Veritas *Variations*

– everything in the world is in constant change and flux; nothing endures;

– that which is "new" is better, simply by being "new"; all that is "old" is past its expiration date, like sour milk;

– all life behind us could not help but be "inferior" as it existed in mankind's "infancy"; modern man is an adult, grown up past the "mewling and puking" baby stages;

– "progress" and "enlightenment" have eliminated the ignorance bred of superstitious religious beliefs;

– "social progress" has freed man from cruelty and backwardness, violence and unkindness; modern man is "nice";

– in the Temple of Science, through the ministrations and advances of wise scientists and researchers, engineers and technocrats, nature has yielded up its mysteries and and has been transformed into a more beneficent force; i.e., God got it wrong

The classical world would have gasped in collective astonishment at such nonsense and then guffawed at the folly of its obviously demented and diminished progeny. Aristophanes' pointed satire would have had sufficient material for a comic masterpiece every day and never run out of targets.

The classical view first appeared (or can first be found) in the works of Hesiod in the 6th Century B.C. (Before Christ, not B.C.E. –" Before the Common Era," whatever that inanity may mean; nevertheless, the destroyers still acknowledge the centrality of the Incarnation as they have no choice but to begin their phony chronicle at that momentous moment.) Hesiod records a Golden Age, a time of peace and harmony and stability, an age that could not endure, as "Nothing gold can stay." That Golden Age declined into the Age of Silver, then to the Age of Bronze. This realistic chronicle of "paradise lost" and decline suggests the inevitable flaws and weaknesses of all men, cultural gravity pulling life downward from

The Voice of the Trumpet

day to day, year to year, century to century. The classical view presents the antithesis of "progress." The wise grey heads are always mocked by youthful optimists for suggesting that "life was better in the old days"; taunting young voices retort "every age has said that." The classical answer from Hesiod to Plato to Ovid would be: "And every age has been correct."

The Book of *Daniel* records the same assessment of human history in God's own Sacred Word, but with a hopeful and triumphant addition. Daniel is called upon to interpret the dream of King Nabuchodonosor and does so by means of Divine Revelation, the vision and the explication being therefore irrefutably true:

> Thou, O King, sawest, and behold there was as it were a great statue. This statue, which was great and high, tall of stature, stood before thee, and the look thereof was terrible.
> The head of this statue was of fine gold, but the breast and the arms of silver, and the belly and the thighs of brass:
> And the legs of iron, the feet part of iron and part of clay.
> Thus thou sawest, till a stone was cut out of a mountain without hands; and it struck the statue upon the feet thereof that were of iron and clay and broke them in pieces.
> Then was the iron, the clay, the brass, the silver and the gold broken to pieces together, and became like the chaff of a summer's thrashing floor. And they were carried away by the wind and there was no place found for them. But the stone that struck the statue became a great mountain and filled the whole earth.

Dan. 2: 31–35.

Daniel interprets the dream, revealing the necessary decline and destruction of the great King's kingdom, hardly a vision of "progress." But Daniel adds a final vision, not found in the classical authors:

> But in the days of those kingdoms the God of heaven will set up a Kingdom that shall never be destroyed: and his Kingdom shall not be delivered up to another people. And it shall consume all these kingdoms: and it shall stand forever.

Dan. 2: 44.

The stone that breaks linear history, the stone that was rejected, the stone that has become the cornerstone will triumph; the rock on which God's Church is built which the gates of hell will not prevail against, existing in time, transcending decline, will lead to victory in time, will lead to a blessed eternity. Not "progress," but "as it was in the beginning, is now, and ever shall be, world without end."

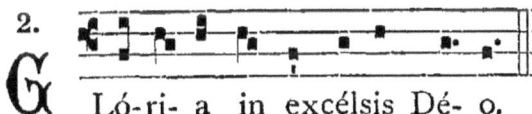
2. Gló-ri- a in excélsis Dé- o.

Dante in the *Inferno* of his *Commedia* (the adjective "Divine" was not attached to the work by the author) uses the verses from the Book of *Daniel*. Canto XIV presents a statue the author calls "The Old Man of Crete," standing in Mount Ida. The great Dante scholar and translator Mark Musa calls the statue "one of the most elaborate and interpreted symbols in the *Inferno*." Dante situates the statue with its back to Damietta, an Egyptian seaport which Musa asserts "represents the East, the pagan world"; the head of the statue looks toward Rome, "the modern, Christian world." Musa continues:

The head of gold represents the Golden Age of Man (that is, in Christian terms, before the Fall). The arms and breast of silver, the trunk of brass, and the legs of iron represent the three declining ages of man. The clay foot (the one made of terra-cotta) may symbolize the medieval Church, weakened and corrupted by temporal concerns and political power struggles. Through the fissure, a crack that runs through every part of the figure except the golden head, flow the Old Man's tears, the sins and sorrows of man through all ages except the Golden Age of Innocence. The tears bore their way down through the mountain, and eventually their course forms the rivers of Hell [Acheron, Styx, and Phlegethon] . . . . His golden head, because it is unblemished, seems to allude to Christ as well as to unfallen Eden, since Christ "is the head of the body, the Church" (Col. 1: 18). In this sense, the Old Man can be said to symbolize fallen humanity unified throughout history in the Church with all its imperfections and sinful "deeds."

Dante's Divine Comedy: Inferno, Vol. 2, *op. cit.*, pp. 203–204.

For the dreamers of utopian dreams, shock and disbelief looms on the horizon; their Godless, half-millennial revolution will soon be coming to an end, crushed by a woman's very high heel.

Veritas *Variations*

Bishop Richard Williamson holds a view of history that reflects both the classical and scriptural visions just presented; he has never been lured to the rocky shores of modern wreckage by the siren song of "progress" and has, in fact, spent much of his teaching and writing focusing on the catastrophe of that alluring false and deadly music. His warnings have proven to be increasingly accurate as the ruined hulks multiply on the wasteland's shore.

He has taught over the years the history of the Mystical Body of Christ itself, delineated in the "Seven Ages of the Church," resulting in the movements of secular history. The source material for his view of the "Seven Ages of the Church" comes from the writings of Venerable Bartholomew Holzhauser, noted priest, confessor and visionary, who lived from 1613 until 1658. Son of a poor but pious shoemaker and one of eleven children, the Venerable Holzhauser from his early years had a love of reading, a deep spirituality and a desire to enter the religious life. He first attended a free school for poor boys in Augsburg, Germany, and supported himself by singing and begging throughout the city. He went on to receive his Doctorate in Philosophy and was ordained to the priesthood in 1639, celebrating his first Mass at Ingolstadt on Pentecost Sunday at the Church of our Lady of Victory. He died at Bingen on the Rhine where he had served as parish priest for many years. He founded an order of priests called the Bartholomites but is remembered today chiefly for his visionary writings which were first presented to Emperor Ferdinand III and Duke Maximilian I, Elector of Bavaria, in 1846. They were published in 1849.

His vision of the "Seven Ages of the Church" derives from his study of the *Apocalypse* and the significance therein of the seven stars and the seven candlesticks, corresponding to the seven churches of Asia Minor, the seven days of creation, the seven ages before Christ and the seven gifts of the Holy Ghost. He suggests that just as all life travels through seven stages ("And each man in his time plays many parts/ His acts being seven . . . "), so God designed seven distinct periods for the history of Holy Mother Church.

Bishop William summarizes Holzhauser's timeline in the following manner:

First Age: 33-70 A.D. The Age of the Apostles. "Going therefore, teach ye all nations, baptizing them in the name of the Father, and of the Son and of the Holy Ghost." Matthew 28: 19.

Second Age: 71-313 A.D. The Age of the Martyrs. The blood of the persecuted martyrs being the "seed of the Church," sealing the foundations of the Church, ending with the Battle of the Milvian Bridge, the vision of the Cross beheld by Constantine and the conversion of Rome.

Third Age: 313-500 A.D. The Age of the Doctors. The devil having failed in his attack on Christian bodies attacks Christian minds through heresies; the Great Doctors of the Church are raised up to combat the heresies of Arianism, Nestorism, Pelagianism, Donatism, Monotheism; Sts. Basil, Athanasius, Gregory Naziaznan, Ambrose, Augustine, Jerome, John Chrysostom all hammer out the responses to these attacks and build the Doctrines of the Church, the Apostles Creed, the Athanasian Creed.

Fourth Age: 500-1517 A.D.: The Glory of Christian Civilization.

Fifth Age: 1517-the Present: The Age of Revolution to the Consecration of Russia to the Immaculate Heart of Mary.

Bishop Williamson firmly believes we live currently in these early years of the 21st Century on the edge of the Abyss. The previous five centuries have been a steady, methodical march to that Abyss, with an ongoing series of revolutions luring men like lemmings – or as Dostoevsky describes the Russian revolutionaries in *Demons*, like the Gadarene swine – to the precipice of a cliff from which the last residuum of the revolutionaries will plummet to smash on the rocks of anarchy, chaos, and bloodletting, a hell loosed on earth. The Age of Revolution will end with the Consecration of Russia to the Immaculate Heart of Mary.

Trumpet Blasts

The rejection of the Catholic Church was the beginning of the collapse of civilization which is reaching its end today.

The past centuries have been a series of revolutions, each revolution making war on the previous one, a war on its predecessor . . . . Once you unhook from the Catholic Church, each revolution is going to undermine its predecessor for society then necessarily becomes unstable.

The problem of the rotten West today is that it is apostate; it keeps searching for substitutes for religion, but there is no mechanism in any substitute to return man to God. To go back to God, to believe in God, to take God seriously, is off modern man's mental map. They cannot even imagine it; they find the idea ridiculous.

For the liberal, liberty is the supreme good. For the liberal, the foundation of truth is liberty; they believe that where you have liberty, you have truth, which is not true at all. Liberty is equally a foundation for lies as for truth.

Revolutionary Virginian aristocrat Thomas Jefferson said, "Just let Truth into the marketplace and it will prevail." This is false, because revolutionary Jefferson did not believe in original sin. You let Truth into the marketplace and it is likely to get trampled on or ignored. Revolutionary Prime Minister Winston Churchill said in a moment of inspiration, "All men meet Truth once in their lives and most walk by."

Liberalism is suicide, a war on the existence of man. Liberals are liars, liberals are murderers. They stand in opposition to the Way, the Truth, the Light; they even stand against Common Sense. Why does the Word of God line up with Common Sense? Because Common Sense lines up with human nature and human nature is the creation of God. People don't want Common Sense because they don't want Reality because they don't want Truth because they don't want God.

Unless men return to Catholic order, society is bound to arrive at the supreme disorder, the Antichrist. This is the ultimate crisis of today's anti-civilization; the Catholic Church bought into the rot of revolution when in the 1960's it held the Second Vatican Council. Archbishop Lefebvre set up a heroic resistance and managed to pull together the remains of the sane Catholic Church; he built his world-wide Society of priests and seminaries and schools that now is being mis-led by revolutionary leadership in exactly the same way.

The coming Third World War will be a massive reality check, the beginning of a Great Chastisement. Anybody who survives will have once more a true fear of God. Speaking of myself, I think I can honestly say that right now in 2012 I do not have a real fear of God. I believe in the God of Mount Sinai who made the mountain thunder and hop so that the Israelites were scared stiff miles and miles away. I believe that is the True God and I believe in the Anger of God but I cannot say I sense it or that I'm properly afraid of it. With the Three Days of Darkness, if I survive, I shall be afraid of the Anger of God. I shall be shaking in my shoes and that will be very salutary. The fear of God is the beginning of wisdom; people today have no fear of God and therefore there is very little 'beginning of wisdom' in today's world. As the world rotted, the Church held firm for the nineteenth and the first half of the twentieth century. When the rot of the world got into the Church and when God's own ministers were indifferent to Him, when they went rotten and began mishandling the Holy Eucharist, then things became deadly serious. That the man of God, that God's own servants should be indifferent to Him – that is a horror! His own privileged servants break the First Commandment and make a monkey of His Church, turning it inside out so that it pleases man and not God – that is the

Veritas *Variations*

ultimate horror and that is what is going to bring down the Chastisement.

We await the Consecration of Russia to the Immaculate Heart of Mary which will put an end to the Fifth Age of the Church.

Venerable Bartholomew Holzhauser writes of the Fifth Age of the Church:

> The fifth period is one of affliction, desolation, humiliation, and poverty for the Church. Jesus Christ will purify His people through cruel wars, famines, plague epidemics, and other horrible calamities. He will also afflict and weaken the Latin Church with many heresies. It is a period of defections, calamities and extermination. Those Christians who survive the sword, plague and famines will be few on earth. Nations will fight against nations, and will be desolated by internecine dissensions.
>
> Are we not to fear, during that period, that the Mohammedans will come again, working out their sinister schemes against the Latin Church?
>
> During this period, many men will abuse the freedom of conscience given to them. It is of such men that Jude, the Apostle, spoke when he said: "These men blaspheme whatever they do not understand; and they corrupt whatever they know naturally as irrational animals do . . . . They feast together without restraint, feeding themselves, grumbling murmurers, walking according to their lusts; their mouth speaketh proud things, they admire people for the sake of gain; they bring about di-

vision, sensual men, having not the spirit."

During this unhappy period, there will be laxity in divine and human precepts. Discipline will suffer. The Holy Canons will be completely disregarded, and the Clergy will not respect the laws of the Church. Everyone will be carried away and led to believe and to do what he fancies, according to the manner of the flesh.

They will ridicule Christian simplicity: they will call it folly and nonsense, but they will have the highest regard for advanced knowledge, and for the skill by which the axioms of the law, the precepts of morality, the Holy Canons and religious dogmas are clouded by senseless questions and elaborate arguments. As a result, no principle at all, however holy, authentic, ancient, and certain it may be, will remain free of censure, criticism, false interpretations, modification, and delimitation by man.

These are evil times, a century full of dangers and calamities. Heresy is everywhere, and the followers of heresy are in power almost everywhere. Bishops, prelates, and priests say that they are doing their duty, that they are vigilant, and that they live as befits their state in life. In like manner, therefore, they all seek excuses. But God will not permit a great evil against His Church: heretics and tyrants will come unexpectedly; they will break into the Church while bishops, prelates, and priests are asleep. They will enter Italy and lay Rome waste; they will break down the churches and destroy everything.

Quoted by Yves Dupont, *Catholic Prophecy*, Rockford, Ill.: Tan Books, 1973, pp. 38–40.

These words accord with the vision of Pope St. Pius X who in 1909 during an audience for the General Chapter of the Franciscan Order suddenly went into a trance-like state; when he emerged from it he stated, "What I have seen is terrifying! Will I be the one or will it be a successor? What is certain is that the Pope will leave Rome and, in leaving the Vatican, he will have to pass over the dead bodies of his priests!" The Pope's vision seems to be in accord with the harsh prediction of Sister Lucia spoken to Father Fuentes in 1957 that many nations will disappear from the face of the earth; with the Akita prophecy given to Sister Sasagawa that fire will fall from the sky and much of mankind will be destroyed; with the prophecies from many Catholic Saints of a coming Three Days of Darkness when the powers of hell will be unleashed upon the earth. We have been warned.

The means by which such devastation can be avoided have been known, but ignored, for many years. Our Lord sent His Blessed Mother from Heaven to give us the preventative: the consecration of Russia to Her Immaculate Heart by the Pope in conjunction with all the Bishops in the world. For many decades now political maneuvering has trumped heavenly help, but we are also assured by Our Lady that the consecration *will* be done, "though it will be late," Russia *will* be converted and a period of peace *will* be granted to mankind. The lion and the lamb can only lie down together with a universal triumph of Our Lady's Immaculate Heart and the universal reign of the Mystical Body of Christ, risen from its fifth period tomb and shining with unimagined brilliance.

Venerable Holzhauser states:

> The sixth period of the Church will begin with the powerful Monarch and the Holy Pontiff . . . and it will last until the revelation of Antichrist [the seventh age]. In this period, God will console His Holy Church for the afflictions and the great tribulation which she has endured during the fifth period. All nations will become Catholic. Vocations will be abundant as never before and all men will seek only the Kingdom of God and His justice. Men will live in peace, and this will be granted because people will make their peace with God.

Ibid., p. 40.

The Voice of the Trumpet

How long this Sixth Age of the Church will last, no one knows. The prophecies suggest something like a return to the Golden Age that has haunted the minds and hearts of men for millennia. What we do know is that as man will still be tainted by original sin and still be subject to temptations of the world and the flesh and the devil, the glorious time will come to an end. As Robert Frost reminds us.

Verbal Music Interlude

> Nature's first green is gold,
> Her hardest hue to hold.
> Her early leaf's a flower.
> But only so an hour,
> So leaf subsides to leaf.
> So Eden sank to grief,
> So dawn goes down to day,
> Nothing gold can stay.

His Excellency Bishop Williamson opines that the Sixth Age may not be lengthy, perhaps, he suggests, twenty-five to fifty years. The memory of modern Fifth Age power and false freedom, convenience and unrestrained concupiscence, miraculous machines and marvels of medicine will be used by the devil to lure mankind back into a trap, a false belief that promises the so-called "glories" of the Fifth Age supported by the arrogant assertion that "this time we will control all this and not allow it to destroy us." Once again, the first temptation, "Ye shall be as gods," will be too alluring and man will take another big bite of the forbidden fruit. The Antichrist will have the way prepared for him and the Seventh Age, a time of persecution worse than the martyrdoms of

Veritas *Variations*

the Second Age and the apostasy of the Fifth Age, both "dress rehearsals" for the nightmarish end of time, will be launched.

We all know how the Seventh Age will end. We have read the book, and like the promise of so many of the best books, the Judge will appear, the God will descend, The Truth shall be revealed, the Evil punished and the Good rewarded. Only this Grand Resolution will *not* be a fiction.

Third Variation – *Conspiracies*

> Conspiracy: 1. An agreement to perform together an illegal, treacherous or evil act. 2. A combining or acting together, as if by evil design.
> —*The American Heritage Dictionary of the English Language*

> [M]ost of the criticism directed at conspiracy beliefs is based on sentimentality about America's political leaders and institutions rather than on unbiased reasoning and objective observation.... The term "conspiracy theory" did not exist as a phrase in everyday American conversation before 1964.... In 1964, the year the Warren Commission issued its report [on the President Kennedy assassination], the *New York Times* published five stories in which "conspiracy theory" appeared. In recent years, the phrase has occurred in over 140 *New*

The Voice of the Trumpet

York Times* stories annually.

> —Lance deHaven-Smith, *Conspiracy Theory in America*, Austin, Texas: University of Texas Press, 2013, pp.2–3

O Lord, thy mercy is in heaven: and thy truth reacheth even to the clouds.

> —Psalm 35: 6

And [they] will indeed turn away their hearing from the truth, but will be turned unto fables.

> —II Timothy 4: 4

The unjust hath said within himself that he would sin: there is no fear of God before his eyes. For in his sight he hath done deceitfully, that his iniquity may be found unto hatred. The words of his mouth are iniquity and guile: he would not understand that he might do well. He hath devised iniquity on his bed: he hath set himself on every way that is not good: but evil he hath not hated.

> —Psalm 35, 2–5

Paranoia becomes common sense as the world goes insane.

> —Norman Mailer

The simple act of an ordinary brave man is not to participate in lies, not to support false actions! His rule: Let *that* come into the world, let it even reign supreme – only not through me . . . . One word of truth shall

Veritas *Variations*

outweigh the whole world.

—Aleksander Solzhenitsyn, *Nobel Prize Lecture*, 1970

Prelude & Fugue

Prelude

Bishop Richard Williamson has believed from the moment of his conversion and reception into the Roman Catholic Church that Jesus Christ is the King of Heaven and Earth. Our Lord's rule does not confine itself to the spaces inside the walls of the Vatican, or Bishops' episcopal palaces or simple residences, or the structures of churches, be they soaring Gothic cathedrals or humble wooden chapels or temporary garages or hotel rooms, or even modern steel and glass eyesores. As King, Our Lord reigns over all of life, every sphere of human existence, every pursuit, every study, every practice, every action, every space. And His Law is the Law of Truth. Those who criticize the Bishop for trespassing into territory not immediately circumscribed by sacred doctrine deny Our Lord's right to claim His Sovereign prerogatives. To confine Catholic Truth and isolate it in a hospital-like "church ward" is to suggest that the highest Truth must be quarantined like a disease, leprosy or the plague, and not wander out into the wide world. "Good fences make good neighbors" as the poet says, but there can be no such enclosures surrounding Christ's Reign, Christ's Rule, Christ's Truth.

The Bishop has therefore always believed himself obligated to present the fullness of truth as part of his episcopal duty as a successor of the apostles, contained in the first admonishment of Our Lord that those men should go into the world and teach all nations. What could be rejected as part of that truthful teaching? As a result, the Williamson apostolate of frank and fearless speech has often outraged the governing secular rulers, themselves governed by the world, the flesh and the devil, as well as sacred rulers, especially those seeking compromise with the world. Even many devout believers who seek to remain above the world, cocooned in a supernatural and impenetrable sphere take issue with His Excellency's outspokenness on these matters. When he states, as in the final minutes of the notorious interview (a trap laid for him on German soil): "I believe that the historical evidence is strongly against, is hugely against, six million Jews having been deliberately gassed in gas chambers as a deliberate policy of Adolph Hitler.... I think that 200,000 to 300,000 Jews perished in Nazi concentration camps but none of them in gas chambers," the world runs mad. "Crucify him!" screams the secular world and the corrupt media; "Excommunicate him again!" shout the conciliar Roman authorities (who do not view denial of the Immaculate Conception, the Virgin Birth, the Resurrection, the Ascension and the Real Presence as excommunicable offenses); "How imprudent! How foolish! How unnecessary!" mutter his confrères. Speaking the truth in the face of the world's unanimous and conforming lies makes the declaimer anathema. We do not currently crucify; we vilify, excoriate, denounce, shun, demean, isolate.

The issue is, however, without a doubt a religious question. Even the revisionist historian Robert Faurisson, an unbeliever who has not only been forced into court on numerous occasions but also had acid thrown in his face for speaking the truth, recognizes the religious import of the controversy:

> The Six Million constitute a lay religion with its own

Veritas *Variations*

dogma, commandments, decrees, prophets, high priests and Saints: St Anne (Frank), St Simon (Wiesenthal), St Eli (Weisel). It has its holy places, its rituals and its pilgrimages. It has its temples and its relics (bars of soap, piles of shoes, etc.), its martyrs, heroes, miracles and miraculous survivors (millions of them), its golden legend and its righteous people. Auschwitz is its Golgotha, Hitler is its Satan. It dictates its law to the nations. Its heart beats in Jerusalem, at the Yad Veshem monument.

Quoted in *Eleison Comments* CCCL.

To speak heresy against this modern false religion will unleash the forces of the Antichrist and drag the truth-teller into a series of kangaroo courts.

Modern man worships in the Temple of Science. Having rejected poetry and its metaphors as venues for exploring the mysteries of life, he has turned not only to the facts of science but also to the metaphors of science to find verities. We enter the revered Modern Edifice of the Temple and visit side chapels of Mathematics, Statistics and Chemistry, with a brief stop to consult with the money-changers, who have no one to drive them out of this "holy place."

Tin Foil Hat Fugue for Two Voices

<u>VOICE 1</u>: Three World Trade Center Buildings in New York City brought down. Pentagon attacked. Weapons – Airliners. Planes seized by young Arabs. Armed with box cutters but with little flight training.

<u>VOICE 2</u>: Six million Jews killed. Gas Chambers. By order.

The Voice of the Trumpet

CHEMISTRY

<u>VOICE 1</u>. Never has a steel-structured building been brought down by fire. Except in New York City on September 11, 2001.

"[The furnishings] in the buildings by code had to be fire resistant, resulting in a limited amount of flammable fuel," says Leslie Young, high-rise architect and former firefighter. "The fire-resistant furnishings as a result burn at about 550 degrees Fahrenheit for approximately 15 minutes." NIST confirms Young's assessment:

> The initial jet fuel fires themselves lasted at most a few minutes.... Fires in WTC 1 were generally ventilation limited ... [and] tended to burn out in about twenty minutes.

National Institute of Science and Technology (NIST), *Federal Building and Fire Safety Investigation of the World Trade Center Disaster: Final Report of the National Construction Safety Team on the Collapses of the World Trade Center Towers*, September 2005 (*"NIST Final Report"*), Part 1, Section 8.3.4, p. 183.

> None of the received steel samples showed evidence of exposure to air temperatures above 600 degrees Fahrenheit for as long as 15 minutes.

Ibid., p.180.

Steel melts at approximately 2500 degrees Fahrenheit. Many eyewitnesses saw and contemporary videos show molten steel flowing down the sides of the World Trade Center buildings. Airplanes with infrared cameras flying over the rubble detected 1400 degree Fahrenheit hot spots burning in the rubble. The self-perpetuating crematorium continued to burn like a demonic votive flame, a man made oven, for six to eight weeks after the event.

Veritas *Variations*

<u>VOICE 2</u>. Typhus, the deadly bacterial disease spread by lice, takes its name from a Greek word meaning "hazy," as the victims of the disease suffer mental disorientation because of the infection. Some believe that as far back as the time of the Peloponnesian War, an epidemic that killed a third of the citizens of Athens resulted from the spread of typhus. Napoleon lost more of his French army to typhus during his assault on Russia in 1812 than were lost in battle. At the same time, an outbreak in Ireland claimed over 100,000 victims. Between 1919 and 1922, the post-revolution Soviet Union lost three million to typhus, an infectious plague that paled compared to the deadly ideological plague being unleashed by the Soviet state against its own citizens, a mass extermination of souls, the numbers of which remain in doubt, ranging from 20 million to 110 million. No one is arrested, fined or imprisoned for debating the numbers.

The Nazi government worried about a new outbreak of typhus as their armies moved to the east. The officials in the Nazi concentration camps sought to prevent typhus outbreaks which spread swiftly in unclean conditions where the population is in close contact. They shaved the heads of prisoners, had them bathe or shower regularly and treated their personal items, bed, clothing and the like, to regular delousing in airtight gas chambers with hydrogen cyanide gas, known by its commercial name Zyklon-B.

In 1988, the leading American engineering expert on state-sanctioned execution chambers, Fred Leuchter, nicknamed "Mr. Death" in a *60 Minutes* profile, travelled to Auschwitz. He visited the site at the behest of the defense team of Ernst Zundel who was being tried in a Canadian court for "holocaust denial." Leuchter tested for residue of the cyanide compound in the chambers known as Krema 1, 2, and 3, as well as one of the delousing facilities. All of the seventeen samples taken from the supposed gas chambers proved to be less than 10 mg/kg. The sample from the delousing facility showed a concentration of 1050mg/kg. Leuchter subsequently testified at the Zundel trial that the three Krema could not have been used as extermination chambers.

The *Leuchter Report* became the subject of controversy. Leuchter not only lost his professional reputation and his employment, but became vilified as a fraud and a liar.

In the early 1990s, German chemist Germar Rudolf went to Auschwitz to repeat Leuchter's experiments under more tightly controlled circumstances. His results confirmed Leuchter's findings. Rudolf published extensive scientific analyses in over a dozen books and articles. The doctrinal student in chemistry was denied his doctorate because his thesis was rejected. He wrote two books of revisionist history, undertaken because his chemical findings led him to further investigation. Both books were first published in Germany, but then all copies were confiscated and burned by German officials. He was sentenced to fourteen months in prison. Seeking refuge in the United States, Rudolf was arrested by immigration officials in 2005 and returned to Germany. In 2007, German courts sentenced Rudolf to two and a half years in prison. The courts ruled he had promoted hatred, committed libel and shown disrespect for the dead. Released from prison in July, 2009, Rudolf currently resides in the United States with his wife and daughter.

In the side chapels of the Temple of Science, things may also be "hazy," not from incense but from the fog of deliberate unknowing.

EPISODE

VOICE 2. The three volume *Report of the Activities of the Red Cross* on its activities during the Second World War was published in Geneva in 1948. German authorities

Veritas *Variations*

reluctantly permitted, according to the *Report*, access to internees in the German camps in central and western Europe, thanks to the 1929 Geneva Military Convention rules which Germany had signed. (The Soviet Union refused to ratify the Convention and denied the ICRC access to its camps, thus isolating their GULAG archipelago islands from any kind of international supervision or inspection.) The ICRC distributed food parcels to major concentration camps in Germany from August 1942 and "from February 1943 onwards this concession was extended to all other camps and prisons" (*ICRC*, Volume III, p. 78). These food packages continued to be distributed until the last months of 1945.

> The Committee was in a position to transfer and distribute in the form of relief supplies over twenty million Swiss francs collected by Jewish welfare organizations throughout the world....

Ibid., Volume I, p. 644.

The American Joint Distribution Committee of New York dispersed the supplies from an office in Berlin until the Americans entered the war, at which time the Germans shut it down. The ICRC expressed their frustration that the roadblocks preventing their attempts to aid Jewish internees came not from Germans, but from the Allied blockade of Europe.

Theresienstadt "where there were about 40,000 Jews deported from various countries was a relatively privileged ghetto" (*ibid.*, Volume III, p. 75).

> The Committee delegates were able to visit the camp at Theresienstadt (Terzin) which was used exclusively for Jews and was governed by special conditions. From information gathered by the Committee, this camp had been started as an experiment by certain leaders of the

The Voice of the Trumpet

> Reich... These men wished to give the Jews the means of setting up a communal life in a town under their own administration and possessing almost complete autonomy... two delegates were able to visit the camp on April 6th, 1945. They confirmed the favorable impression on the first visit.

Ibid., Volume I, p. 642.

Not only was the Committee prevented from "sending anything whatsoever to Russia" (*Ibid.*, Volume II, p. 62), but when the Soviets took control of Romania, they terminated the aid the Committee had been extending to close to 200,000 Romanian Jews.

> In the chaotic condition of Germany after the invasion during the final months of the war, the camps received no food supplies at all and starvation claimed an increasing number of victims. Itself alarmed by this situation, the German government at last informed the ICRC [of the crisis] on February 1st, 1945.... In March, 1945, discussions between the President of the ICRC and General of the S. S. Kaltenbrunner gave even more decisive results. Relief could henceforth be distributed by the ICRC, and one delegate was authorized to stay in each camp....

Ibid., Volume III, p. 83.

PHYSICS

<u>VOICE 1</u>. The top sections of both World Trade Center Towers (as well as World Trade Center Building 7) fell at close to free fall speed, as if in their precipitous descent they had no obstacles whatsoever below them. Each tower took 10–12 seconds to collapse to the ground; an absolute free fall would have taken slightly over 9 seconds. Each top section somehow had sufficient energy to destroy 80,000 tons of structure below it while it also

Veritas *Variations*

accelerated to free fall speed. Gravity alone could not make this possible; the law of conservation momentum will not allow this. There cannot have been any vertical structure below them as the Towers collapsed.

> Since the stories below the level of collapse initiation provided little resistance ... the building section above came down essentially in free fall.

NIST Final Report, Part 1, Section 6.14.4, p. 146.

Roland Angle graduated from University of California – Berkeley with a B.S. in Civil Engineering, served in the U.S. Army Special Forces, where he trained in the use of explosives, and became a licensed civil engineer in California. His fifty years of engineering experience has included designing and testing blast-hardened missile launch facilities and designing naval explosive containers, harbor terminal facilities, earth foundation systems, and hydraulic systems. In addition, he has owned three construction companies and taught engineering subjects to high school students.

Mr. Angle makes the following observations: NIST is telling us that the structures below the top of the Towers ceased to exist for the first few seconds of the collapse.

> Well, things in physics just don't cease to exist and cease to resist the forces that are on them .... That's impossible. That's a violation of the fundamental laws of physics that says for every action there's an equal and opposite reaction.
>
> This is high school physics and our whole society is being led to believe that these fundamental laws of physics – hard science – don't apply any more, and that, I think, should frighten all of us.

Mr. Angle is one of the nearly 3000 architects and engineers who make up the group *Architects and Engineers*

The Voice of the Trumpet

for 9-11 Truth. His comments and those of 2990 others may be found at their website.

Perhaps high school physics is now as badly taught as high school grammar, literature, history, languages and mathematics, but that cannot eliminate the laws of physics. Perhaps the United States Supreme Court overturned the Laws of Physics as part of their abolition of Natural Law (long since having overthrown Divine Law).

> And I was frightened. He said, Marie,
> Marie, hold on tight. And down we went.

MATHEMATICS

<u>VOICE 2</u>. Plaque at Auschwitz, put in place at the end of World War II:

> FOUR MILLION
> PEOPLE SUFFERED
> AND DIED HERE
> AT THE HANDS
> OF THE NAZI
>   MURDERERS
> BETWEEN THE YEARS
> 1940 and 1945

The statistics came from the Soviet authorities, and the world well knows what sticklers for truth they were. After the collapse of the Soviet Union in 1991 when the Soviet archives were opened and actual statistics became available, a new plaque replaced the former one:

> FOR EVER LET THE PLACE BE
> A CRY OF DESPAIR
> AND A WARNING TO HUMANITY
> WHERE THE NAZIS MURDERED
> ABOUT ONE AND A HALF

Veritas *Variations*

MILLION
MEN, WOMEN, AND CHILDREN,
MAINLY JEWS
FROM VARIOUS COUNTRIES
OF EUROPE.
AUSCHWITZ – BIRKENAU
1940–1945

Math Problem #1:
Question: 4,000,000 minus 1,500,000 = ?
Answer: 2,500,000
Math Problem #2:
Question: 6,000,000 minus 2,500,000 = ?
Answer: 3,500,000
Modern Math Problem #3:
Question: 6,000,000 minus 2,500,000 = ?
Miracle Answer: 6,000,000
2 + 2 = 5

EPISODE

VOICE 1. MODERN SCIENTIFIC PROPHETIC MIRACLE.
4:10 p.m., EST, September 11, 2001. CNN reporter Aaron Brown informs viewers, "We are getting reports now, one of the other buildings [Building 7] is on fire and is collapsing or has collapsed."
4:57 p.m. CNN reporter Aaron Brown verifies for viewers that the Solomon Brothers building [Building 7] has collapsed.
5:10 p.m. BBC reporter Jane Standley on the scene in New York City reports in a live video feed that Building 7 of the World Trade Center Complex has collapsed. Building 7 stands proudly upright and unimpaired, not smoking, not blazing, not shaking, without a wobble, without a tremor, in full view over her left shoulder.

The Voice of the Trumpet

5:15 p.m. The screen goes blank. The BBC reporters in London announce the satellite feed has for some unknown reason been lost.

5:20 p.m. The top stories of Building 7 descend to the ground in 12.25 seconds. In free fall. The Laws of Physics are having a bad day.

The owner of the World Trade Center Complex, Larry Silverstein had insured the buildings in July of 2001. After a series of disputes with insurers, the court awarded Silverstein $4.55 billion dollars. Silverstein later stated in an interview he had decided with fire officials to "pull" (demolish) Building 7 that afternoon to avoid any additional loss of life. Another technological and engineering miracle. Building 7 was wired and prepared for implosion in a few hours – an obvious new record, worthy of inclusion in the Guinness Book of World Records or the Catalogue of Scientific and Engineering Miracles.

VOICE 2. STATISTICAL PROPHECY.

"There are 6,000,000 living, bleeding, suffering arguments in favor of Zionism" (Rabbis Gottheil and Wise, *New York Times*, June 11, 1900, p. 7).

"Startling reports of the condition and future of Russia's 6,000,000 Jews were made on March 12 in Berlin . . . . Dr. Nathan paints a horrifying picture of the plight and prospects of his co-religionists, and forecasts at any hour renewed massacres . . . . He left St. Petersburg with the firm conviction that the Russian Government's studied policy for the 'solution' of the Jewish question is systemic and murderous extermination" (*New York Times*, March 25, 1906, p. SM6).

"In the world today there are about 13,000,000 Jews, of whom more than 6,000,000 are in the very heart of the war zone; Jews whose lives are at stake and who today are subjected to every manner of suffering and sorrow . . . " (*New York Times*, January 14, 1915, p. 3).

Veritas *Variations*

"The American people, Jews and non-Jews alike, will soon be asked to lend or contribute $1,000,000,000 to carry out plans for the reconstruction of the Jewry of the entire world . . . . 6,000,000 Jews need help" (*New York Times*, October 18, 1918, p. 12).

Felix Warburg, Chairman of the Joint Distribution Committee of American Friends for Jewish War Sufferers: World War I "reduced to tragically unbelievable poverty, starvation and disease about 6,000,000 souls, or half the Jewish population of the earth" (*New York Times*, November 12, 1919, p. 7).

"Jewish war sufferers in Central and Eastern Europe, where six millions face horrifying conditions of famine, disease and death . . . " (*New York Times*, May 7, 1920, p. 11).

"Authenticated reports point to 2,000,000 Jews who have already been slain by all manner of satanic barbarism, and plans for the total extermination of all Jews upon whom the Nazis can lay their hands. The slaughter of a third of the Jewish population in Hitler's domain and the threatened slaughter of all [$3 \times 2,000,000 = 6,000,000$] is a *holocaust* without parallel." (*New York Times*, December 13, 1942, p.12).

STRETTO

VOICE 1. "After the 1993 attack [on the World Trade Center], bomb-sniffing dogs had patrolled the towers; on Thursday [September 6, 2001] bomb-sniffing dogs were abruptly removed" (*Newsday*, September 12, 2001).

On September 8th and 9th, 2001, for the first time in thirty years, all the security systems in the World Trade Center Towers became useless at the same time. All security disappeared – security badges, locks on doors, security cameras all ceased operating. The given reason – a "re-cabling exercise."

The Voice of the Trumpet

VOICE 2. Fourteen countries have enacted or expanded anti-"holocaust" laws – Austria, Belgium, the Czech Republic, France, Germany, Liechtenstein, Lithuania, Luxembourg, Poland, Portugal, Romania, Spain, and Switzerland; all claim to uphold the right of free speech and inquiry.

VOICE 1. "We are unable to provide a full explanation of the total collapse." —Catherine S. Fletcher, Management and Organization Division, NIST, September 27, 2003.

VOICE 2. Germany has stated that "holocaust denial" will "corrupt the youth." "[Socrates], thou shouldst be living at this hour."

VOICE 1. On September 10, 2001, Secretary of Defense Donald Rumsfeld announced that two point three trillion dollars ($2,300,000,000,000) was unaccounted for in Defense Department records. The flying object that hit the Pentagon the next day conveniently targeted the Accounting Offices. But it was a bad day all around. Airport security failed four times at three different airports – Logan International Airport in Boston, Washington Dulles International Airport, Newark International Airport; the U. S. Air Force for the first time in its history could not get one interceptor jet fighter into the air.

VOICE 2. In March, 2017, internet retailer Amazon under pressure from Jewish groups stopped selling three "holocaust denial" books: *Holocaust: The Greatest Lie of the Twentieth Century* by Eleanor Wittakers; *The Hoax of the Twentieth Century* by Arthur Butz; *Did Six Million Really Die?* by Richard Harwood. The Jewish groups asserted that Amazon provided a platform for anti-semites.

VOICE 1. During the week preceding September 11, 2001, wise investors shorted airline stocks, i.e., they made a bet that those stocks would soon decrease in value. On some days, "put options" exceeded their usual volume by up to 100 times larger than normal. They did

Veritas *Variations*

not have to wait long for an astonishing return on their investments. Airline stocks fell precipitously, almost as rapidly as the Towers themselves. The 9-11 Commission studied the peculiar trading and stated the increase was "coincidentally innocuous."

<u>VOICE 2</u>. In 1979, the International Red Cross released records from Arolsen, West Germany, recording that organization's figures for the number of total deaths in the concentration camps during World War II. According to their estimates, 272,000 persons total died in the camps, half of whom were Jews. Bishop Williamson stated that he believed 200,000 to 300,000 perished in the camps, a number in accord with the number put forth by the International Red Cross. His remark landed him in the German Courts. The International Red Cross has not yet been arrested and charged.

CODETTA

> One of the differences between Bishop Williamson and other bishops is his political courage. This was in emulation with [sic] Archbishop Lefebvre, who every year laid a wreath at the tomb of Maréchal Pétain, praised Franco, Salazar, and even Pinochet.... Bishop Williamson did not teach the political nature of our religion out of a mere fancy, nor a desire to posture himself as an anti-liberal, but because Satan uses a political framework to bind souls to himself and throw them into hell. Both in him and the Archbishop there is the certainty that when God straightens things out in the *res publica*, millions of souls will benefit, and that is why Catholic men must keep a careful watch of the political situation with respect of the Rights of God. Moreover, when a Catholic allows or keeps silent on the trampling of the Rights of God, as perhaps $7/8^{ths}$ of all Catholics are prone to do, traditional no less than conciliar, he is already a liberal and his Catholic life is

in jeopardy, even if he can keep a nice façade for some time.

Hence, find missteps along the path of Bishop Williamson if you must, but do not tell me he betrayed Christ, his King, because he had to pay the price for it on several occasions, and was a relentless teacher and defender all his life, of the Rights of God.

Fr. François Chazal, *Oportet Christum Regnare*, Spring, 2016, pp. 3–4.

> A Saint once complained to Our Lord after a temptation was past, saying: "Where were You, O my loving Jesus, during this horrible tempest?" Our Lord replied: "I was in the midst of your heart, and was pleased to see you combat so bravely."
>
> —St. John Vianney

These matters are not doctrine; they are questions of history and facts and reality, and thus ultimately questions of truth. Consider the sources, the consequences following from various assertions and the ultimate goal. If some skepticism as to media-promoted premises may arise in your thoughts, then, reader, you may have begun to earn a tinfoil hat. Wear it as you inquire with curiosity and apprehension until your end and it may assist you in attaining a heavenly crown.

Fourth Variation – *Betrayal*

Passacaglia

> My bowels, my bowels are in pain, the
> senses of my heart are troubled within me.
> I will not hold my peace, for my soul hath

Veritas *Variations*

heard the sound of the trumpet, the cry of battle.

—Jeremiah 4: 19

And I appointed watchmen over you, saying: Harken ye the sound of the trumpet. And they said: We will not harken.

—Jeremiah 6: 17

NOVEMBER, 1988

[I]f I live a little while, supposing that Rome calls for a renewed dialogue, then, I will put conditions . . . . I will place the discussion on the doctrinal level: 'Do you agree with the great encyclicals of all the popes who preceded you? Do you agree with *Quanta Cura* of Pius IX, *Immortale Dei* and *Libertas* of Leo XIII, *Pascendi Gregis* of Pius X, *Quas Primas* of Pius XI, *Humani Generis* of Pius XII? Are you in full communion with these Popes and their teachings? Do you still accept the entire Anti-Modernist Oath? Are you in favor of the social reign of Our Lord Jesus Christ? If you do not accept the doctrine of your predecessors, it is useless to talk! As long as you do not accept to correct the Council, in consideration of the doctrine of these Popes, your predecessors, no dialogue is possible. It is useless.

Archbishop Marcel Lefebvre, Interview, *Fideliter*, November-December, 1988.

JANUARY, 1992

Not many months after the death of Archbishop Lefebvre, a hypothetical offer comes from Rome to the SSPX with tentative tendrils of offers for a reconciliation. Then Superior General of the Society, Father Franz Schmidberger rejects the offer in an unpublished private letter to the Holy See. Bishop Williamson paraphrases the letter's content as saying that as long as Rome remains sunk in conciliarism, no fruitful collaboration between the SSPX and Rome seems possible.

JULY, 1994

The General Chapter of the SSPX meets at Écône to select a new Superior General. Bishop Bernard Fellay is put forward as the candidate. He expresses his reluctance to assume the position for the Founder of the Society had stated explicitly in 1988 that the Superior General of the Society should not be one of the four Bishops. Fr. Schmidberger and others convince Bishop Fellay to accept the position.

AUGUST, 1994

In his Rector's Letter of August, 1994, Bishop Williamson defends the election of Bishop Fellay by saying the following:

> [S]ince 1988, negotiations with Rome have not yet reopened, because the Society has refused to abandon the old religion, and Rome has refused to abandon the new religion, and no amount of diplomacy or subjective good will on either side can bridge the widening objective gulf between the two religions. In this situation the Society no longer felt obliged to spare the susceptibilities of Rome, [the possibility of "excommunication," such "excommunication" having taken place immediately after the June, 1988 consecration], so if the best man it had was one of those "excommunicated" in 1988, it felt free to elect him....

Letters from the Rector, No. 129.

The Bishop in his abundant charity cannot imagine this "best man" could become the willing architect of an unsafe bridge across a "great gulf fixed."

Veritas *Variations*

1995

The former French ambassador to Japan (1985–1987) and to the Italian government (1988–1992), Gilbert Pérol, writes an article that seeks to propose "good offices" between the SSPX and the Vatican. He himself cannot bring to fruition his dream of establishing friendly relations and dialogue for he dies on March 8, 1995, the 55th birthday of Bishop Richard Williamson. His Excellency will later comment on the Pérol proposal:

> Not being a theologian, Pérol says he thinks that the present situation of the Church and world requires that the problem of the divisions between Catholics following on the Council 'should be stated in entirely new terms.' It is rather as a diplomat that he proposes that on the one side Rome should admit that it gravely mistreated the Tridentine rite of Mass, and it should suspend the excommunications of 1988, while on the other hand the SSPX must not totally reject the Council and it must recognize that Rome is still the highest authority in the Church.
>
> In other words as a diplomat Pérol proposed that if only there were a little give and take on each side, then the agony could be emptied out of the clash between the Council and Tradition, and all Catholics could once more live happily ever after. Thus he and millions of other Catholics would no longer be faced with having to either abandon Rome for the sake of Tradition, or abandon Tradition for the sake of Rome. Lovely! Back to the comfort zone of the 1950's! but the 1950's are gone, and gone forever. Then where is the flaw in his thinking?
>
> It is at the very outset when he says he is no theologian. True, he may have been no professional theologian, but *every Catholic must be an amateur theologian,* or, better said, must know his catechism, because only in the light of its doctrine can he judge questions of the Faith. Our Lord's warning to discern between sheep and wolves (Mt. VII, 15–20) was not addressed only to professional

theologians! So Pérol's renouncing "theology" in favor of diplomacy is yet one more example of modern man's failure to grasp the importance of doctrine.

Eleison Comments CCXCIV.

NOVEMBER, 1995

Bishop Fellay, the Superior General of the SSPX, quashes all rumors of talks with Rome and states there have been no contacts with Vatican authorities, nor would he approve of any such contacts.

DECEMBER, 1996

> You cannot dialogue with persons who share none of your basic principles. Right up until the spring of 1988, Archbishop Lefebvre charitably assumed that the Roman churchmen wanted to defend the Catholic Faith of souls, and so he engaged for thirteen years in face-to-face discussions with them, but when in the summer of 1988 their actions made it clear beyond doubt that the unchanging Faith of souls was not their concern, then he gave up discussing, and took definitive action to guarantee the Faith's interim defense, God willing, until Rome comes to its Catholic senses. The disagreement had finally showed itself to be too basic for dialogue to be continued....
>
> [I]f all men were, extraordinarily, to abandon the Truth, then Our Lord says the stones in the street would cry out (Lk. 19: 40). The problem is neither leaders, nor politics, nor egos, nor canon law, nor personalities, nor diplomacy, nor misunderstandings, nor lack of dialogue, but the clash between, on the one side, the Way, the Truth and the Life, and on the other side the Father of Lies, Satan. Men may shift in that clash from one side to the other, but the clash is eternal and it is not matter for any kind of conciliation.

Letters from the Rector, No. 157.

1997

Madame Huguette Pérol, the widow of Gilbert Pérol, remaining a devoted wife to her deceased husband, seeks to revivify her husband's dream.

1998

A working organization is founded to promote a rapprochement between Modern Rome and the SSPX. Known as GREC, "Groupe de Réflection Entre Catholiques" [Group for Reflection Among Catholics], the group's design comes also from Father Michel Lelong, a staunch supporter of the Second Vatican Council, especially its promotion of inter-religious dialogue, evidenced in the priest's work in dialoguing with Muslims. GREC states straightforwardly its primary aim – to interpret Vatican II in the light of Tradition, or, more realistically, to insert round pegs into square holes. An early supporter of GREC, Father Alain Lorans, spokesman for the SSPX District of France, receives permission from Bishop Fellay to join the discussions, designed to find a meeting ground between the Society of Priests founded by Archbishop Lefebvre and the Conciliar Church spawned by Vatican II, or to discover where the sky and the sea could become one. A modern organization, GREC forms many small committees, attracts like-minded supporting members, holds discussions and dialogues and small conferences, though these gatherings assemble with little fanfare as the cells remain private and the talk remains confidential so as to avoid reaction from the two "communities." The GREC participants know with certainty any leaked information might spark fire-storms in both groups.

Bishop Fellay stays fully informed of the ongoing discussions, but keeps his knowledge under close wraps. The other three SSPX Bishops are not apprized.

Archbishop Lefebvre: "We do not have the same outlook on a reconciliation [that Rome has] . . . . We see it as a return of Rome to Tradition. We do not agree; it is a dialogue of death."

MAY 23, 2000

GREC holds its first public meeting to which Fr. Lorans, Rector of the SSPX INSTITUTE in Paris, contributes. One hundred and fifty people attend. More meetings follow subsequently with more SSPX priests attending.

AUGUST, 2000

The SSPX holds a pilgrimage to the Basilicas in Rome. 4,500 pilgrims line the Via della Conciliazione leading to St. Peter's and then fill the Basilica itself. One Italian journalist remarks that for the first time in the Church's history, thousands of "excommunicated" Catholics filled St. Peter's to pray for the Pope.

AUGUST, 2000

Seizing the opportunity of the presence of the four "excommunicated" bishops being in Rome, Cardinal Castrillón Hoyos proffers a luncheon invitation. Three of the four bishops who are able to attend, accept. The meeting is cordial. Yet just a few weeks before the luncheon the Cardinal had made a move against tradition in the Fraternity of St. Peter by removing four of their chosen leaders and replacing them with four new men chosen by Rome.

AUGUST, 2000

Bishop Fellay concludes the Meeting of the Superiors of the SSPX in Albano by commenting, "Firmness pays off. It is Rome which is wrong. We have no reason to back down. We must continue as we have done. Has Rome changed? See what they told St. Peter's: 'Traditionalists must recognize that there is only one rite of Mass in the

Church, and that rite is the new rite.' So Rome is hardening its position. Under pressure it may make a few exceptions for the old Mass, but its principles are unchanged" (*Letters from the Rector*, No. 200).

YEAR'S END, 2000

Rome reopens contacts with the SSPX. Bishop Williamson comments:

> [S]o long as any organization like the Society has the Truth while Rome has not, then the Society is in the driving seat *for all Catholic purposes*, and any behavior, shape, size or form of negotiations which would allow this Rome to get back into the driver's seat would be tantamount to a betrayal of the Truth.

Ibid.

MARCH, 2001

The SSPX announces that all contacts with Rome have ceased. No negotiations have taken place.

MAY, 2001

Zenit.org reports that Bishop Fellay is engaging in talks with Cardinal Castrillón Hoyos.

In Germany and/or Switzerland. A Swiss news agency also reports that the men met in Germany and Switzerland. SSPX headquarters deny the reports. The Swiss news agency apologizes a few days later, saying a source in Rome itself had provided them with the information.

MAY 11, 2001

Cardinal Castrillón Hoyos traveling in Germany has a dinner meeting with representatives from the Fraternity of St. Peter and the Pro Missa Tridentina association. During the discussion, the Cardinal confides that "there are difficulties with Bishop Williamson, but Bishop Fellay assures us that he is humble and will obey."

MAY 11, 2001

La Liberté, a periodical published in the Canton of Valais in Switzerland, reports that Bishop Fellay has stated: "To accept the Council is not a problem for us . . . . we go along with 95% of it. It is more a spirit that we oppose, an attitude before the change came which postulates that everything in the world changes, therefore the Church must change."

JANUARY, 2002

The Traditionalist clergy in Campos, Brazil, strike a deal with Rome. They are granted an "apostolic administration," thus becoming a diocese directly under the Pope and subject to their own Bishop Rangel, who is dying of cancer. They are promised that they may continue celebrating the Mass of All Time. Father Cottier, the Pope's own theologian in Rome states in an interview on January 20, "Little by little we must expect other steps, for example that they [the Campos priests] also participate in concelebrations of the reformed rite. However, we must not be in a hurry. What is important is that in their hearts there should no longer be rejection. Communion found again in the Church has an internal dynamism of its own that will mature." He proves himself to be prophetic. On September 8, 2004, the newly consecrated Bishop Rifan, who has replaced Bishop Rangel, concelebrates the *Novus Ordo* Mass at the National Basilica of Our Lady of Aparecida near Sao Paulo, Brazil. At the same ceremony, three women distribute communion. A photo exists of one of the women giving communion to a priest.

MARCH, 2002

> What kind of Rome do we have when it can sign an agreement with Campos and in the same week can do something like Assisi II [second gathering of world

religions]? They definitely will not say "We recognize Tradition" in any universal sense. But Campos is contented because Rome has recognized Tradition in Campos. But has it, really? If Rome truly recognized Tradition anywhere it wouldn't be able to have an Assisi II, the very contrary of Tradition. It is impossible to see in the recognition of Campos a recognition of Tradition....

[The Society of St. Pius X] position is that there is only one truth, the eternal truth. This truth is exclusive. Truth will not allow its contradiction to be made equal to it. In mathematics, it's clear. Any student who would say, "Two plus two equals five," would fail, but ecumenism says, "It is whatever figure you like." We say, "No, it is four, period." Only one number is the true one. We say all other religions are wrong, only one is true. This truth is exclusive. It is the only one by which we can be saved. All the others are just cheating the people. They cannot lead to God. And, I may say, just looking at Assisi II helps us to see the enormous problem in the Church today. The Society is not the problem; the problem is in Rome.

Bishop Fellay, Conference, Kansas City, Missouri, March 5, 2002.

Archbishop Marcel Lefebvre: "No practical agreement without a doctrinal agreement."

APRIL, 2003

Rumors come from Rome that three of the four SSPX Bishops will be "re-incommunicated" into the Church at a public ceremony. The one shepherd who will *not* be received back into the fold is the one that Rome fears most, the one Archbishop Lefebvre had named in 1988 when Rome had held out the possibility of the SSPX having its own bishop. Rome recognizes the true son of Archbishop Lefebvre and does not want another intractable Traditional hard-liner in their midst. A second rumor says that the Traditional Mass Indult will be extended to all priests. No such actions immediately ensue.

AUGUST, 2003

Bishop Williamson, having declined Bishop Fellay's directive in 1999 to leave the United States and become District Superior of Asia in 1999, in 2003 accepts the proposal of Bishop Fellay that he leave the Seminary in Winona and assume the position of Rector of the La Reja Seminary outside of Buenos Aires, Argentina. One wit states that Bishop Williamson thus will find himself a short distance away from Cardinal Bergoglio, Archbishop of Buenos Aires, but light years away in true Catholic doctrine.

The departing Bishop writes his final "Letter from the Rector" and concludes with a warning and a poem:

> [W]hile subjective sincerity cannot change objective reality, it can be deceiving, highly deceiving. Thus the more innocent or ignorant – "sincere" – these Romans are in what is objectively their deluded fight against Catholic reality, the more dangerous any contacts or negotiations with them can be. The SSPX, like any other defender of the objective Catholic Faith, must today and tomorrow beware like the plague of "nice guys" in Rome. As Teresa of Avila said, "I do not need my confessor to be a Saint, I *do* need him to know his *Catholic doctrine.*"
>
> Should then the SSPX have no contact at all with the Romans? No. Even if a man's mother is a leper, he stays by her bedside, while taking care not to catch the illness which would put an end to his being able to look after her. In May I said that the Romans, as holding authority over the Church, have huge influence and responsibility for millions of souls, and they are not necessarily impervious to the Truth – while there is life, there is hope. To which one can add that if by the grace of God the SSPX possesses the Truth, it is the

Veritas *Variations*

SSPX's duty to make that Truth – prudently – available and accessible to the churchmen who so need it. Also, that Truth will have the effect of discerning the spirits in Rome, and of dividing the Romans who are truly in good faith from those who are not. But how can the little stone of truth bring down the giant of error (Dan. 2: 34, 35) if there is no contact?

My dear friends, let us all persevere in the Truth, however much more difficult yet that may become in the next several years. For if we do persevere, our reward in heaven will go far beyond anything we can imagine. Let us pray for one another. I will not forget the United States. I send you all my blessing as a bishop. Please support my successor in Winona.

> So, dear friends, after one and twenty years
> I leave the United States, with many tears.
> At sixty-three, I've given what I can,
> It's time to yield my place to a younger man.
> When I came here, I came with heavy heart,
> And now with equal sadness I depart.
> For when I came, I did not want to leave
> Where I had been before. So now I grieve
> To quit the scene of one third of my life,
> Laden with priestly toil and happy strife.
> Yet clearly I remember when I came,
> To three companions on the aeroplane
> I said, "I shall in the USA have fun!"
> And that proved true. So now my time is done,
> I might expect the same fun where I go,
> Except – America's unique, and so
> The fun-ny third of my career must end,
> As to a serious land my way I wend.
> My friends may shed a tear, but not my foes
> Who think my leaving terminates their woes.
> But let them not exalt! "I SHALL RETURN"
> As bishop, to ordain and to confirm!
> So if the liberals dare to rise again
> I'll thunder, growl, and strike with might and main!

The Voice of the Trumpet

Nor let me hear of women growing S-L-A-C-K,
Or instantaneously I will be back!!
And if they're S-L-A-C-K-ING off when I am dead,
My ghost will come and haunt them, fierce and dread!
Meanwhile, dear US ladies, girls, God bless
Your being so docile with your feminine dress!
Never have men so needed women true!
In Europe they would learn a thing or two
From Yankee gals, in gracious dresses dressed!
Well done! – by your own children you'll be blessed
Who learn what is a mother – NOT A MAN!
Alas, it's difficult to make a plan
For future newsletters. They hardly fit
In countries lacking ripe old Yankee . . . wit!
But trust that I support you from afar.
Men, be good fathers. In the home you are
By God's design the head. Do not wimp out!
Not only women are meant to be devout!
Be full of God, and lead against the world –
By Catholic men the Devil must be hurled
Back into Hell! Pray hard! Pain's on the way
With shrieks and howls of grief, nor is that day
Far off. Then gird your loins, be strong, stand tall –
Tomorrow has no room for spirits small.
Flee electronics. Stay with real life.
Give time, love, and attention to your wife.
Forget "The Sound of Music," silly stuff
Of which the world has had more than enough.
So ends the last Newsletter I shall write.
Soon I must fly far South into the night.
Ah, my dear friends! – I feel like I could cry! –
SO LONG! FAREWELL! AUF WIEDERSEHEN! GOOD BYE!

+ Richard Williamson

GOOD SHEPHERD SUNDAY, 2004

A Traditional Catholic lady believes the Blessed Virgin Mary has spoken to her and has given her a message to

Veritas *Variations*

pass to Bishop Fellay: the SSPX is to lead the faithful in a Rosary Crusade for the Consecration of Russia to her Immaculate Heart. The lady in humility and shyness hesitates to convey the message.

AUGUST, 2005

Pope Benedict XVI receives Bishop Bernard Fellay at Castel Gandolfo. Also in attendance are Cardinal Castrillón Hoyos and Fr. Schmidberger. The discussions include the present state of the Church and the SSPX, the Society's concerns regarding Modernism, the possible permission for "freeing" the Tridentine Mass and the possible recognition of the SSPX by the Holy See.

Archbishop Lefebvre: "No practical agreement without a doctrinal agreement."

JUNE, 2006

The lady gives the message to Bishop Fellay but still hesitates from shyness to say that it has come to her from the Blessed Virgin Mary in a locution. Bishop Fellay takes up the idea of a Rosary Crusade but ignores the Blessed Mother's stated request. He decides to apply the fruits of the crusade to the "liberation" of the Tridentine Mass, already hinted at in his discussions with Pope Benedict XVI.

JULY, 2006

Bishop Fellay announces the commencement of the Rosary Crusade for the following intentions: 1) to give the Pope strength to "free" the Traditional Mass; 2) for the Social Reign of Christ the King; and 3) for the Triumph of the Immaculate Heart of Mary.

AUGUST, 2006

The Blessed Virgin Mary in another locution to the lady says to inform Bishop Fellay the request has come from the Mother of God; she will bless the Crusade as a sign that she is the source of the message – with the reminder that her original request has not been fulfilled.

OCTOBER, 2006

Bishop Fellay sends the spiritual bouquet of two and a half million rosaries to the Pope.

JULY 7, 2007

Pope Benedict XVI issues the Moto Proprio *Summorum Pontificum* in which he states that the Tridentine Mass was "never abrogated," confirming what the traditionalists had been stating for decades. In the accompanying letter to clergy, he also states that Pope John Paul II in his Apostolic Letter *Ecclesia Dei* of 1988 "primarily wanted to assist the Society of Saint Pius X to recover full unity with the Successor of Saint Peter and sought to heal a wound experienced ever more painfully. Unfortunately this reconciliation has not yet come about." From the Seminary in La Reja, Bishop Williamson sends a letter to the faithful in which he discusses the Motu Proprio. Among his comments: "[E]ven just a partial setting free of the traditional Mass would be a great step forward for the Universal church. The powerful grace contained in the Mass, presently strangled as it were by the rite of Paul VI, would start to flow again all over the world. However, it would take much more than just restoring the true rite of Mass to solve the crisis of faith in the Church." This letter becomes the first of the weekly letters of the Bishop to the faithful, *Eleison Comments*, which will over the years cover a multitude of topics and become a source of disputation with a fellow Society bishop.

JULY 7, 1591

Father Roger Dickenson and Ralph Milner, yeoman, martyred at Winchester.

Veritas *Variations*

DECEMBER, 2007

The Blessed Virgin Mary tells the lady to write again to Bishop Fellay to remind him of her stated desire that a second Rosary Crusade be properly dedicated to the Consecration of Russia to her Immaculate Heart, her original request.

JANUARY, 2008

The requests become more urgent as the Blessed Virgin Mary knows that Bishop Fellay has his own intentions for a second Rosary Crusade, intentions having nothing to do, for a second time, with her request. Our Lady directs the lady to inform Bishop Fellay not to use the Crusade for the "lifting of the 'excommunications'"; if he does so, it will be fatal for the SSPX and she will not bless such an effort, as she had the first substitute intention. She will use the rosaries for other intentions.

HOLY SATURDAY, MARCH, 2008

Our Lady says the lady should tell Bishop Fellay that he cannot move any closer to Rome, no matter how well intentioned the Holy Father may seem to be. She also repeats the Second Crusade is not to be used for the "lifting of the 'excommunications.'"

MARCH 22, 1602

Father James Harrison and Anthony Bates, layman, martyred at York.

JUNE, 2008

Cardinal Castrillón Hoyos summons Bishop Fellay to Rome. Bishop Fellay is ordered to accept a five-point ultimatum that Rome seeks to impose on the SSPX. Four concern the submission to and respect for the Holy Father; the fifth demands a response by the end of the month. Bishop Fellay responds in a letter to the Pope on

June 28, 2008. The contents of the response have never been made public.

JUNE 28, 1654
Father John Southworth, martyred at Tyburn.

OCTOBER 23, 2008
In a "Letter to Friends and Benefactors," Bishop Fellay announces a new Rosary Crusade to be undertaken from November 1 to Christmas. The intention of the Crusade will be "to obtain the withdrawal of the decree of excommunication [sic] through [Our Lady's] intercession."

OCTOBER 23, 1680
Father Thomas Thwing, martyred at York.

NOVEMBER 1, 2008
Bishop Richard Williamson is interviewed for 90 minutes by a Swedish media reporter, Ali Fagan. The interview, to be shown on Swedish television, takes place at the Zaitzkofen Seminary in Germany. Bishop Williamson takes the interviewer to be a man of good faith and intelligence so "I told him the truth." Out of his deep charity, the Bishop once again shows himself vulnerable to thinking often too well of people. When the camera stops rolling, His Excellency goes to two members of the television team and asks them to please be discreet about what he has said. They make no promises. Ali Fagan will later boast that they got away from the seminary with the tapes, suggesting a deliberate trap had been set.

2008
The SSPX forms an association with Corporation Lawyer Maximilian Krah. He offers legal assistance to the SSPX and joins the board of Della Sarto, Inc., which manages the assets of the SSPX.

Veritas *Variations*

JANUARY 17, 2009

Bishop Fellay receives from Cardinal Castrillón Hoyos a copy of the official Decree, dated January 21, lifting the "excommunications."

JANUARY 21, 2009

Swedish Television broadcasts only the final minutes of the interview, making clear their original malevolent intention. The timing is clearly meant to undermine the lifting of the "excommunications."

JANUARY 21, 1586

Father Edward Strancham and Father Nicolas Woodfen, martyred at Tyburn.

JANUARY 21, 1642

Father Thomas Reynolds and Alban Roe, Order of St. Benedict, martyred at Tyburn.

LATE JANUARY, 2009

Lawyer Maximilian Krah telephones Bishop Williamson in Argentina and informs him that the remarks made in the interview are blowing up. The Bishop responds, "Oh, dear, . . . sure enough. You cannot expect any more from journalists." The lawyer will later use these words to claim that Williamson knew what he was "in for" when he responded to the interviewer's question. Bishop Williamson will deny that assertion, saying he should have known better, but did not at the time. He was asked a question and he responded truthfully.

JANUARY 27, 2009

Bishop Bernard Fellay: "[I]t must remain clear that those comments do not reflect in any way the attitude of our community. That is why I have forbidden Bishop Williamson to issue any public opinion on any political or historical matter until further notice."

The Voice of the Trumpet

St. Paul: "I speak the truth in Christ. I lie not, my conscience bearing me witness in the Holy Ghost that I have great sadness and continual sorrow in my heart. For I wished myself to be an anathema from Christ for my brethren . . . " (Rom. 9: 1–3).

JANUARY 28, 2009

Bishop Williamson writes to Cardinal Castrillón Hoyos:

> Your Eminence,
>
> Amidst the tremendous media storm stirred up by imprudent remarks of mine on Swedish television, I beg of you to accept, only as is properly respectful, my sincere regrets for having caused to yourself and to the Holy Father so much unnecessary distress and problems.
>
> For me, all that matters is Truth Incarnate, and the interests of His one true Church, through which alone we can save our souls and give eternal glory, in our little way, to Almighty God. So I have only one comment, from the prophet Jonas, 1, 12:
>
> "Take me up and throw me into the sea; then the sea will quiet down for you; for I know it is because of me that this great tempest has come upon you."
>
> Please also accept, and convey to the Holy Father, my sincere personal thanks for the document signed last Wednesday and made public on Saturday. Most humbly I will offer a Mass for both of you.
>
> Sincerely yours in Christ
> +Richard Williamson

JANUARY 29, 2009

The BBC reports that the Chief Rabbinate of Jerusalem has broken off all official ties with the Vatican. He expects Bishop Williamson to publicly retract his remarks before links can be renewed.

JANUARY 29, 2009

Official Vatican Spokesman Federico Lombardi states:

Veritas *Variations*

"[W]hoever denies the Shoah knows nothing of the mystery of God or the Cross of Christ."

FEBRUARY 4, 2009

That Vatican announces that Bishop Richard Williamson must absolutely and publicly distance himself from his positions on the Holocaust or he will not be allowed to serve as a Catholic bishop.

Had he denied the Immaculate Conception, or the Virgin Birth, or Our Lord's Miracles, or the Resurrection or the Ascension of Our Lord, or Our Lady's Assumption, as have many princes of the Church, the Bishop could have remained in good standing. The Vatican of the "New Springtime" holds firm to a few modernist dogmas and the imprudent Bishop had denied one of the most sacred.

FEBRUARY 4, 2009

Note from the Secretariat of State concerning the four prelates of the Society of St. Pius X:

> [T]he Decree of the Congregation for Bishops, dated 21 January 2009, was an act by which the Holy Father responded benevolently to repeated requests from the Superior General of the Society of Saint Pius X . . . . His Holiness desired to remove an impediment which was prejudicial to the opening of a door to dialogue. He now awaits a corresponding gesture from the four bishops expressing total adherence to the doctrine and discipline of the Church . . . . A full recognition of the Second Vatican Council and the Magisterium of Popes John XXIII, Paul VI, John Paul I, John Paul II and Benedict XVI himself is an indispensable condition for any future recognition of the Society of Saint Pius X.

Archbishop Lefebvre: "No practical agreement without a doctrinal agreement."

FEBRUARY, 2009

The world press blasts the opinion of a single individual on a detail in secular history into a world-shattering event. The rage against the modern secular apostate crescendos. Crowds of reporters surround the La Reja Seminary in Argentina. The Seminary becomes a fortress, with the Rector and the seminarians imprisoned inside. As the howls from the media mouths increase, Bishop Fellay listens with trepidation to the cacophony of frenzied caterwauling. He sends Father Pfluger, a believer in the "holocaust," to Argentina. The envoy relates the frightening effect the remarks could have on the SSPX in Germany, the fear of colleagues, the loss of chapels, the closure of schools. The Argentinian government, claiming entry irregularities for the British citizen, demands Bishop Williamson leave the country.

FEBRUARY 9, 2009

Bishop Williamson speaks out of the whirlwind to the German magazine *Der Spiegel*. The magazine prefaces the interview with the statement that the Bishop's "denial of the Holocaust has done serious damage to the Catholic Church."

> Williamson: "Throughout my life, I have always sought the truth. That is why I converted to Catholicism and became a priest. And now I can only say something, the truth of which I am convinced. Because I realize that there are many honest and intelligent people who think differently, I must now review the historical evidence once again. I said the same thing in my interview with Swedish television: Historical evidence is at issue, not emotions. And if I find this evidence, I will correct myself...."
>
> *Spiegel*: "Your position on Judaism is consistently anti-Semitic."
>
> Williamson: "St. Paul put it this way: The Jews are

Veritas *Variations*

beloved for the sake of Our Father, but they are our enemies for the sake of the gospel."

Spiegel: "Do you seriously intend to use Catholic tradition and the Bible to justify your anti-Semitism?"

Williamson: "Anti-Semitism means many things today, for instance, when one criticizes the Israeli actions in the Gaza Strip. The Church has always understood the definition of anti-Semitism to be the rejection of Jews because of their Jewish roots. This is condemned by the Church. Incidentally, this is self-evident in a religion whose founders and all important individuals in its early history were Jews. But it was also clear, because of the large numbers of Jewish Christians in early Christianity, that all men need Christ for their salvation – all men, including the Jews"

FEBRUARY 20, 2009

From the *Jewish Telegraphic Agency*:

> Fifty Catholic Democrats in the U.S. House of Representatives pressed Pope Benedict XVI to fully repudiate the views of a Holocaust-denying bishop.
>
> "Your Holiness Pope Benedict XVI, As Catholic Members of Congress, we are writing to express our deep concerns with your decision to reinstate Bishop Richard Williamson to communion with the Catholic Church at the same time that Bishop Williamson publicly denies that the Holocaust occurred or that such was the policy under Adolf Hitler," they wrote in a letter sent last month after Williamson's reinstatement was announced. "We do not question your reasons for revoking the excommunication of Bishop Williamson or your right to do so, but we fail to understand why the revocation was not accompanied by an emphatic public rejection of his denial of the Holocaust...."
>
> The letter was spearheaded by U.S. Reps William Delahunt (D-Mass.) and Rosa DeLauro (D-Conn.), who is married to Stanley Greenberg, a leading Dem-

ocratic pollster who is active in Pro-Israel circles....

These "Catholic Members of Congress" hold no such "deep concerns" over the slaughter of innocent children in the womb, nor has any condemnation against them come from Rome.

FEBRUARY 20, 1592

Father Thomas Pormort, martyred in St. Paul's Churchyard, London.

FEBRUARY 25, 2009

Bishop Williamson, seeking anonymity and avoiding the piranha press by wearing a baseball cap and dark glasses, arrives at the Buenos Aires airport to depart for England. The wall-eyed febrile man-eaters spot him and swarm about him, shouting questions, circling for a kill, ready to feast on his person, hoping for headlines. One television reporter surges forward with bared microphone, demanding a scoop; an episcopal fist is raised in the intruder's face, and the object of the feeding frenzy pushes past, sending the media minnow into a pole. This "big catch" makes the headline splash for the day.

As the SSPX speedily distances itself from their media star of the hour, Father Morgan, District Superior for England, arranges for protectors to guard the Bishop when he arrives in London and to see that he travels safely to the Society House in Wimbledon where he will take refuge. Also meeting him at the London airport is Lady Michele Renouf who has brought with her a legal team to defend the Bishop should an attempt be made to detain him at the airport.

FEBRUARY 26, 2009

A second public statement from Bishop Williamson:

> The Holy Father and my Superior, Bishop Bernard

Fellay, have requested that I reconsider remarks I made on Swedish television four months ago, because their consequences have been so heavy.

Observing these consequences I can truthfully say that I regret having made such remarks, and that if I had known beforehand the full harm and hurt to which they would give rise, especially to the Church, but also to survivors and relatives of victims of injustice under the Third Reich, I would not have made them.

On Swedish television I gave only the opinion ("I believe . . . " "I believe . . . ") of a non-historian, an opinion formed 20 years ago on the basis of evidence then available, and rarely expressed in public since.

However, the events of recent weeks and the advice of senior members of the Society of St. Pius X have persuaded me of my responsibility for much distress caused. To all souls that took honest scandal from what I said, before God I apologize.

As the Holy Father has said, every act of unjust violence against one man hurts all mankind.

+Richard Williamson

London, 26 February, 2009

FEBRUARY 26, 1607

Father Robert Drury, martyred at Tyburn.

FEBRUARY 27, 1601

Father Mark Barkworth, Father Roger Filcock, and Anne Line, widow, martyred at Tyburn.

Shakespeare's poem "The Phoenix and the Turtle," published in 1601, very likely memorializes the holy love of Anne Line and her husband Roger Line. Roger Line's Catholic devotion resulted in his banishment to Flanders where he died in 1594. The poem may have been recited following the secret Requiem Mass held for the widow, martyred for harboring a priest, or may have been written to memorialize that ceremony. It concludes with a beautiful "Threnos," a song of lamentation.

> Beauty, truth, and rarity,
> Grace in all simplicity,
> Here enclosed in cinders lie.
> Death is now the phoenix' nest,
> And the turtle's loyal breast
> To eternity doth rest,
> Leaving no posterity;
> 'Twas not their infirmity,
> It was married chastity.
> Truth may seem, but cannot be;
> Beauty brag, but 'tis not she;
> Truth and beauty buried be.
> To this urn let those repair
> That are either true or fair;
> For these dead birds sigh a prayer.

FEBRUARY 28, 2009

Lady Renouf in an interview with a reporter for the *Daily Telegraph*, states: "[O]ur concern is not Holocaust denial but debate denial. People should have freedom to question the accepted view of what happened. That questioning is part of our culture."

The Bishop some years later remarks,

> If the SSPX in Germany had stood tall, they would have rallied many Germans, Catholics and non-Catholics; they would have rallied them to the Catholic flag by standing for Truth. The price to pay may well have been the loss of chapels and schools, but the Truth is more important than buildings . . . it is the Jewish world view against the Catholic world view. The SSPX have no alternative to teaching the "holocaust" in SSPX schools in Germany or we lose the schools. I say the SSPX might have made a breakthrough. The Catholic

Church got credit for one minute with large numbers of souls all over the world because one dumb Catholic Bishop told a bit of truth.

MARCH 10, 2009

Letter of Pope Benedict XVI to the Bishops of the Catholic Church:

> [A]n unforeseen mishap for me was the fact that the Williamson case came on top of the remission of the excommunication. The discreet gesture of mercy toward four bishops ordained validly but not legitimately suddenly appeared as something completely different: as the repudiation of reconciliation between Christians and Jews, and thus the reversal of what the Council had laid down in this regard to guide the Church's path. A gesture of reconciliation with an ecclesial group engaged in a process of separation thus turned into its very antithesis: an apparent step backwards with regard to all the steps of reconciliation between Christians and Jews taken since the Council – steps which my own work as a theologian had sought from the beginning to take part in and support.... I was saddened by the fact that even Catholics who, after all, might have had a better knowledge of the situation, thought they had to attack me with open hostility. Precisely for this reason I thank all the more our Jewish friends, who quickly helped to clear up the misunderstanding and to restore the atmosphere of friendship and trust which – as in the days of Pope John Paul II – has also existed throughout my pontificate and, thank God, continues to exist.

OCTOBER 25, 2009

A German court in Regensburg holds a hearing on the Williamson case. The court finds him guilty of "Holocaust denial" and the female judge fines Bishop Williamson 12,000 Euros. The Bishop appeals.

<u>OCTOBER 25, 1415</u>

English forces in France facing insurmountable odds win a great victory at the Battle of Agincourt.

> This day is called the Feast of Crispian.
> He that outlives this day and comes safe home
> Will stand a-tiptoe when this day is named
> And rouse him at the name of Crispian.
> He that shall see this day and live old age
> Will yearly on the vigil feast his neighbors
> And say, "Tomorrow is Saint Crispian."
> Then will he strip his sleeve and show his scars
> And say, "These wounds I had on Crispin's Day."
> Old men forget; yet all shall be forgot,
> But he'll remember with advantages
> What feats he did that day. Then shall our names,
> Familiar in his mouth as household words –
> Harry the King, Bedford and Exeter,
> Warwick and Talbot, Salisbury and Gloucester –
> Be in their flowing cups freshly remembered.
> This story shall the good man teach his son;
> And Crispin Crispian shall ne'er go by,
> From this day to the ending of the world,
> But we in it shall be remember-ed –
> We few, we happy few, we band of brothers,
> For he today that sheds his blood with me
> Shall be my brother; be he ne'er so vile
> This day shall gentle his condition.
> And gentleman in England now abed
> Shall think themselves accurst they were not here,
> And hold their manhoods cheap whiles any speaks
> Who fought with us upon Saint Crispin's Day.

Henry V (4.3.40–67).

Veritas *Variations*

NOVEMBER 9, 2009
Regensburg court rules that Williamson must stand trial for inciting "racial hatred."

NOVEMBER 9, 1610
Father George Nappier martyred at Oxford.

NOVEMBER 13, 2009
Doctrinal discussions begin in Rome between theologians from the SSPX and representatives from the Vatican.

JANUARY 12, 2010
SSPX lawyer Maximilian Krah receives permission from Bishop Fellay to bring two *Der Spiegel* reporters from Germany to Wimbledon to interview Bishop Williamson . . . again. Lawyer Krah seeks to "coach" Williamson before the proposed interview. A priest residing in the District House researches articles written by the two reporters who will arrive the next day at the house and leaves the material for the Bishop to read in the morning.

JANUARY 13, 2010
Williamson reads the material and realizes the reporters are left-wingers and anti-Catholic. Remembering the distortions in the earlier *Spiegel* interview, he informs Krah not to come with the reporters. Krah ignores the Bishop's wishes and arrives at the SSPX District House with the two reporters. Williamson refuses to speak with them.

FEBRUARY 1, 2010
The reporters publish an article for *Spiegel* headlined: "Embarrassment for the Catholic Church: BISHOP WILLIAMSON UNREPENTENT IN HOLOCAUST DENIAL."

The journalists report that "Both the obstinate bishop's refusal to abandon his preposterous Holocaust theories and the trial in Regensburg are as embarrassing to the SSPX as they are to the Vatican, which is currently in direct talks with the fundamentalists.... Left-leaning and liberal theologians like Hans Küng have spent their lives dreaming in vain of such an encounter."

From the article, "Bishop Bernard Fellay, the Superior General of the SSPX, likens Bishop Williamson to uranium: 'It's dangerous when you have it', he says, 'but you simply can't leave it by the side of the road'.... Bishop Fellay, Williamson's Superior, looks distressed as he sits in his office at Schwandegg in Menzingen, Switzerland. He fervently hopes 'that Williamson won't explode.... We have lost one of our four bishops.... We can't use him for anything any more.' He is struggling with himself and history, trying to find the right words and the appropriate amount of distance to the matter. He finds the whole thing 'incredibly unpleasant,' and says that he had believed that 'the bishop had understood things better in the meantime.' But unfortunately Williamson did not understand. Fellay says his personal belief is that the Holocaust is 'obviously' a fact.... On the other hand, the whole debate has had its advantages. Because of Williamson, the SSPX has acquired a level of notoriety unprecedented since its establishment in 1969 by the renegade French Archbishop Marcel Lefebvre. Ultra-conservatives have always loved the Pius Brothers, and now they are becoming heroes of the right-wing, anti-modernist movement. What should a Superior General like Fellay do about this? 'We have an appeal for extremists, whom we don't even want,' says Fellay, for whom questions of faith are ultimately the most important issues."

In the same article, Fr. Pfluger refers to Bishop Williamson as a "ticking time bomb" and suggests that the man has been suffering from Parkinson's disease for many years.

Veritas *Variations*

FEBRUARY 1, 1645

Father Henry Morse, martyred at Tyburn.

Father Morse's dying words: "Come, my sweetest Jesu, that I may be inseparably united to Thee in time and in eternity. Welcome ropes, hurdles, gibbets, knives and butchery. Welcome for the love of Jesus my Saviour."

APRIL 10, 2010

L'Osservatore Romano, page one:

> It's true [the Beatles] took drugs, lived life to excess because of their success, even said they were bigger than Jesus and put out mysterious messages that were possibly even Satanic . . . . They may not have been the best example for the youth of the day but they were by no means the worst. Their beautiful melodies changed music and continue to give pleasure . . . . Forty years later the Beatles still astound with their originality and they are a consolation against the continual assault on music lovers by the record industry.

Pope Benedict XVI approved the commentary.

FEBRUARY 7, 2018

Jazz musician Quincy Jones:

> [The Beatles] were the worst musicians in the world . . . . Paul was the worst bass player I ever heard. And Ringo? Don't even talk about it.

APRIL 16, 2010

Full hearing in German court on the "Williamson case." Bishop Fellay tells Bishop Williamson not to attend as his presence would result in a media circus and further shake the SSPX in Germany; Williamson obeys. Lawyer Krah has chosen as Williamson's defense attorney Matthias Lossmann, a liberal whom Williamson characterizes as "left of the Green Party." The Bishop does call his lawyer conscientious and kind, saying that Lossmann behaves decently at the hearing; however, Lossmann states before the court that he "believes in the Holocaust," and consequently defends his client without strong conviction. Maximilian Krah takes the stand as the main defense witness and defends the SSPX rather than Williamson, labelling the Bishop a typical British eccentric and suggesting that while the Bishop would not deliberately lie, his ability to perceive the truth is severely impaired. The court in Regensburg, the home of Pope Benedict XVI, finds the Bishop guilty of inciting racial hatred, but reduces the fine to 10,000 Euros.

MARCH 22, 1991

The SSPX learns that Archbishop Lefebvre has lost his appeal to the French court in a case brought against him by LICRA (*Ligue Internationale Contre le Racisme et l'Antisémitisme*). The priests decide not to inform the dying man. Three days later the Archbishop dies, never knowing he has been convicted of "racism" and "antisemitism" by a court of his native land. To assert in public hard truths and the rights of Christ the King in a Christ-hating age is to be nailed to a modern legal gibbet – as in the case of the spiritual father and that of his spiritual heir.

NOVEMBER 15, 2010

The German court after learning that the Bishop has appealed the April ruling sets November 29 for another hearing. The Bishop finds a more energetic defense attorney, Wolfgang Nahrath from Berlin, an advocate who holds similar views on the historical event that has caused the uproar. Matthias Lossmann refuses to work with lawyer Nahrath and the media erupts yet again, accusing the Bishop of hiring a "neo-Nazi" to defend him,

Veritas Variations

an obvious bit of nonsensical exaggeration as any actual "neo-Nazi" would not be practicing law in Berlin but would be serving time in a German prison.

NOVEMBER 19, 2010

Bishop Fellay, learning mid-week of the new lawyer and shaken by the new media hubbub, orders Williamson to drop Nahrath as his attorney or face expulsion from the SSPX. He even sends an SSPX priest who is a close friend of the Bishop to appeal to him to change his mind and find another lawyer. The Bishop, facing the choice of staying in the SSPX by accepting a "namby-pamby" new lawyer or keeping a strong defense attorney and being expelled from the SSPX, "my family, my life," agrees to drop Nahrath as his lawyer. On this Friday of the same week, the Bishop tells his priest friend that Nahrath will be replaced, informs Nahrath of the decision and e-mails Bishop Fellay that he has complied with the order and will find a new attorney. Bishop Fellay responds the same day to the e-mail thanking Williamson and saying the SSPX will have no problem with paying the fine.

NOVEMBER 20, 2010

On Saturday morning, Bishop Fellay, knowing that Williamson has dropped Nahrath, issues the following press release:

> On November 20, 2010, the General Headquarters of the Society of Saint Pius X published the following communication concerning the Bishop Richard Williamson's appeal to the court of Regensburg, which was to take place on November 29. The Superior General, Bishop Bernard Fellay, has learnt by the press of Bishop Richard Williamson's decision, just ten days before his trial, to dismiss the lawyer charged with his defense, in favor of a lawyer who is openly affiliated to

The Voice of the Trumpet

the so-called neo-Nazi movement in Germany, and to other such groups. Bishop Fellay has given Bishop Williamson a formal order to go back on this decision and to not allow himself to become an instrument of political theses that are completely foreign to his mission as a Catholic bishop serving the Society of Saint Pius X.

Disobedience to this order would result in Bishop Williamson being expelled from the Society of Saint Pius X.

Menzingen, November 20 of 2010

A new lawyer is engaged and the date for the hearing is delayed. The new advocate tells Williamson that he must now go before the court and say that he believes in the "holocaust." Williamson refuses and another lawyer is sought. Edgar Weiler and his son Benjamin agree to be attorneys for the defense and Bishop Fellay approves. He also says that Williamson may attend the trial. At ordinations in Écône before the trial, rescheduled for July 11, 2011, the Bishop tells a good young German priest that he has not yet decided whether or not to appear for the hearing. The young priest simply appeals, "Please don't . . . ," and that decides the issue. Williamson does not attend the trial.

Father and son lawyers Weiler work diligently for their client and begin preparing a strong and appropriate defense.

DECEMBER 27, 2010

In an interview in New Caledonia with the publication *Les Nouvelles Calédoniennes*, Bishop Fellay states,

> the Pope returns to traditional ideas. He sees very well that there is a deviation and that he must correct it. We are perhaps a little closer to the Pope than it seems . . . . Anyway, the Pope said that it is only a problem of canonical discipline. An act by Rome will suffice to say

Veritas *Variations*

it is finished and we will return to the Church. It will come. I am very optimistic.

WINTER, 2010–2011

Bishop Fellay orders Bishop Williamson to shut down the weekly *Eleison Comments* e-mails.

Bishop Williamson asks why there is a problem. The weekly Letters are

> a little voice of truth in a world of lies. A number of souls find the short weekly letter a help to their faith and to their world view. To defend the downtown, you must defend the suburbs. If you lose the suburbs, you lose the downtown; the suburbs are the world view, the downtown is the faith. The *Eleison Comments* attempt to present a harmonized, integrated faith and world view that is politically incorrect on many points, but which present in this gigantic crisis of the faith, the Church and the world, a little voice needed by a number of souls. The faith of these souls and their eternal salvation is more important than an order even from a legitimate superior.

The Bishop says he fears Bishop Fellay does not understand, but asks Bishop Fellay to please inform him, the author of the Letters, which specific letters have been particularly objectionable. Bishop Fellay never responds to this request.

JULY 10, 2011

The doctrinal discussions with Rome having concluded, Bishop Alfonso de Galarreta, one of the participants, issues *Reflections about the Roman Proposal*. He states that Rome's offers to the SSPX were

> confusing, misleading, false and essentially bad . . . . Given the circumstances, it is certain that at the end,

after long discussions, we arrive at absolutely nothing.... There is no change in the doctrinal point of view from Rome that would justify ours. On the contrary, the discussions have shown they will not accept anything in our criticisms. It would be absurd for us to go in the direction of a practical agreement after the result of discussions and findings.... Such an approach would show a serious diplomatic weakness on the part of the Fraternity, and indeed, more than diplomatic. It would be a lack of consistency, honesty and firmness, which would have effects like loss of credibility and moral authority we enjoy. The mere fact of going down this path will lead us to distrust and division.

Archbishop Lefebvre: "We do not agree; it is a dialogue of death."

JULY 11, 2011

The ruling of the lower court of Regensburg is upheld. The fine is reduced to 6,500 Euros.

OCTOBER, 2011

Bishop Fellay meets with the superiors of the SSPX in Albano, Italy to discuss the status of negotiations with Rome. Bishop Fellay excludes Bishop Williamson from the meeting because of Williamson's refusal to shut down the *Eleison Comments*.

FEBRUARY 22, 2012

On appeal, the German higher court dismisses the conviction of Bishop Williamson on the grounds that the charges were "inadequately drawn up."

APRIL 7, 2012

Bishops Alfonso de Galarreta. Bernard Tissier de Mallerais, and Richard Williamson send a letter to the General Council of the SSPX, of which they are not members. In the letter, soon speeding across the Internet, the three Bishops express their opposition to a proposed Roman

Veritas *Variations*

proposal for a practical agreement with the Society. They reassert the fact that the doctrinal discussions from 2009 to 2011 have made clear that no doctrinal agreement is possible with a Rome still entrenched in the confusion, ambiguities and errors of the Second Vatican Council. In their letter of protest and warning, they quote the words of the Founder who feared present-day Rome only

> maneuvers to separate us from the largest number of faithful possible. This is the perspective in which they seem to be always giving a little more and always going very far. We must absolutely convince our faithful that it is no more than a maneuver, that it is dangerous to put oneself into the hands of Conciliar bishops and Modernist Rome. It is the greatest danger threatening our people. If we have struggled for twenty years to avoid the Conciliar errors, it is not in order, now, to put ourselves in the hands of those professing these errors.

The letter concludes by asking those in authority to "listen again to your Founder. He was right 25 years ago. He is still right today. On his behalf, we entreat you: do not engage the Society in a purely practical agreement."

APRIL 7, 1595

Fathers Alexander Rawlins and Henry Walpole, martyred at York.

APRIL 7, 1606

Father Edward Oldcorne and lay-brother Ralph Ashley, martyred at Worcester.

APRIL 13, 1642

Fathers John Lockwood (age 87) and Edmund Catherick (age 35), martyred at York.

Father Lockwood, having studied at Douay and Rheims and ordained at Rome, was sent to England where he offered the sacraments in secret for 44 years to persecuted Catholics. On arriving at the gallows he gave money to the two "priest-catchers" who had uncovered him and thanked them for bringing him "to this happy place." Seeing that the younger priest Father Catherick displayed signs of fear at the prospect of being the first to be hanged, old Father Lockwood insisted, "The place is mine, I am his senior by many years, and therefore with leave I challenge it as my right to mount the ladder first." He then, according to an eyewitness, exhorted Father Catherick to be courageous and said, "O let us run in spirit to our Savior in the Garden, and call upon Him in his Agony and bloody sweat." He then tried to climb the steps to the gallows but failed due to his infirmity and age. He excused himself to the onlookers with a smile and said such a climb was "hard service for an old man of four score and seven." Two men coming forward helped him up the stairs and he thanked them and gave them a shilling each. He looked below to Father Catherick and asked how he felt and the younger cleric answered, "In good heart and ready to follow, strengthened by God's grace and your good example." Father Lockwood was hanged, followed immediately by Father Catherick. The court's sentence demanded that the priests be "drawn and quartered" after the hanging. The executioner scrupled at the butcherly part, and for a time flatly refused it; he even threatened to hang himself rather than carry out the full sentence. He was finally persuaded by "a wicked woman" in the crowd and "like a madman" disemboweled and quartered the martyred priest, cutting the entrails to bits and flinging them into the crowd. Father Lockwood's severed head was fixed on the north gate of York Castle, near the King's palace. King Charles I could not exit his palace without viewing the old martyr's now lifeless "dome of Thought, palace of the Soul." The King's own head would soon be removed by an act of Parliament.

Veritas *Variations*

APRIL 14, 2012

The General Council – Bishop Bernard Fellay, Fathers Niklaus Pfluger and Alain-Marc Nély – responds to the letter from the Bishops, saying their letter "is lacking in supernatural spirit and in realism." The responders wonder "if you still believe that the visible Church with its seat in Rome is truly the Church of Our Lord Jesus Christ.... One has the impression that you are so scandalized that you no longer accept that that could still be true." They say the reality is that "the present situation in April of 2012 is very different from that of 1988 .... one may observe a change of attitude in the Church, helped by the gestures and acts of Benedict XVI towards Tradition."

Archbishop Lefebvre: "[T]hey [Conciliar Rome] seem to be always giving a little more and always going very far."

Perhaps the most interesting words in the response are the following: "You cannot know how much your attitude over the last few months – quite different for each of you – has been hard for us. It has prevented the Superior General from sharing with you these great concerns, which he would gladly have brought you in to, had he not found himself faced with such a strong and passionate lack of understanding." Opposition becomes "lack of understanding"; the Superior General's desire to find common ground with Modernist Rome dating back to 1998 and his approval for Fr. Lorans to engage in "talks" to reach a resolution has become "the last few months"; the comments make clear that the Superior General has for many years engaged in negotiations in the dark, keeping secret from his three fellow Bishops his work toward finding an "agreement" with the Conciliar authorities.

APRIL 15, 2012

Bishop Fellay presents a Doctrinal Preamble to Rome on behalf of the SSPX.

Among many curiosities, the Preamble contains the following:

> [I[t is legitimate to promote through legitimate discussion the study and theological explanations of the expressions and formulations of Vatican II and of the Magisterium which followed it, in the case where they don't appear reconcilable with the previous Magisterium of the Church.

A practical agreement is possible *before* a doctrinal agreement. Such discussions would *not* be "a dialogue of death." Archbishop Lefebvre is thrown under the bus.

It is *not* "absurd for us to go in the direction of a practical agreement after the result of our [doctrinal] discussions and findings." Bishop de Galarreta is thrown under the bus.

Bishop Williamson has not been informed of the Doctrinal Preamble ahead of its submission to Rome.

MAY 25, 2012

Father François Chazal:

> I remember asking Bishop Fellay in Cebu, before Assisi III, if he could make some big statement and gesture, like the Archbishop did for Assisi I. All I got was an angry NO, on account of our work of dealing with Rome now. Just as we are nice to Benedict XVI, good priests and bishops resisting reconciliation are facing growing threats, a perfect repeat of Vatican II: "If you don't agree with the official stance of the Society, leave the Society." Well, the duty of a priest of the Society is not necessarily to uphold the position of the Society, especially if it has just changed all of a sudden one good morning in May 2012. The duty of the priest of the Society is to protect the Catholic Faith, as long as the official Church is overrun by modernism.

Veritas *Variations*

JUNE 13, 2012

Bishop Fellay reports in the Summer 2012 SSPX internal document *Cor Unum* that

> [t]he 13 June interview with Cardinal Levada well and truly confirmed that the Vatican has proposed for us "a canonical arrangement" based on "my letter of 14 April 2012" whereby "we would have to say at the same time that we were in agreement and not in agreement." This extremely delicate letter seems to have been approved by the Pope and the Cardinals.

Modernist agreement: $2 + 2 = 4$ *and* $2 + 2 = 5$. "To be *and* not to be...."

The document delivered to Bishop Fellay by Cardinal Levada on June 13 contains additional demands joined with the original text, reportedly added by Pope Benedict XVI, regarding the Magisterium, Vatican II and the Mass of Paul VI. The new demands make acceptance impossible. The Vatican, fully aware of the April 7 letter from the three other SSPX Bishops, knows now that sweeping up all of the Society into their conciliar net will not be possible; Bishop Fellay knows that the added requirements make a consensus with the SSPX impossible.

JUNE 13, 1573

Father Thomas Woodhouse, martyred at Tyburn.

During his time in the Fleet prison, awaiting execution, Father Woodhouse wrote papers persuading men of the true faith, signed his name, tied them to stones and threw them out of the prison window into the street.

JUNE 17, 2012

Bishop Fellay writes to Pope Benedict XVI:

> Unfortunately, in the current context of the Society,

the new declaration will not be accepted . . . . I committed myself, despite rather strong opposition within the ranks of the Society, and at the expense of significant troubles. And I do intend to continue to make every effort to pursue this path in order to arrive at the necessary clarifications . . . . May your Holiness deign to believe my filial devotion and dearest desire to serve Holy Church.

Father Olivier Rioult, *The Impossible Reconciliation*, 2013, p. 39.

JULY 11-14, 2012

General Chapter Meeting of the SSPX. Participants vote 29-6 in support of Bishop Fellay's decision to exclude Bishop Williamson from the meeting.

LATE AUGUST, 2012

At the request of Traditional Catholics in Brazil, Bishop Williamson travels to the Monastery of Santa Cruz to confirm and to give conferences; he does not first request approval from Bishop Fellay.

SEPTEMBER 3, 2012 - FEAST OF ST. PIUS X

> HONOR AND GLORY TO BP. WILLIAMSON
> Dom Thomas Aquino
>
> In this dramatic moment in the life of the Holy Church, a moment in which the Faith is most gravely threatened, an episcopal voice rises and confirms the faithful in the faith of their Baptism. Whose is this voice but the Bishop persecuted, slandered, accused of rebellion, etc., etc., etc.? And why is he persecuted, slandered, accused? Precisely because he defends the Faith and this crime has no forgiveness in the modern world. The modern world accepts everything; it even accepts Tradition, as long as that Tradition accepts the modern world. The modern world is a highly concentrated solvent. It accepts everything it can dissolve,

except the indissoluble Catholic Faith, except the integral, pure and immaculate Catholic doctrine, and this is what is at stake in this dramatic moment for Tradition. Are we going to divide the Faith as Solomon proposed to the two women vying for a child? Modernist Rome says: "Yes, let's divide the Faith, let's do a bargain. Why not?" Bishop Williamson says: "No, non possumus," and we are with him: "Non possumus!." Like Saint Peter we say to the Pharisees: "We cannot stop preaching in the name of Our Lord Jesus Christ! Judge yourselves whether it is better to obey God than men." The child must live, as in the judgment of Solomon. In the present case, it is not the child who should live, but the mother, Our Mother the Holy Church. To divide her by giving a piece to the modernists and a piece to the traditionalists? Never!

For all these reasons we say and proclaim: "Honor and glory to Bishop Williamson and to all priests who defend the Faith without compromise with the enemies of the Catholic Faith." Some may be scandalized by the mere fact of speaking about enemies in this terrible battle. If this is your case, dear reader, remember that the Church here on earth is called militant, because it militates against three cruel enemies, as states the *Catechism of the Council of Trent*, which are the devil, the world and the flesh. Also remember the prayer: "By the sign of the Holy Cross, deliver us, from our enemies, O Lord our God." Remember also the words of St. Pius X, whom we celebrate today. The enemies of the Church are currently in the veins of the same Church.

These enemies are in Rome, unfortunately, this Rome that wants to make a deal with Tradition, i.e., the modernist Rome which wants to make a deal with eternal Rome. To what end? Even if the intention in the heart of Benedict XVI is not known, it is not difficult to know how all this will end if this agreement (whose bitter fruits are already being felt, even before completion) takes place. The fruit, which already can be seen, is the silence of Tradition, but as St. Gregory the Great said, "The Church would rather die than be silent." Then She, the real mother, will not shut up, will not make this shameful agreement, but will continue to speak, preach and work for the salvation of their children. This is what the brave priests are doing, this is what Bishop Williamson is doing. For this reason we say: "Honor and glory to Bishop Williamson, successor to the Apostles and confessor of the Faith."

Honor and glory to the Bishop who administered 99 confirmations in eight days and directed his apostolic word fifteen times to different audiences, which together represent more than 300 people in this vast Brazil, evangelized by the Portuguese and now by a Bishop from the former "island of saints."

Our Monastery of Santa Cruz and the faithful of Rio, Salvador, Vitoria, Campo Grande, Maringa and Novo Friburgo thank the solicitude of a true son of Archbishop Lefebvre, faithful to his teachings, who came to confirm, not only with the sacrament, but also with his deep understanding of revealed doctrine, of the modern errors and of the medicine for today's illness, among which stands out the Holy Rosary, which Bishop Williamson recommends the faithful pray every day. May the Virgin Mary obtain for us the grace to watch and pray to avoid falling into the temptation of agreements and to defeat the infernal serpent that wants to destroy Tradition.

OCTOBER 4, 2012

The deadline having passed by which time Bishop Williamson was to declare his submission to his superiors, a submission meaning he would no longer speak in public or offer the sacraments without specific approval, the Superior General and the General Council expel him from the Society of St. Pius X. In their public statement issued subsequently they quote Archbishop Lefebvre: "This is the destruction of all authority. How can authority be

Veritas *Variations*

exercised if it needs to ask all members to participate in the exercise of authority?"

In his comments, the Archbishop obviously refers to the dissolution of authority in the Conciliar Church, an authority he himself would ignore for the sake of a higher good – the Traditions of the Faith in its doctrines and highest truths. Bishop Williamson some years later would offer comments that shine a clear light back on the feeble excuse used for his expulsion: "Truth remains the purpose of Authority and Authority is not the purpose of Truth. Authority is the indispensable defender and guarantee of Truth, but it comes after Truth and not before." The Archbishop certainly would have agreed with the observations of his faithful disciple.

An offer is conveyed by the District Superior in England to Bishop Williamson that if he will shut down *Eleison Comments*, he will be given a pension and a residence "for a time." The Bishop asks for the promise in writing. His request is refused.

Bishop Williamson, after 36 years of service to the SSPX, is expelled without a pension or a place to reside.

OCTOBER, 2012 – DECEMBER, 2014

Bishop Williamson accepts an offer to take up residency at an apartment in Epsom, Surrey. The weekly *Eleison Comments* continue. The Bishop, now responsible for the first time in many decades for his own upkeep, dines regularly on bread and cheese, like the proverbial church mouse. The Scottish strand in his DNA has him saving for later, much like his used stationery and envelopes, used pasta water. He is advised for health reasons to discontinue drinking pasta water.

Over the next few years, the Bishop travels to France (five trips), the USA (four trips), Canada (two trips), Mexico (two trips), as well as Austria, India, Spain, and Brazil, continuing to give conferences ("teach all nations") and confirming ("baptising them in the name of the Father, Son and Holy Ghost").

OCTOBER 19, 2012

Bishop Williamson writes an "Open Letter to Bishop Fellay on an "Exclusion":

> The reasons you give for your decision to exclude your servant are, you tell me, the following: he has continued to publish the "Eleison Comments"; he has attacked the authorities of the Society; he has exercised an independent apostolate; he has given support to rebellious colleagues; he has been formally, obstinately and pertinaciously disobedient; he has separated himself from the Society; he no longer submits to any authority.
>
> May not all these reasons be summed up in disobedience? No doubt in the course of the last 12 years your servant has said and done things which before God were inappropriate and excessive, but I think it would be enough to point them out one by one for him to make the apology called for in all truth and justice. But we are no doubt agreed that the essential problem found in these details can be summed up in one word: disobedience.
>
> Then let us at once point out how many more or less disagreeable orders of the Superior General have been unfailingly obeyed by your servant. In 2003 he left behind an important and fruitful apostolate in the United States to go to Argentina. In 2009 he left his post as Seminary Rector and left behind Argentina to moulder in a London attic for three and a half years, with no episcopal functions because they were denied him. All that was left him by way of ministry was virtually the weekly "Eleison Comments," the refusal to interrupt which constitutes the large part of the "disobedience" of which he stands accused. And ever since 2009 it has been open season for the Society Superiors to discredit and insult him to their hearts' content. And Society members all over the world have been encouraged by

their example to do the same if they wished. Your servant hardly reacted, preferring silence to scandalous confrontations. One might go so far as to say that he obstinately refused to disobey. But let that go, because that is not the real problem....

[I]f the rebellious bishop took upon himself – for the first time in nigh on four years – an independent apostolate, how can he be blamed for having accepted an invitation, coming from outside the Society, to give the sacrament of Confirmation and to preach the word of truth? Is that not the very function of a bishop?...

So if he does seem for years to have been separating himself from the Society, the truth is that he has been distancing himself from the conciliatory Society, and not from that of the Archbishop. And if he seems insubordinate to any exercise of authority on the part of Society leaders, the truth is that that applies only to orders running counter to the purposes for which the Society was founded. In fact how many other orders are there at all, besides the order to close down the "Comments," which he can be blamed for having disobeyed in a "formal, obstinate and pertinacious" manner? Is there even one other such order? Since Archbishop Lefebvre refused to obey only acts of authority of Church leaders which were of a nature to destroy the Church, his disobedience was more apparent than real. Likewise refusing to close down the "Comments" is a disobedience more apparent then real....

In brief, your Excellency, you may now go ahead and exclude me, because the arguments above are not likely to persuade you, but the exclusion will be more apparent than real. I have been a member of the Archbishop's Society ever since my perpetual engagement. I have been one of its priests for over 36 years. I have been one of its bishops, like yourself, for nearly a quarter of a century. That is not all wiped out with one stroke of a pen. Member of the Archbishop's Society I therefore remain, and I wait....

The Voice of the Trumpet

OCTOBER 19, 1595

Philip Howard, Earl of Arundel, convert, dies in the Tower after ten years imprisonment.

As he lay dying, he requested of Queen Elizabeth that he be allowed to see his wife and children. "Good Queen Bess" responded, "If he will but once attend the Protestant Service, he will not only see his wife and children, but be restored to his honors and estates with every mark of royal favor." The Earl replied, "Tell Her majesty, if my religion be the cause for which I suffer, sorry I am that I have but one life to lose."

Inscription cut into the wall of the Tower by Philip Howard:

"The more affliction we endure for Christ in this world, the more glory we shall obtain with Christ in the next. To be bound on account of sin is a disgrace; but to sustain the bonds of prison for Christ's sake is the greatest glory."

JANUARY 16, 2013

Having had the conviction of Bishop Williamson dismissed on appeal by a Superior German Court on the grounds of an "inadequately drawn" charge, the prosecutors (persecutors) take the Bishop to court a second time and now win a conviction. Bishop Richard Williamson is again convicted of having incited "racial hatred." The fine is reduced to 1600 Euros as the convicted man is currently unemployed.

JANUARY 16, 2013

Cardinal Cañizares quoted in *Rome Reports*: "On one occasion, Bishop Fellay, who is the leader of St. Pius X, came to see me and said, 'We just came from an abbey that is near Florence. If Archbishop Lefebvre had seen how they celebrated there, he would not have taken the step that he did'.... The missal used was the Paul VI Missal in its strictest form."

Bishop Fellay responds by saying "a phrase has been badly interpreted."

MARCH 28, 2013

Bishop Williamson puts out a special *Eleison Comment* "Open Letter to the Priests of the Society of Society of St. Pius X":

> Reverend Fathers, whoever studies the [Doctrinal Declaration of 15 April] in the original text can only conclude that their author or authors have given up the Archbishop's fight for Tradition, and have gone over in their minds to Vatican II. Do you wish yourself and your flock to be moulded by such superiors?
>
> Nor let it be said that the first two and last three of the ten paragraphs are broadly taken from the Archbishop's own Protocol of 5 May 1988, so that the Declaration is faithful to him. It is well known that on 6 May he repudiated that Protocol because he himself recognized that it made too many concessions for the Society to be able to continue defending Tradition.
>
> Another error is to say that the danger is over because the Declaration has been "withdrawn" by the Superior General. The Declaration is the poisoned fruit of what has become a liberal mind-set at the top of the Society, and that mind-set has not been recognized, let alone retracted.... The problem is less the agreement than the desire of any agreement that will grant to the Society official recognition, and that desire is still very much there. Following the whole modern world and the Conciliar Church, the Society's leadership seems to have lost its grip on the primacy of truth, especially Catholic Truth.

MARCH 28, 1600

Father Christopher Wharton, martyred at York.

SEPTEMBER 23, 2013

Bishop Williamson refuses to pay the fine assessed by the court in January, 2013; he again appeals.

OCTOBER 12, 2013

Bishop Fellay speaks of Pope Francis as a Modernist: "We may not have the entire picture at this point, but we have enough to be scared to death."

DECEMBER 13, 2013

Bishop Fellay and his assistants travel to Rome at the request of the *Ecclesia Dei* Commission for a meeting. Following the meeting while lunching in the refectory of St. Martha's House, Archbishop Pozzo introduces Bishop Fellay to Pope Francis. Pope Francis says that he is glad to meet the Superior General of the SSPX; Bishop Fellay responds that he is praying a lot; Francis says, "Pray for me." Such is the extent of the impromptu meeting.

SPRING, 2014

With the generous assistance of benefactors, Bishop Williamson purchases a residence in Broadstairs, northeast Kent, England. In *Eleison Comments* CCCLXII, he describes it as "spacious . . . a delightful refuge, five minutes on foot from the sea which God created, and which the liberals cannot touch." Broadstairs and vicinity has hosted many famous folk, including the painter J.M.W. Turner, poet Samuel Taylor Coleridge of *Rime of the Ancient Mariner* fame, and T.S. Eliot, who wrote a section of the most influential poem of the twentieth century *The Waste Land* in nearby Margate. The most famous visitor was Charles Dickens, who not only enjoyed visiting Broadstairs but found the town by the sea a congenial place in which to write, turning out many pages of his most acclaimed novels there, including *The Pickwick Papers* and *David Copperfield*.

Veritas *Variations*

The Bishop admits only heaven knows how the house will be used in the future. The "Resistance," a small group of priests fighting to maintain the vision and the strength of Archbishop Lefebvre, are welcome at the aged three-story modest former hotel, and many visit. Many traditional Catholics, unhappy with the Bishop's recognition that present circumstances prevent the establishment of a new "Society" such as the Archbishop founded nearly half a century earlier, believe the Bishop refuses to fight through growth. The Bishop recognizes the impossibility of such action and supports the idea of an independent network of parishes, bound together by a common faith and a common cause. Even then, the protestant revolution, having permeated every aspect of worldly and spiritual life, continues to cause divisions even among those holding the Faith. As the conciliar Church pursues community and fellowship in the world with the supper table and the worship of man by man, the traditional movement fragments into quarreling small groups, each with its own solution to the Church's agony, and the squabbles and divisions separate believing soul from believing soul, creating Catholics divided by a common religion. Only God at this juncture can end the dissolution and restore His Church. In the meantime, Bishop Williamson teaches through the weekly letters and travels far and wide providing the sacraments.

<u>APRIL 10, 2014</u>

The National Court of Karlsruhe refuses Bishop Williamson's appeal, saying the appeal is not serious. The case reverts to the Court at Regensburg.

<u>APRIL 11, 1608</u>

Father George Gervase, martyred at Tyburn.

APRIL 24, 2014

The Court upholds the conviction as the review by the higher court "did not reveal any procedural errors" and so rejected the appeal. Bishop Williamson is convicted of "inciting racial hatred" and the fine of 1800 Euros remains in place. The Bishop has only a few days to make a last appeal to the European International Court of the Rights of Man in Strasbourg. He does so, and there the case remains, lodged in bureaucratic machinery.

JUNE 5, 2014

The *Australia Jewish News* alerts the Australian government authorities of a planned visit by Bishop Williamson to the Traditional Catholic communities in Australia. The Australian government leaps into action, cancelling the Bishop's visa.

SEPTEMBER 23, 2014

Officials of the Congregation for the Doctrine of the Faith meet with representatives of the SSPX. The Holy See Press Office reports: "[I]t was decided to proceed gradually and over a reasonable period of time in order to overcome difficulties and with a view to the envisioned full reconciliation."

SEPTEMBER 23, 1544

Father John Ireland, martyred at Tyburn.

   Archbishop Lefebvre: "No practical agreement without a doctrinal agreement."

MARCH 19, 2015 – FEAST OF SAINT JOSEPH, PATRON OF THE UNIVERSAL CHURCH

Bishop Richard Williamson consecrates Father Jean-Michel Faure in Novo Friburgo, Brazil, at the Monastery of Santa Cruz. On this occasion of being raised to the episcopacy, Fr. Faure, who left the SSPX in 2013 in disagreement with their movement toward Conciliar Rome, assumes the title first offered to him by Archbishop Lefebvre in 1988. At that time, Fr. Faure expressed gratitude to the Archbishop but refused the offer. Rome proclaims Bishop Williamson "automatically excommunicated" but, as His Excellency explains in the CDII *Eleison Comments*, "as in 1988 this declaration is false, because by Church Law whoever commits a punishable act does not incur the normal penalty, e.g. excommunication for consecrating a bishop without Rome's permission, if he acted *out of necessity*."

JUNE 28, 2015

Bishop Williamson provides the Sacrament of Confirmation in Mahopac, New York. Answering questions following a subsequent conference for the faithful, the Bishop responds to a woman who says that though she has the Traditional Mass on Sundays, on weekdays, trying hard to maintain her faith, she attends the *Novus Ordo Missae* said by a good priest; is she wrong to do so?

The Bishop's response is used as a cudgel by traditionalists opposing him; they claim he has asserted that one may attend the new mass.

Here are excerpts from his actual response to the question:

> There's the principle and there's the practice. In practice the New Mass is a key part of the new religion, which is a major part of the worldwide apostasy of today....
>
> Archbishop Lefebvre, in public, would say stay away. Keep away from the New Mass....
>
> In certain circumstances, like those you mentioned, exceptionally, if you're not going to scandalize anybody....
>
> The conclusion many of them [who see you attending] are going to come to is that the New Mass is okay....
>
> The principles are clear, and the wrongness of the

Novus Ordo mass is clear....

The Archbishop said if you want to look after your faith, stay away from the New Mass....

The new religion is false, and it strangles grace....

But I hope it is clear that I don't therefore say that the *Novus Ordo Missae* or the Novus Ordo religion are good; that's obviously not the case....

Generally, it's a tremendous danger because the new religion is very seductive . . . and it's easy to go with it and lose the faith....

Stay away from the Novus Ordo, but exceptionally, if you're watching and praying, even there you may find the grace of God....

But it does harm in itself, there's no doubt about it....

It's a rite designed to undermine the Catholic faith.

In response to the uproar his misreported and misunderstood comments unleashed, the Bishop in *Eleison Comments* CCCCLIIVI explains:

> The principle is clear in theory: to follow Our Lord we need, in the immortal words of St. Augustine, to "slay the errors but love the erring." That means that we should never so slay the errors as to also slay the erring (i.e. those who are in error, unless they are dangerous and incorrigible), and we should never so love the erring as to love also their errors. In practice it can be all too easy to slide from slaying the error into slaying the erring, or to slide from loving the erring into loving their error. In different words: "The Church is uncompromising in principles because she believes, she is tolerant in practice because she loves. The enemies of the Church are tolerant in principle because they do not believe, and uncompromising in practice because they do not love."

<u>JUNE 28, 1654</u>

Father John Southworth, martyred at Tyburn.

With his last breath he vowed:

I was brought up in the truly ancient Roman Catholic Apostolic religion, which taught me that the sum of the only true Christian profession is to die. This lesson I have heretofore in my life-time desired to learn; this lesson I came here to put in practice by dying, being taught it by our Blessed Saviour, both by precept and example. This gallows I look on as His Cross, which I gladly take to follow my dear Saviour. My faith is my crime, the performance of my duty the occasion of my condemnation.

SEPTEMBER 1, 2015

Pope Francis in announcing the forthcoming Jubilee Year of Mercy announces that the faithful may receive validly and licitly the Sacrament of "Reconciliation" from the priests of the SSPX.

MARCH 4, 2016

Blasting Tuba – Piping Piccolo Duet

Bishop Fellay appears on a television show called *Comfort Zone: Confronting the Powerful* which airs on this date. He is interviewed by intrepid and unyielding liberal host Tim Sebastian. Highlights:

Tim Sebastian: "You said, 'Jews are those who over centuries have been enemies of the Church.' Why did you say that?"

Bishop Fellay: "I think the phrase has made a lot of controversy."

TS: "And you knew it would."

BF: "No, because it was absolutely not my intention. My intention was that the Jews would look at the Church as an enemy. It was not an expression of the other side. Maybe I was not expressing myself correctly..."

TS: "Rome slapped you down. A Vatican spokesman said, 'It is impossible to speak of Jews as enemies of the Church....'" The Anti-Defamation League called you 'an unrepentant anti-semite.'"

BF: "[B]ecause of all the background with the story of Bishop Williamson . . . . I totally disagree with his position on the Jewish question."

TS: "This is the man who minimized the holocaust . . . a holocaust denier, in fact."

BF: "I think so."

~

TS: "In 1990, Marcel Lefebvre, the co-founder [sic] of your organization was convicted of defaming the Muslim community. He had to pay a 500 Franc fine. That's not the best advert for your group, is it? . . . you have that in your history."

BF: "And that is so marginal a thing, unhappy things . . . "

TS: "Why is it marginal? It matters a lot to the people who were defamed."

BF: "[It was] just a warning about not all Muslims, again . . . they are really side issues. They are not our thing, not what we do."

TS: "But they cause outrage . . . . I don't think I could find a single apology you made, apart from Bishop Williamson."

~

TS: " 'Woman can never be man's equal," [Pope Pius X] said, "and cannot therefore enjoy equal rights. Few women would ever desire to legislate and those who did would only be classed as eccentrics."

BF: "You have to distinguish things when you speak of rights."

TS: "You go along with that?"

BF: "I'm making distinctions. Many things can be cleared if you distinguish things. And here on that question of women and men, it is clear a man is not a woman and a woman is not a man.."

TS: "But that is not the point he was making."

BF: "Each one has, so to say, abilities or qualities that make them fit or better for doing some works, not only works but operations, actions"

TS: "So you stand by what he said all those years ago, a century ago. You stand by what he said."

BF: "I am explaining what it means."

TS: "He says, 'Few women would ever desire to legislate.' Parliaments around the world are full of women who legislate."

BF: "Today they are full, yes."

TS: "So you can't stand by that statement, can you? You can't continue to say . . . it's out of date, isn't it? It's out of date."

BF: "The understanding. What did he mean? Let's say, he made an application for that time, but the fundamental meaning, this distinction between men and women as human beings . . . they are absolutely equal. I maintain that and Pius the Tenth would have said that too. As human beings they have exactly the same rights."

TS: "My point is – these statements and these attitudes that you cling to as part of traditionalism need updating, don't they?"

BF: "To a certain point, yes."

In under thirty minutes, Bishop Williamson, Archbishop Lefebvre and Pope St. Pius X – traditionalism itself – all thrown under the modernist bus.

MARCH 4, 1590

Father Christopher Bales, martyred in Fleet Street.

Alexander Blake, layman, martyred in Gray's Inn Lane.

Blake, a poor hostler in Gray's Inn Lane, was arraigned and hanged because he lodged a priest in his house.

Nicholas Horner, tailor, martyred at Smithfield.

Horner was arraigned and condemned for having made a jerkin for a priest. While his diseased leg was being cut off in prison, he being made to sit on a form neither bound nor held by any violence, neither offered to stir nor used any impatient screech or cries, but wringing his hands in very good order, often said, "Jesus, increase my pains, and increase my patience."

The Voice of the Trumpet

MARCH 19, 2016 – FEAST DAY OF SAINT JOSEPH PATRON OF THE UNIVERSAL CHURCH

Bishop Richard Williamson and Bishop Jean-Michel Faure consecrate Father Tomas Aquino in Novo Friburgo, Brazil, at the Monastery of Santa Cruz. In *Eleison Comments* CDLIII, the Bishop quotes Professor Carlos Nougué who provides background on the new Bishop. Having been resident in France at the Monastery of Le Barroux under Dom Gérard, Tomas Aquino decided to return to his native Brazil and found an extension of the French monastery in Novo Friburgo. When Dom Gérard broke his promise to Archbishop Lefebvre that he would support the consecrations of 1988 and instead made an agreement with Rome, Dom Tomas broke with Le Barroux and declared the Monastery in Brazil to be independent. The Monastery continued to have the support of the SSPX until 2012 when Dom Tomas wrote Bishop Fellay and notified the Bishop that he and the monks of Novo Friburgo could not follow him in any attempted reconciliation with conciliar Rome. The Society responded by informing Dom Tomas that if he did not leave the Monastery within fifteen days, all support, including access to the Sacrament of Holy Orders, would cease. Professor Nougué wrote Bishop Fellay and expressed his outrage at such an injustice. Bishop Fellay responded by saying that Dom Tomas had a mental problem and the decision would not be reversed. Bishop Williamson on learning of the threat promised continuing support, both sacramental and financial for the Monastery. As of this day, the Sacrament of Holy Orders includes raising the Superior of the Monastery to the episcopacy of the Roman Catholic Church... again, clearly out of necessity.

APRIL 1, 2016

Bishop Fellay meets with Pope Francis in the Vatican at his *Domus Sanctae Marthae* residence. It is later announced "it was decided that the exchanges would continue... without haste."

> [I]t is true to say that Conciliar Rome is occupying the structures of Catholic Rome, but to say that the Conciliar Church is therefore the Catholic Church is as foolish as to say that a cuckoo is a nightingale because it occupies a nightingale's nest.

Eleison Comments CCCLXXXIV.

MAY 9, 2016

Interview of Pope Francis appearing in *La Croix*.

LA CROIX: On April 1, you received Bishop Bernard Fellay, Superior General of the priestly Fraternity of St. Pius X. Is the reintegration of the Lefebvrists into the Church again under consideration?

POPE FRANCIS: In Buenos Aires, I often spoke with them. They greeted me, asked me on their knees for a blessing. They say they are Catholic. They love the Church. Bishop Fellay is a man with whom one can dialogue. That is not the case for other elements who are a little strange, such as Bishop Williamson or others who have been radicalized. Leaving this aside, I believe, as I said in Argentina, that they are Catholics on the way to full communion. During this year of mercy, I felt that I needed to authorize their confessors to pardon the sin of abortion. They thanked me for this gesture. Previously, Benedict XVI, whom they greatly respect, had liberalized the use of the Tridentine Rite Mass. So good dialogue and good work are taking place.

Archbishop Lefebvre: "We do not agree; it is a dialogue of death."

MAY 9, 1679

Thomas Pickering, lay-brother, O.S.B., martyred at Tyburn.

The Voice of the Trumpet

> The tyme hath been we had one faith,
> And strode aright one ancient path;
> The thym is now that each man may
> See newe religions coyned each day.
> Sweet Jesu, with Thy Mother mylde
> Sweet Virgine Mother with thy chylde,
> Angells and Saints of each degree
> Redress our countree's miserie.
>
> —William Blundell, 1560–1638.

And, please God, our Church's "miserie."

JULY 4, 2016

Bishop Fellay calls for yet another Rosary Crusade for the following intentions: 1) to establish devotion to the Immaculate Heart of Mary; 2) to advance the eventual triumph of her Immaculate Heart; 3) to move the Pope and the bishops to consecrate Russia to her Immaculate Heart; and 4) to protect the Society of St. Pius X and all other traditional communities. *See* MARCH, 2008, and HOLY SATURDAY, 2008.

MAY 11, 2017 – FEAST OF STS. PHILIP AND JAMES

Bishops Williamson, Faure and Tomas de Aquino raise Father Gerardo Zendejas to the episcopacy in a Consecration Ceremony held at St. Athanasius Church in Vienna, Virginia, the independent Traditional Catholic parish shepherded for many decades by Father Ronald Ringrose.

> Authority is the indispensable defender and guarantee of Truth, but it comes after Truth and not before. Take for example one of Our Lord's last instructions to Peter before He will leave Peter behind to govern the Church (Lk. XXII, 31–32): "Simon, Simon, behold Satan hath desired to have you (plural), that he may sift you as wheat. But I have prayed for thee (singular) that

thy faith fail not (Truth); and thou, being once converted (Truth), confirm thy brethren (Authority)." And when on Palm Sunday a few days beforehand the Pharisees had attempted to rebuke Our Lord for the joyful noise being made by His disciples, so necessary is the adoration of God in Truth that Our Lord replied (Lk. XIX,40): "I say to you that if these shall hold their peace, the stones will cry out."

In today's Newchurch, Authority is mixing Conciliar error with Catholic Truth in the engine of the Church, which is like mixing water with gasoline (petrol) in the engine of a motor car – the car is crippled, the Church is crippled. And whereas Archbishop Lefebvre defied that crippling, not least of all but rather above all, by his consecrating of four bishops to maintain a Catholic authority that would protect God's Truth, his successors at the head of what was once his Society are doing their utmost to submit his protection of Truth to the crippled and crippling Authority of Rome! If these successors seriously think that once they are "inside the official Church" they will be in a position to convert the neo-modernists, they are essentially naïve. Already they are holding their fire on Vatican II. Just when do they imagine they will be able to open fire again?

In these quite exceptional circumstances, there must be disciples of Our Lord who tell the Truth – so as to spare the stones the effort! These disciples may not be united as they would be beneath true Authority (always allowing for human weakness). They may be "straitened and cast down," they may suffer "tribulation and persecution" (cf. II Cor. IV, 8–9)., but they must be there for as long as Truth is held in captivity. Will that be a long time? God knows. Many of us expected Him to intervene long ago, but God has a very long fuse. However, intervene He will, if anything at all is still to be saved. Patience.

Eleison Comments DIV.

OCTOBER 28, 2017

In May, following the First Mass of Bishop Zendejas in Vienna, Virginia at St. Athanasius Church, the four bishops made an Act of Consecration to the Immaculate Heart of Mary, in their way giving evidence to their belief in her request at Fatima for a Consecration of Russia to her Immaculate Heart.

In Late October, the four bishops traveled to Fatima and made the same act of Consecration on the site where the request was first made.

This Act showed their Faith in her message, their Hope that one day the Pope in conjunction with all the bishops in the world will make a similar Consecration of Russia to her Immaculate Heart, and their Charity, as this Act of Consecration lifted the hearts of believing Catholics, providing them with the fortitude to trudge on through the modern mire.

Here is the Act of Consecration prayed on those two occasions:

> Most Holy Mother of God, Immaculate Heart of Mary, Seat of Mercy, Seat of Goodness, Seat of Pardon, sure door by which souls are to enter Heaven, see on their knees before you four sons of Archbishop Lefebvre, four bishops striving to do what they can to help you to obtain from the Pope and bishops of your Divine Son's one true Church that Consecration of Russia to your Sorrowful and Immaculate Heart which can alone obtain peace for mankind, now in the shadow of a frightful Third World War. In Fatima, Portugal, one hundred years ago, you first warned mankind of the Second World War to come, of famine and persecutions, if people would not cease offending God. To prevent these disasters, you promised to return to ask for the Consecration of Russia to your Immaculate Heart, and for the Communion of Reparation on Five First Saturdays. If your requests were heeded, Russia would

Veritas *Variations*

be converted, and there would be peace. If not, disasters would follow and Russia would spread its errors throughout the world. Within the next 12 years you returned as you had promised, and you made the double request.

However, trusting in human means to solve the Church's grave problems, the Catholic churchmen did not immediately do what you had requested. Two years later your Divine Son Himself warned mankind through Sister Lucy of Fatima, that since His ministers were delaying to carry out His command, they would suffer grave consequences: Russia would spread its errors throughout the world, causing wars and persecutions of the Church, and the Pope would suffer greatly. Still the Pope preferred his human means of dealing with Russia.

In 1936 Our Lord explained to Sister Lucy that Russia's conversion depended upon its consecration to your Immaculate Heart because He wanted the whole Church to recognize that that conversion was a triumph of your Heart, so that devotion to your Heart would rank alongside devotion to His own Sacred Heart.

Still the churchmen hesitated, so that in 1939 the terrible Second World War broke out, and all over the world Communism extended its power. Immediately after the war your pilgrim statues of Fatima had great success, but still the churchmen would not do exactly as you had requested, and so in 1957 before Sister Lucy was silenced by the churchmen, she expressed your own sadness that neither good people nor bad people had paid attention to the message of Fatima. You said that the good people gave it no importance, while the bad cared nothing about it. But you warned us once more that a terrible punishment was imminent.

Just three years later that punishment began with the churchmen's refusal to make public the third part of your Secret Message of Fatima, which you had asked them to publish at the latest in 1960. By an almost unpardonable lie they pretended that you had told them, that from 1960 onwards they might publish it, and this effort of theirs to stifle your message of Fatima has continued ever since, culminating in the year 2000. But you have never given up your attempts to save us, while the churchmen were even more severely punished by the blindness which overwhelmed them at the Second Vatican Council. In the third part of the Secret it is most likely that you had warned against exactly the errors which prevailed at that Council. And now the entire Church is in darkness, and the world is on the brink of the third and most terrible World War.

Immaculate Heart of Mary, most Holy Mother of God, we cry to you in our distress. Help of Christians, Refuge of Sinners, Comforter of the Afflicted we trust in you. Queen of the Most Holy Rosary, Mother of the Church, we implore your most loving, maternal and Immaculate Heart to have mercy upon us poor sinners, your children; hear and answer our plea. We beg of you to obtain from your Divine Son, the graces necessary for the Holy Father and the bishops to fulfil without further delay the long-standing command of Heaven, by consecrating with the bishops of the entire world, Holy Russia to your Immaculate Heart, as was requested and in the manner requested by you, on behalf of the Most Holy Trinity so long ago, and which has yet to be accomplished.

Immaculate Heart of Mary, you know how much suffering mankind would have avoided over the last 90 years if only one of the Popes during that time had heeded your request for the Consecration of Russia. Mother of God, you and your Divine Son alone know what a frightful chastisement is now hanging over the heads of mankind if the Popes, for whatever inadequate human reasons, still refuse your request. If it depends upon them, they are liable to prevaricate, although you told us one hundred years ago how much that would make them suffer. Mother of God, your Divine Son can refuse you nothing that you ask of Him.

Veritas *Variations*

He wishes the Consecration to depend on you, because He wishes your Immaculate Heart to be honoured as the source of the Consecration's triumph. Holy Mother of God, most humbly upon our knees we beg of you to obtain those graces needed by the Pope to perform the Consecration.

Meanwhile before you here today, we commend, we entrust, and we do whatever lies within our own power, to consecrate Russia to your Immaculate Heart, not because we can remotely take the place of the Pope and the bishops of the whole world, but because we wish to honour your requests as far as we can. If only Holy Russia became Catholic once more, the Eastern Church might resurrect the Western Church, presently devastated by materialism and atheism. Mother of God, we commend our own selves also to your protection and to your all-powerful intercession with Our Lord Jesus Christ, who is the Lord of Lords and the King of Kings, but who is at the same time a Son who infinitely loves His Mother, and will do anything she asks. Beloved and Blessed Mother, we have not a shadow of doubt that in the end your Immaculate Heart will triumph.

And, in Truth, it will.

Le Moulin du Pin, July 6, 1990.

Le Treilhou Caussade, August 1990.

"And I appointed watchmen over you, saying: Hearken to the sound of the trumpet. And they said: We will not hearken."

—Jeremias 6: 17

Coda

In 1968, Paul McCartney had a dream. In the dream his mother, Mary, appeared to him. His mother, a Roman Catholic who lived her life in Liverpool, had Paul baptized as a Catholic. Despite her assurance that her children would be reared as Catholic, her agnostic husband, James, refused, not even allowing the children to attend Catholic schools. She died in 1956 of breast cancer on the day she was to have surgery. Her last act was to lay out her children's clothes for the day so they would be properly dressed if she should not return.

In the dream, she spoke to her son and told him, "It will be all right, just let it be." "Let it be" became the title of the song released in March, 1970, the final Beatles' single. It was released before McCartney announced his departure from the group. Written and sung by him, the song with its hymn-like and organ-accompanied melody possesses an aura of the spiritual, despite McCartney's avowed lack of faith. This aura so permeates the song that John Lennon mocked it during the recording session by smirkingly announcing, "and, now, 'hark the herald angels' come...."

The song proved popular and climbed to the number one position on the pop charts quickly. Many fans who came to love the song asked McCartney if the song referred to the Virgin Mary and he replied the reference was to his mother, Mary. He added, the listeners could interpret the song however they pleased.

So....

"Let It Be" Original Lyrics – Troped

When I find myself in times of trouble
Mother [of God] Mary [Most Holy] comes to me
[Seat of Wisdom], Speaking words of wisdom, [trust in God], let it be.

And [now] in my hour of darkness [and then at the hour of my death]
She is [and will be] standing right in front of me
Speaking words of wisdom, let it be
Yeah, let it be [God is in control]....
Whisper words of wisdom, let it be [His Will be done].

When the broken-hearted people
Living in the world agree
[When after the consecration of Russia by the Pope and bishops]
There will be an answer [when my Immaculate Heart triumphs with a period of peace]
Let it be.
For though [poor sinners] they may be parted

Coda

There is still a chance that they will see [that only I can help them]
There will be an answer [consecrate Russia to my Immaculate Heart]
Let it be [done soon].

And when the night is cloudy
[When Rome loses the Faith and becomes the seat of the anti-Christ]
There is still a light that shines on me
[My Son, the Light of the World]
Shine on until tomorrow [and forever . . . .]
Let it [God's Will] be [done].

I wake up to the sound of music [!]
[Sleepers, awake!]
Mother Mary, [Queen of Heaven and of Earth], comes to me
Speaking words of wisdom, let it be.
There will be an answer [the consecration of Russia], let it be.
You know there's going to be an answer [though it will be late]
Oh, let it be [on earth as it is in heaven].

God can turn all things to good.

Let It Be

The *deus ex machina* or "the god from the machine" is a dramatic device in which insoluble plot complications are suddenly and surprisingly resolved by the appearance of a character or a message or an external event that brings about an unexpected happy ending. The name comes from Greek tragedy where an actual machine

The Voice of the Trumpet

sat atop the *skene*, the permanent stage structure before which the action played out. In many Greek plays, a god would descend from above on the machine and resolve the complex and seemingly insoluble human situation through divine intervention. The first known use occurs in the *Eumenides* of Aeschylus, and Euripides makes use of the device in both his *Medea* and *Alcestis*. Shakespeare makes use of the device in his romances, even to having Jupiter descend from above seated on an eagle in Act Five of *Cymbeline*. Molière uses the plot device in *Tartuffe* and John Gay in his popular *The Beggar's Opera*.

At the conclusion of Beethoven's only opera, *Fidelio*, a masterpiece he wrestled with for twelve years, this dramatic device is used with especially powerful force as it has musical accompaniment. The villainous Don Pizarro, the governor of the prison where the hero Florestan has been unjustly held, arrives to see that the good man's execution is carried out according to his orders. Rocco, the decent jailer, hesitates and as Florestan accuses Pizarro of being a vile murderer, Don Pizarro pulls his dagger to do the evil deed himself. Leonore, Florestan's wife who has been working in the prison disguised as the boy Fidelio, reveals her true identity and brandishes a pistol to defend her husband. At this moment of crisis:

Man hört die Trompete auf dem Thurm
[The sound of the trumpet is heard from the tower]

"O, was ist das? Gerechter Gott!"
["Oh, what is that? Just God!"]

Man hört die Trompeten stärker
[The trumpet sounds louder]

"Gerecht, o Gott! Ist dein Gericht!"
["Oh, God! How just is Thy Judgment!"]

Coda

Don Fernando, the good minister of the good King arrives in time, evil is put down, good triumphs, happy ending ... set to some of the most magnificent music ever penned.

Deep in the hearts of the faithful, trust in God dwells. The *deus ex machina* on the stage grows out of a genuine fact in human knowledge. As God sent his patriarchs and prophets to guide and warn His chosen people, as He sent His Son to redeem mankind, as He sent His Blessed Mother to console and direct the faithful, He will be the God of Rescue and simultaneously the God of Justice to bring us out of the dark pit, the abyss, the chasm in which we now dwell. "End will be simple, sudden, God given." We must trust in the God of Rescue who will come to us and help us again, as always; we must remember He is also the God of Judgment before whom we will stand when the Last Trumpet sounds who will judge us and reward or punish us as we have deserved.

St. John Vianney began the hearing of confessions at the unlikely hour of one o'clock in the morning, and it has been reported that he spent from 13 to 17 painful hours a day in the cramped, stifling confessional.

Completely exhausted by apostolic labors and by the additional penances he inflicted on his thin, sickly body, the Saint died peacefully on August 4, 1859, after receiving the final consolations of his religion. Forty-five years later, on June 17, 1904, his body was exhumed because of his impending beatification and was found dried and darkened, but perfectly entire. Only his face, which was still perfectly recognizable, suffered a little from the effects of death. After the viscera were removed, "the precious remains were wrapped in bands of fine linens and clothed in the following vestments: a tunic of white watered silk, a black cassock, a rochet edged with fine lace, and a stole of cloth of gold embroidered with lilies and roses of the same material. A rosary of jasper beads was twined around the darkened fingers, and the face was covered with a wax mask which reproduces the features of the servant of God. When on April 2, 1905, the old men of Ars, who had known M. Vianney well, were shown the relic as it is seen today by pilgrims, they burst into tears and exclaimed with one voice: 'Oh, how truly like him!'"

During the year of his beatification, his perfectly preserved heart was removed and enclosed in a beautiful reliquary, which was placed in a separate building called The Shrine of the Curé's Heart.

The magnificent reliquary that contains the body of the Saint was donated by priests around the world and is situated above an altar of the basilica . . . . "

Joan Carroll Cruz, *The Incorruptibles*, Charlotte, North Carolina: Tan Books, 1977, pp. 258–259.

Pilgrims come from around the world to the Basilica of Ars to pray before the incorrupt body of the Holy Saint; priests come to offer Mass in the Basilica at the altar where the Patron Saint of Priests rests, awaiting the Resurrection. Those who cannot make the journey may visit the shrine and pray from their distant homes as a webcam from inside the Basilica broadcasts live 24 hours a day. The lens of the camera is focused on the altar and on the tabernacle and on the Saint. Modern technology and timeless worship are wed here so that all the world, or the many who seek to find their way, may view, may pray, may rejoice.

Coda

7. B E- á- ti e- stis Sancti De- i o- mnes

> Let there be a trumpet in thy throat like an eagle upon the house of the Lord: because they have transgressed my covenant, and have violated my law.
>
> —Osse 8: 1

What then composed this English Bishop? What was his essence that shaped his existence? Who had God wrought in bringing out of nothing such a soul in the wasted final years of the age of revolution and the modernist derangement.

First and foremost, he believed the doctrines of the Catholic faith and knew in his bones and to the depth of his soul that doctrines must be restored and honored. He knew this would happen in God's good time and that God's Truth would be restored. Then, and appropriately for a vassal, he believed in Authority. He knew exactly what he had been granted at his episcopal consecration in 1988. He had no jurisdiction, but he had been graced with the mandate to teach and to offer the sacraments: "Going therefore, teach ye all nations: baptizing them in the name of the Father and of the Son and of the Holy Ghost. Teaching them to observe all things whatsoever I have commanded you . . . " (Matt. 28: 19-20). His teaching began in retreats, then to the seminaries, then in his monthly Rector's Letters and sermons and conferences, and then in his weekly *Eleison Comments*, not to mention his voluminous correspondence through paper or electronic means with countless questioning, troubled, despairing or thankful souls.

The Voice of the Trumpet

What he would not do was take onto himself an authority he did not possess. Avoiding the protestant temptation of striking out on his own independent path and determining his own organized movement, His Excellency waited patiently, trusting in God and waiting for God's good time. Many traditional Catholics excoriated him for not "doing something," as if human effort could clean the filthy revolutionary stables of five hundred years of muck, refuse and lies. Bishop Richard Williamson holds fast to the words of the Blessed Mother who stated precisely that the only remedies that remain for mankind are the Holy Rosary and devotion to her Immaculate Heart. As he waits, he follows his own advice, repeatedly offered in all his public teaching and in private to a myriad of souls – "Watch and pray, watch and pray, Fifteen Mysteries every day."

The Bishop thus follows the example of the beloved disciple St. John. As Our Lord's physical body expired in agony on the cross, St. John remained close to the Blessed Mother, sharing her sorrow and undoubtedly praying; so Bishop Williamson, viewing the horrifying crucifixion of the Mystical Body of Christ, the Holy Catholic Church, stands with Our Lady, participating in her pain and praying as she asked. He waits for word of the miraculous Resurrection.

> She [Mary Magdalene] ran therefore and cometh to Simon Peter and to the other disciple whom Jesus loved [John]and saith to them: They have taken away the Lord out of the sepulcher: and we know not where they have laid him.
>
> Peter therefore went out and that other disciple: and they came to the sepulchre.
>
> And they both ran together: and that other disciple did outrun Peter and came first to the sepulchre.
>
> And when he stooped down, he saw the linen cloths

Coda

lying: but yet he went not in.

Then cometh Simon Peter, following him, and went into the sepulchre: and saw the linen cloths lying,

And the napkin that had been about his head, not lying with the linen cloths, but apart, wrapped up into one place.

Then the other disciple also went in, who came first to the sepulchre: and he saw and believed.

John 20: 2–8.

Having arrived at the tomb where the Mystical Body of Christ, Holy Mother Church, appears dead, Bishop Richard Williamson waits. Devout Catholic Bishop that he is and fully aware of hierarchy and authority, he knows that only a Pope, after the Consecration of Russia to Our Lady's Immaculate Heart, may "enter first," and then recognize and proclaim the mystery of the Resurrected Mystical Body. And he believes a pope, in conjunction with all the bishops, will pronounce the necessary words, bringing the full restoration. (Perhaps after this pontiff at a future date confesses to the great conciliar betrayal and emulates the first Pope: "And Peter wept.")

But the Bishop waits with charity, knowing the pain and confusion roiling the hearts and souls of countless faithful as in these days of seeming defeat, for the Mystical Body is seemingly lifeless and cold in the darkened and sealed tomb of modernism. Bishop Richard Williamson may seem to some severe and to others neglectful, to some too harsh and to others too lenient, but any soul who has had contact with his person recognizes his public face of proper episcopal dignity is melded with an unfailing Christ-like sympathy and living charity, though never separated from Truth. His heart had been educated in old school humanities before his head cleared and absorbed the fullness of Catholic reality. This cruciate intersection of worldly wisdom and divine aspiration stands as an inspiration to many.

What has informed his entire life is a deep appreciation for motherhood, from his own mother who made a nest for her fledglings and first passed on wisdom of the heart, to a deep devotion to his Blessed Mother who has guided his priestly life. On the brink of her inevitable Triumph over Satan, the Bishop insists her Rosary is the "most powerful weapon in the world." She will soon crush the serpent's head and usher in the Sixth Age of the Church under the Queenly Reign of Her Immaculate Heart; her role as co-redemptrix, long held dear by centuries of Catholic souls, will likely be officially and dogmatically proclaimed.

And so he constantly reminds women of their special role and warns them not to be tempted by the forbidden fruit allurements of the modern world that seek to confuse and distort their unique and precious gift, the conception, the birthing, the nurturing of life. The Blessed Mother is their perfect model and inspiration, and when the enemy's voice calls to them "Ye shall be as men" – universities, public prominence, workplace advancement, slacks, sterility, abortion – their best defense is to invoke and imitate the Blessed Mother. The voice of the trumpet calls them to this battle; their field of battle is their home with their families, their neighborhood with their close acquaintances, their parishes with their fellow souls in need of love, consolation and support, and their prayer life where they are united to their paragon in charity and service.

And he reminds men that their neglect and impotence has created this catastrophe. They must again assume their rightful place and become defenders of the family and the moral order.

Bishop Williamson calls our age a "dress rehearsal" for the final Seventh Age, the coming of the anti-Christ,

Coda

but in the present age, his voice reminds us that each soul will face the inevitable and necessary end of its particular earthly existence. Our end will come one day, as one day the end will come for the world itself. "The readiness is all."

> So, when the last and dreaded hour
> This crumbling pageant shall devour,
> The Trumpet shall be heard on high,
> The dead shall live, the living die,
> And music shall untune the sky.

At the piano in La Reja, Argentina, Dec., 1985.

www.ingramcontent.com/pod-product-compliance
Lightning Source LLC
Chambersburg PA
CBHW071259110526
44591CB00010B/720